POPULAR TELEVISION IN BRITAIN

TV TIMES October 7, 1955. Vol. I. No. 3.
Registered at the G.P.O. as a newspaper.

The only paper giving **NEW TV** programmes in full   No. 3   4ᵈ

TV TIMES

OFFICIAL PROGRAMMES   SUNDAY **OCT 9**—SATURDAY **OCT 15**

	Page
Viewing Guide and Play Bill...	3
Looking Around..................	4-5
Jack Hylton—Master Showman	9
Meet the Visionettes...........10-11
The Pajama Game.................	12
Should Parliament be Televised? by W. J. Brown...	13

COVER PICTURE

RICHARD GREENE (above), whose flashing smile and dark good looks are known to millions of cinemagoers, plays the part of Robin in " The Adventures of Robin Hood " —the serial which appears every Sunday at 5.30.

See story—pages 6-7.

	Page
Sportscreen......................	14
Fashions with an Irish lilt........	15
The stories of the Hallé.........	17
A Goon's-eye view..............	19
When the camera goes visiting	20-21
Charm in the Morning...........	22
The Young View.................	23
Double-Crossword................	38

And all the Programmes—Pages 24 to 37

POPULAR TELEVISION IN BRITAIN

· STUDIES IN CULTURAL HISTORY ·

EDITED BY
JOHN CORNER

bfi

BFI Publishing

First published in 1991 by the
British Film Institute
21 Stephen Street, London W1P 1PL

Reprinted 1997

British Library Cataloguing in Publication Data
Popular television in Britain: studies in cultural history.
1. Great Britain. Television programmes, history
I. Corner, John
791.450941

ISBN 0-85170-269-4 (h/b)
0-85170-270-8 (p/b)

Cover design by Geoff Wiggins
Cover photograph by V.B. Cole

Set in Plantin by
Fakenham Photosetting Limited,
Fakenham, Norfolk
Printed in Great Britain by
Ebenezer Baylis & Son Limited,
The Trinity Press, Worcester, and London

Contents

Notes on Contributors   vii

General Introduction: Television and British Society in the 1950s   1
JOHN CORNER

Before the Golden Age: Early Television Drama   22
JOHN CAUGHIE

Documentary Voices   42
JOHN CORNER

Every Wart and Pustule: Gilbert Harding and Television Stardom   60
ANDY MEDHURST

'Hancock's Half Hour': A Watershed in British Television Comedy   75
PETER GODDARD

Television and Pop: The Case of the 1950s   90
JOHN HILL

Wise Scientists and Female Androids: Class and Gender in Science Fiction   108
JOY LEMAN

Banging In Some Reality: The Original 'Z Cars'   125
STUART LAING

Filth, Sedition and Blasphemy: The Rise and Fall of Television Satire   145
ANDREW CRISELL

Television Memories and Cultures of Viewing 1950–65   159
TIM O'SULLIVAN

'Grandstand', the Sports Fan and the Family Audience   182
GARRY WHANNEL

All Bark and No Bite: The Film Industry's Response to Television   197
EDWARD BUSCOMBE

Index of Proper Names and Programmes   209

Acknowledgments

The contributors whose work is collected here have indicated in their essays where their own acknowledgments are due in terms of institutional, library and personal support. I would like to thank the photographic libraries of the BBC, Granada Television and the BFI for their help in illustrating the book, and Ed Buscombe and Roma Gibson for their enthusiasm for the project from the beginning and their editorial advice in its later stages.

Notes on Contributors

EDWARD BUSCOMBE is Head of Trade Publishing at the British Film Insitute. His most recent publication is the *BFI Companion to the Western* (André Deutsch, 1988).

JOHN CAUGHIE lectures in Drama, Film and Television at the University of Glasgow. He has written on aspects of film and television theory, history and analysis in a number of books and journals, including the journal *Screen*, of which he is now an editor. Among his books is the edited collection, *Theories of Authorship* (RKP/BFI, 1981).

JOHN CORNER is a lecturer in the School of Politics and Communication Studies at the University of Liverpool. He has written extensively on media topics in books and journals. He co-edited *Communication Studies* (Third Edition, 1989), edited *Documentary and the Mass Media* and co-authored *Nuclear Reactions: Form and Response in 'Public Issue' Television*. He is an editor of the journal *Media, Culture and Society*.

ANDREW CRISELL is Principal Lecturer in Communication at Sunderland Polytechnic. He spent a year working in the BBC and is the author of *Understanding Radio* (Methuen, 1986). He has published in book collections, journals and magazines, including *The Listener*, and is currently planning a volume of essays on contemporary developments in sound broadcasting.

PETER GODDARD lives in Liverpool and is completing doctoral research into the development of British television comedy in the 1950s.

JOHN HILL is a Senior Lecturer in Media Studies at the University of Coleraine. He is the author of *Sex, Class and Realism: British Cinema 1956–63* and the co-author of *Cinema and Ireland*.

STUART LAING is currently Dean of the School of Cultural and Community Studies at the University of Sussex. His publications include *Representations of Working Class Life 1957–64* (1986) and the co-authored *Disorder and Discipline: Popular Culture 1950 to the Present* (1988).

JOY LEMAN lectures in Film and Television Studies at the London College of Printing, which is part of the London Institute. Her interest in broadcasting history arises from work done for her M. Phil thesis on 'Radio programmes for women in wartime Britain'.

ANDY MEDHURST teaches Media Studies and Popular Culture at the University of Sussex. He writes on media and cultural issues for *The Listener*, *Marxism Today* and *Gay Times*. His volume of the BFI's History of the British Film series, covering the period 1945–58, is due to be published in 1992.

TIM O'SULLIVAN is a lecturer in Media and Cultural Studies at the Polytechnic of Wales. His research and publication interests have largely concerned developments in media education. Current research includes work on the domestic acquisition of satellite television and compact disc technologies.

GARRY WHANNEL works as a lecturer and writer/researcher specialising in television sport. He is the author of *Blowing the Whistle: The Politics of Sport* (Pluto, 1983) and co-editor of *Five-Ring Circus: Money, Power and Politics at the Olympic Games* (Pluto, 1984) and of *Off the Ball: The Football World Cup* (Pluto, 1984). He has also recently co-edited *Understanding Television* (Routledge, 1990) and is working on a book on television sport.

General Introduction
Television and British Society in the 1950s

JOHN CORNER

The essays in this volume are all concerned in one way or another with television programmes in Britain during television's formative years as a popular medium. That is to say, roughly, from the early 1950s through to the innovations of the early 1960s. Some writers have gone back earlier, to discuss the immediate post-war scene or even aspects of the pre-war television service, while others have continued further into the 1960s in order to give their generic or thematic topic better coherence.

Politically, the lengthy period covered by the book involves three broad phases. First of all, the attempts by the post-war Labour Governments to reconstruct British economy and society within a particular version of social democratic welfare capitalism. These attempts led to significant structural change and provided the basis for 50s growth, though the Government met with a degree of popular disenchantment in the face of continued material shortages and budgetary instability. Then, the return of a commercially expansionary but welfarist Conservatism in 1951, which was carried through into the long-running Tory project of a 'New Britain' to be characterised by increasing 'affluence', the central ideological as well as economic theme of the times. Over a series of governments, this project itself became subject to increasing difficulties, as unanticipated global economic changes brought acute balance of payments problems and exacerbated a loosening of the consensus of domestic politics. Finally, in 1964 the Labour Party returned to government under Harold Wilson, with the themes of modernisation and technology to the fore and a revised perspective on the principles and practice of socialist change.

Economically, the move is essentially one from the circumstances of shortage and restriction in the immediate post-war economy to a steady rise in the general standard of living, accompanied by changed patterns of work and of leisure. The basis for this was improved terms of foreign investment and a substantial increase in domestic investment. In a useful, culturally oriented overview of the larger part of the period under examination, John Hill quotes Pinto-Duchinsky on this uninterrupted growth:

> During these years (1951–64) there was uninterrupted full employment, while productivity increased faster than in any other period of comparable length in the twentieth century.[1]

Hill notes, too, that during this period average earnings (allowing for inflation) increased by 30 per cent. Within the area of leisure, in terms both of time-use and household expenditure, it was television – as the chief agency of domestic recreation and, directly and indirectly, as a key promoter of increased consumption in other spheres – which began to hold the central place.

Culturally, the period is one in which there occur a number of radical shifts in the class, gender and generational character both of culture in its broadest sense and of the popular arts. New tensions and aspirations around individual identity and the possibilities for community are worked out within the still dominant framework of an 'official', class-secure social system and its attendant inequalities. The alliances and contradictions between the terms of this older cultural order and some of the cultural dynamics and themes projected through the intensified activities of the market, massively reorganising the contours, thematics and forms of the 'popular' as a category of consumption, undoubtedly provide the major focus for analysis. They are the concern of many of the pieces which follow.

As a collection of essays in cultural history, the book is designed to meet, in some measure at least, the urgent requirement that now exists for a more detailed and connected understanding of television's role in shaping British post-war culture. Such a requirement has both specialist academic and also more general origins.

Academically, the rise of media studies as an element of undergraduate, and now secondary level studies has been almost entirely focused around the analysis of contemporary phenomena. Study of film has been an exception to this, working often from a canon of established classics which, although it has thereby provided historical texts for discussion, has nevertheless often followed literary studies by framing this discussion within the terms of an ahistorical, desocialised aesthetics. In the study of broadcasting, historical questions, where they have featured at all, have mostly been present as a swiftly covered 'background'.[2] Given the lack of primary research in the area, this situation is to some extent understandable, as is the pull towards working with the detailed textual instances of today, rather than distanced, second-hand and often unengagingly generalised accounts of past forms and contexts. However, the result has too often been a foreshortening and simplifying of perspective, in which the questioning of television's textuality and sociality today has been limited by ignorance about the details of its institutional and formal development as this has proceeded alongside larger shifts of polity and culture.

But 1990 suggests other than simply academic reasons for coming to terms more fully with the culture of television in Britain, with its often subtly interactive relationship between 'official' and 'popular' discourses, its unparalleled mixing of 'high' and 'low' forms and the play-off between its democratising accessibility and its vulnerability to abuse by the powerful. At the time of writing, a new Broadcasting Bill is in Parliament[3] which will certainly have the effect of changing quite radically the institutional contexts and working assumptions within which British television has, with a surprising degree of continuity, been produced and broadcast since the post-war recommencement of the fledgling BBC

2

service on 7 June 1946. The new measures will affect not only the funding and regulatory structures of broadcasting, but also, largely through these, its address to the audience, its range, its forms and its political, social and cultural disposition. With the threat (or, as some see it, the promise) of a more intensive commodification of the television product, a new and strategic debate about 'quality' has begun, with that term often being used to cover a variety of different and conflicting aesthetic, social and professional values and criteria.

This is, then, a good time for a retrospective cultural analysis. Though necessarily selective, such an analysis can get some way beyond the bland narratives of historical background, at the same time as it can provide the scholarship with which to temper current tendencies towards either seeing imminent change simplistically, as the end of a 'golden age' or, equally simplistically, as the triumph of democracy over élitism.

In this introduction I want first of all to develop an account of what seem to me to be salient events and circumstances within, or affecting, the British television industry during the period with which the majority of these essays are concerned. I then want to continue to map this period by reference to four interconnected themes. This I hope will provide a coherent and useful gateway to the articles themselves, whose different topics, approaches and methods I shall then attempt to identify and relate on the map.

The First Phase of Television in Britain: Public Institution and Popular Culture

When the BBC resumed its limited television service after the war (transmissions had begun in 1936), it was still very much the case that radio was the dominant medium and many people in broadcasting thought it likely to remain so for a long time. In 1948, after a year and a half of transmissions, the number of licences had reached 45,564 (in a population of approximately 50 million). The price of a 'budget model' television set was then around £50, in relation, for instance, to an average industrial wage of just under £7 a week.[4]

The BBC enjoyed considerable security as the sole agency of broadcasting. It had emerged from the war even further confirmed as a national institution. Consideration of the renewal of its licence, and of the possibility of its monopoly being discontinued, had in 1946 been deferred for five years in the context of more immediate and pressing political tasks. This latter decision had, however, not been made without considerable argument. Churchill had challenged the Labour Government on the idea of extending the licence without inquiry, and indications that the BBC's monopoly would be a principal point of conflict – economic, cultural and political – were widespread. In a letter to the The Times on 26 June 1946, Sir Frederick Ogilvie, Director-General of the BBC from 1938–42, made a case for the benefits of competition in terms which, at points, have considerable current resonance. 'Freedom is choice', he claimed, and warned of the dangers inherent in the 'nationalisation of the infinitely precious things of the mind and the spirit'.[5] At the same time, anxiety about the real motives behind the attack on the BBC's monopoly was expressed in several quarters. It was thought by the *Manchester Guardian* that many of the stated points of Conservative critique were spurious and that behind them was 'the sulpherous smell of the political and commercial pit and not a distinterested attempt to secure ... the best possible broadcasting service'.[6]

These early exchanges were, of course, primarily about the future of the radio services. However, after the Conservatives came into office in 1951 and rapidly reframed the dominant terms of debate, such exchanges finally came to a head in the arguments and sustained campaigning which led up to the introduction of Commercial Television via the Television Act of 1954. The BBC was widely regarded at this time as being too committed to a radio perspective to give television the planning attention and the budget that it needed. This helped the case of those who thought that another agency of broadcasting was required to realise fully the potential of the new medium. By then, television had already begun to show the sort of appeal that would make it, with its commercial expansion and reconstructed notions of the 'popular', the most influential single factor in British post-war culture. Television licences (actually *combined* TV and radio licences) had climbed steeply to just under 5 million by 1955, and this first growth curve of monochrome set-ownership would continue right through to the late 60s, when it got close to 16 million.[7]

An event cited by many commentators as a milestone in this development (though perhaps not quite constituting its *origins*, as some have claimed) was the televising of the Coronation of Queen Elizabeth in 1953. Whatever the final degree of significance given to this in the formation of a British television culture, the viewing figures are hugely impressive in their indication of a society united in national public ceremony via the means of live 'secondary participation'. Fifty-six per cent (over 20 million) of the adult population of Great Britain are judged to have watched the service on television, and the assessment of *where* they watched it gives some idea of the stage of development of the popular viewing audience at the time. Nearly 8 million watched it in their own homes, but well over 10 million watched at the homes of friends.[8] Owners of sets at this time could often combine the pleasures of viewing with that of hospitality to the extended family or to neighbours, by inviting regular or 'special occasion' visits.

Significantly, the television audience for the Coronation was far in excess of those listening to the radio – television was now in the process of becoming the principal instrument both of public information and of national cultural identity. Regularly scheduled programmes like the panel game *What's My Line?* projected 'celebrity-ness' into the front room with a captivatingly novel mixture of showbiz glamour and cosiness. This programme (starting in 1951) steadily became an anticipated point of reference in the popular experience of weekly routine, generating secondary texts of news items, guest appearances and gossip quite unprecedented at the time, though prefigurative of later developments.

In July 1954, after a long and sometimes very heated period of debate both in Parliament and in the country at large, the Television Bill of 1954 passed its Second Reading by the margin of 296 to 269 votes. Many of those who had objected to the initial idea of 'Commercial Television', including several prominent Conservatives, had been made less anxious about the fate of the national culture as a result of two measures which had been introduced into the planning.[9]

4

First of all, there was to be a public authority – the Independent Television Authority (ITA) – to regulate the activities of the newly 'independent' sector of broadcasting (independent of precisely *what*? was a question asked by many critics, who also noted the contradistinctive implication that the BBC was state-controlled). The Authority itself, not the companies, would own (and rent) transmission facilities. Many planned features of this body closely resembled those of the BBC, conferring on the newcomer an immediate aura of responsibility and institutional rectitude. This encompassing of commercial activities within the broad principles and regulations of established 'public service' provision seemed, to many of the strongest advocates of ITV, immediately to involve a disappointing curtailment of market possibilities. 'This is not competitive TV', remarked one advertiser, 'this is a miniscule BBC operating under handicaps which even that august body has never had to face'.[10] But the measure also won over several of those in Parliament and sectors of the establishment who had previously been opposed to the Bill.

Secondly, it was made clear that advertising would be conducted primarily through 'spot ads' introduced at 'natural breaks' in the programmes and *not*, as in the United States, by programme sponsorship. This separation of programme material from advertising allowed the term 'editorial television' to be used to describe a situation in which, despite gaining revenue from advertisers, the programme-makers could themselves claim to be free from commercial manipulation. Since a very large part of the campaign for the *prevention* of Commercial Television had drawn on examples illustrating the extent to which American programme material had been skewed in theme, content and treatment by direct commercial pressures,[11] this restriction to 'spot ads', coupled with the ITA idea, had the effect of undermining the 'anti' position in its most popular and self-evident aspects.

It was also clearly the case that the arguments of the 'anti' lobby, notably here those of the Labour Party, had not been much helped by Lord Reith's own statements on the matter. Reith had been the first Director-General of the BBC, and continued to play a role as the idiosyncratic and very strong-willed conscience of national broadcasting values. Giving evidence in 1950, before a Committee chaired by Lord Beveridge which was then investigating the future of broadcasting, he observed that:

> . . . it was the brute force of monopoly that had enabled the BBC to become what it did and to do what it did . . . if there is to be competition it will be of cheapness not of goodness.[12]

Subsequently, during the passage of the Bill through the House of Lords, he likened the arrival of commercial broadcasting to 'Smallpox, Bubonic Plague and the Black Death'.[13] Such an explicit and emphatic commitment to the promulgation of a single set of standards by the denial of choice had the effect of making it difficult for other arguments against competition to evade the taint of undemocratic élitism, a fact which Tory propagandists were quick to note in their liberationist claims to be 'setting television free'.[14] The Conservative MP Selwyn

Lloyd, himself a member of Beveridge's investigatory committee, had seized on this vulnerability in his own writings on the question. In a way which became influential in the later conduct of the debate, he placed Reith's unfortunate phrasing quite clearly in the context of primary political principles:

> I am not attracted by the idea of compulsory uplift achieved by 'the brute force of monopoly' to use Lord Reith's phrase. If people are to be trusted with the franchise, surely they should be able to decide for themselves whether they want to be educated or entertained in the evening?[15]

The arrival of competition radically altered the terms in which programmes were conceived of and scheduled, as many of the articles in this collection demonstrate in detail. It is worth noting, however, that the national networking system which became ITV's principle mode of operation had the effect of limiting this competition to being one between the network and the BBC, whereas much pro-ITV argument had focused on the benefits of inter-company *rivalry* to produce quality programmes for the network.[16] What had not been foreseen was the ease with which what had been planned as a mechanism of bracing, internal competition (the network) became a device for comfortable trade-offs.

Although it went through an early financial crisis in its launch phase (one which led to severe economies in production budgets and a reduction in serious outputs)[17], ITV soon proved a highly profitable and very popular option with viewers, whose numbers were now rising rapidly. The ownership or rental of a television set was, by 1956, passing through and out of the stage of being a marker of status within the working class. TV was on the way to becoming a standard feature of every home, re-structuring domestic patterns and social habits in a way which in some aspects resembled, but in others significantly departed from, the shaping influence which radio had exerted upon everyday life and household activities in an earlier period.

Senior BBC staff had been prepared for a drop to just under a 40 per cent share of the audience following the start of competition, considering that still to be sufficient to guarantee the continuation of the licence fee. But splits as dramatically low as 21/79 were cited for a short time (though not without debates as to method of calculation)[18], as new-style ITV entertainments attracted sections of the BBC's once captive audience. Even before competition began, some BBC producers had been alarmed by the possibility of being caught in a trap whereby inability to maintain a sizeable slice of the national audience would almost certainly lead to Conservative schemes to end the licence-fee system, or at least to reduce the level of support, while attempts by the BBC to retrieve their position by aggressively popular programming would lead to criticisms of it abandoning its national cultural responsibilities.[19] This would not be the last time that the BBC would be caught in the 'cleft' of the quality/popularity opposition, as assessed by dominant cultural criteria which it had, itself, done much to reinforce and propagate as a national and a 'natural' standard. Grace Wyndham Goldie, at that time a senior member of the BBC's Television Talks and Current Affairs Department, remembers the change in attitude which the new conditions necessitated on the part of at least some producers:

> A number of experienced television producers were then honourably – but perhaps a trifle myopically – mainly interested in creating programmes of cultural importance designed for minorities and it was vital that they should realise that unless their programmes were popular as well as valuable their chance of producing valuable programmes in the future might vanish altogether.[20]

Within the modified structures constituted by continuing (though reduced) economic and educational inequality, commercial expansionism and changing relations of social class and of cultural aspiration, the 'democratic' and the 'popular' began to be identified in new and sometimes conflicting ways within broadcasting. The Director of BBC Television, Gerald Beadle, addressing himself to the problem of the Corporation's falling ratings at the time, seemed to be working with an implicit view of the audience as unflattering as that which his competitors were accused of using when he noted that:

> The one big strategic weapon, the hydrogen bomb of television competition ... is the lowering of the proportion of intelligent programmes in main viewing hours below the level of one's competitor.[21]

He went on to remark, however, that this lowest common denominator 'hydrogen bomb' should not be used but that, instead, the BBC should strive to give expression 'to the advancing tastes and aspirations, or the perplexities, of an educated democracy in the making'.[22] It is interesting how this remark, despite its continuity with an established BBC ethos, adopts the reflective/expressive view of broadcasting rather than what was now the far more vulnerable cultural leadership perspective. It is also clear that the comment is in some degree of tension with his earlier assumptions about the *effectiveness* of the 'hydrogen bomb' plan.

The BBC's fight back, a slow one throughout the late 50s, was largely conducted through an increase in the output of television drama and the development of innovative forms of popular programming in a range of genres, 'serious' and 'light'. For instance, *Tonight*, an early evening news magazine presented by Cliff Michelmore, started in 1957 and quickly developed a regular audience of 8 million viewers.[23] This programme is significant, not only for the philosophy informing its development, but also for the shifts in journalistic modes of address it brought about. At the end of 1956, the Postmaster General allowed an extension of broadcasting hours and ended the so-called 'toddler's truce' – a period without transmissions from six to seven in the evenings. With this hour now available for scheduling, it became a focal point of the ratings war, since it was thought to be vital to the success of programmes later in the evening that viewers were tuned in early on the 'right' channel. The BBC's response was to allow an already successful programme unit under Donald Baverstock to develop the

Tonight idea as a daily opener to the BBC's evening offerings, running for fifty minutes and finishing at 6.55 pm.

Tonight (a title which, though relatively quiet, was clearly just about as immediate as it could be) contained a number of elements which show the re-articulation both of the notion of the viewer as citizen and of the category of the popular during this period. In relation to then dominant BBC conventions, it carried with it a projection of irreverence which was to be developed much further in the 1960s, as a number of pieces in this collection show. It mixed serious and light items – for instance, political interviews, filmed features, occasional sketches and topical calypsos – with unprecedented confidence. Baverstock commented later:

> The notion then that television programmes should be *either* serious *or* entertaining struck us as false and rather insulting to the audience.[24]

Perhaps most significantly of all, through its presenter Cliff Michelmore, the programme developed a modality of easy, familiar address which seemed to resonate perfectly with emerging ideas about social conventions and public values across a wide class spectrum. The eventual press response to him indicates something of the particular way in which the TV personality phenomenon, the assimilation of schedules within national domestic life and a broader shift in social and cultural values were interconnectedly at work. The *Evening Standard* called him the 'John Bull of the Small Screen', going on to note that:

> This avuncular pink-faced, middle-brow with middle-class accent, occasional squeak in the voice and mild-as-cocoa manner has a very warm place in the hearts of millions of Britons.[25]

A more precise, if also professionally prescriptive, account of the cultural relationships which the programme was seeking to make is offered by Grace Wyndham-Goldie:

> *Tonight* with Cliff Michelmore was rapidly becoming the voice of the people ... Such an identification between the public mood and a television programme does not happen by accident. All television producers must, to some extent, have an affinity with the public for which they are producing programmes. During the preparation and rehearsal of a programme they must wince where the public is bound to wince, they must resent condescension which the public is bound to resent ... But *Tonight* carried this normal requirement a stage further. *Every spoken word was scrutinised to ensure that it was part of the process of identification.* (my emphasis)[26]

This is, however, to take one programme, albeit a pivotal one in terms of mode of address, as an example of a more general development extending beyond the BBC's own productions (and such different but popular programmes as *Hancock's Half Hour* (1956), *Six-Five Special* (1957), David Attenborough's *Zoo*

Quest (1956) and *Grandstand* (1958)) to the ITV companies. It was, after all, these companies' efforts to seek out and capture new popular audiences which had largely instigated the shift in broadcasting's new sensitivity towards, and indeed anticipation of, popular culture in its class, regional and generational variety. It was not just a question of popular blockbusters like *Sunday Night at the London Palladium* (1955) or the bright and often condescendingly matey address of the game shows (such as *Take Your Pick* and *Double Your Money*). However loosely the companies chose to interpret their declared commitments to their regions, a stronger sense of different voices, of previously unaccessed experience, came through the filter of their programme formats than had hitherto managed to penetrate through the sieve of metropolitan-centredness which habitually, if unconsciously, was used by the BBC in fashioning its images of the nation. In ATV's Armchair Theatre, put out nationally from 1956, ITV brought about a decisive shift in the terms of serious drama too, scheduling in a regular slot one-off plays which had been conceived of, written and produced *as television* right from the start.[27]

Although, with the passing of the 1954 Act, the question of national television development had slid off the Parliamentary agenda, the appearance of the Pilkington Committee Report on Broadcasting in 1962 caused the cultural politics of broadcasting once more to become a major issue of public debate. The literary critic and cultural analyst, Richard Hoggart, was an influential member of the Committee. The Report's foregrounding of the emancipatory but also the exploitative potential of broadcasting within a broader framework addressing questions of social and educational inequality was picked up as controversial. And by openly opposing 'quality' to 'commerce' in many of its most considered formulations, it was actually controversial in a more focused and fundamental way than the debate about the introduction of ITV had been.[28]

In most respects the BBC (which had prepared long and thoroughly for the Committee) came out better than the Independent companies, whose representatives could not have expected, only six years after the success of the ITV launch, the thoroughgoing critique of commercial debasement which the Report contained. In a statement which uncompromisingly identified a gap between 'quality' and 'popularity', the Report noted that:

> The disquiet about, and dissatisfaction with, television are, in our view, justly attributed very largely to the service of independent television ... This is so despite the popularity of the service, and the well-known fact that many of its programmes command the largest audiences.[29]

As one might expect, there was a strong backlash both from the popular press, the ITV companies and many Conservative supporters. Peter Cadbury, Chairman of Westward Television, held a bonfire party at which the Report was burnt in effigy, while the *Daily Mirror* (an ATV shareholder) interpreted the Report's message thus: 'Pilkington tells the public to go to hell'. The *Daily Sketch* feared the approach of 'Big Brother' and noted, 'If they think you're enjoying yourself too much – well, they'll soon put a stop to that'. Perhaps the most emphatic piece of populist response came from the *Sunday Pictorial*'s columnist, Woodrow Wyatt (also a Labour MP), who converted the Report's language into a direct attack on the ordinary viewer:

> You 'trivial' people, to borrow the Pilkington Committee's favourite phrase. How dare you prefer watching commercial television to looking at what Auntie BBC so kindly provides for you? ... The ITV programmes are 'naughty' and 'bad' for you. They are produced by ordinary men and women who like the same things as you do ... Pilkington is out to stop all this rot about you being allowed to enjoy yourself ... You trivial people will have to brush up your culture.[30]

This piece of over-the-top ventriloquism nevertheless catches at the way in which the terms of the Pilkington Report, particularly the uses of 'trivial' and of 'moral', were far too easily reducible (albeit by conscious distortion) to the sort of explicit paternalism that could no longer find support or deference quite so available as might have been the case a decade earlier. In fact, I think in many ways the Pilkington Report can be seen to mark the last serious attempt (and possibly one of the first too!) to bridge the gap between the terms of parliamentary and public debate on national culture and the terms of a more analytically thorough-going cultural critique developing within the arts and social science disciplines of the universities. Despite its strength of humanistic social vision, it was a misguided project in many respects, intellectually flawed by its fudging of the political relationship between economic and cultural inequality and tactically flawed in the vulnerability of its tone and language. Though little legislation followed *directly* from its submission, the Report, together with the responses to it, nevertheless mark an important moment in the history of post-war national culture, revealing stress lines, fracture points and also convergences, with more than usual clarity and detail.[31]

The Director-General who had steered the BBC through Pilkington was Hugh Greene, appointed in 1960, and it was within the terms of his up-dated perspective on 'public service' television in a changed cultural climate that the innovative current affairs, drama and entertainment shows of the mid-60s appeared, some of which are referred to in the essays collected here.[32] These innovations cross-fertilised with the work of the major independent companies as the audience split became a more balanced one and as British television stabilised institutionally within the terms of 'duopoly'.

Having used this condensed and highly selective narrative to consider a few general features of the first decade of popular television in Britain, I want now to work briefly within the terms of a more focused conceptual agenda. Though this refers downwards to phenomena often inseparable within the social processes of TV's development, such a schema offers points of focus around which to organise analysis and theoretical inquiry of the kind pursued in the articles. Four themes which I think have this kind of usefulness are Institution and Culture, World and Home, Schedule and Genre and Value and Popularity. Each is a couplet which, while not indicating a straight opposition, catches at a tension – the precise

10

articulation of which seems to take analysis directly into questions about British television and cultural change.

Institution and Culture

The relationship obtaining in broadcasting between cultural producers, artefacts and audiences is, both at the present time and during the period with which this study is concerned, one heavily mediated by institutional factors. In this respect, television clearly has something of the bureaucratic cultural character of sound broadcasting and may be contrasted with the other principal media of industrialised public culture – the press and cinema – in its degree of vertical integration. The very high costs of producing television, the distribution directly into the home via the airwaves, the organisation around service, schedule and channel rather than discrete programme, all these have served to make television's relation to national cultural life one which has been administratively overseen, and indeed 'policed', at a number of levels. Some of the Kafkaesque undertones around the BBC's hallowed maxim for producers of 'referral upwards' connect with this sense of a multi-layered filtering process not likely to provide too much by way of accident, chance and risk.

Under Lord Reith, the first Director-General, the BBC was quickly regarded, both by itself and by many members of the political and artistic establishment, as an 'embassy of the national culture', one with weighty constitutional obligations.[33] Reith's zealous bureaucratic ambitions for using sound radio as an instrument for national improvement were caught, like many similar ambitions, across the contradictions between what were in practice the very different improving perspectives of top-down cultural management on the one hand ('promulgating standards') and, on the other, of an emancipatory accessing of voices and releasing of energies from below. The two approaches sometimes became fused in a distinctively British (Arnoldian–Leavisian) discourse of *cultural enlightenment* which, in its defining contradictions, might be characterised as the didactic-emancipatory (and to which Selwyn Lloyd's deft critical phrase about 'compulsory uplift' damagingly refers).

Not surprisingly, given the political overdeterminations at work, cultural management tended to win, at least in overall institutional tendency if not always in achieved consequence. Although the terms of this discourse continue to haunt British liberalism's (and part of the British Left's) perspectives on the arts, education and the whole concept of a public realm, in its Reithian version it could not survive for long in the post-war cultural climate. Certainly, after the loss of the BBC monopoly, its time was up. Even its very translatability from the terms of address of radio to those of television may be questioned, without thereby falling into technological essentialism.

After the introduction of competition in 1955 there was, as noted earlier, an important de-metropolitanisation of broadcasting as 'regional' cities such as Manchester, Birmingham (and later) Newcastle, Plymouth, and Norwich became production centres, as also did Glasgow, Cardiff and Belfast. This devolutionary effect was to some extent offset by the extensive networking agreements which the 'Big Four' ITV companies worked out and which inevitably led to an emphasis on programme-making which could deliver a large national audience to advertisers. Towards this end, successful US models of TV entertainment (*I Love Lucy* featured on the cover of the first edition of the Independent network's *TV Times*) were as important as indigenous, local variety. Both had the effect of shifting the nation's nightly viewing further away from paternalist framings, towards that enticement and satisfaction of viewer pleasures which were, for the new network, *institutionally* necessary for survival.

World and Home

Although radio had preceded it in many of its 'public sphere' functions, television reworked the relations between the 'public' and the 'private' which sound broadcasting had installed at the heart of polity and culture. It was a further, crucial contribution to that privatisation of leisure which a number of commentators have identified as an accelerated cultural tendency in post-war Britain.[34] Central to this reworking was, of course, its apparent capacity to *show* people what was happening rather than to mediate it through spoken description. The combined advantages over radio (vision) and cinema (liveness) gave a uniquely high level of 'co-presence' to television programming, the viewer often being put in the position of a witness, *alongside* the broadcasters, to the anterior realities depicted on the screen. Programmes varied in the extent to which this electronic magic was fantasy-framed as a journey (taking the viewer, armchair and all, on a trip 'out there'), or, conversely, as an act of delivery (the exotic, the exciting and the previously unrecorded brought into your own front room). The former mode is well illustrated in this comment from the *Radio Times* in 1955:

> People want to be taken everywhere, so we take them there. During this year's General Election we took you to 20 different points in one night. We have even taken you underground, into ships at sea and even to see aircraft flying on and off a carrier at sea ... The next on the list is submarines.[35]

Starting in 1953, the BBC's *Panorama* was content with the relatively modest and conventional metaphoric status of a 'weekly window on the world'.

Just as the viewer contemplated the various 'worlds' passing before the camera lens from her or his own separate space, that of the living-room, so the broadcasters at regular intervals appeared to contemplate them from a matching space, the space of the studio, with its times co-extensive with the 'night's viewing'. The possibilities for relaxed informality, for a rhetoric of *understatement*, of the *self-evident* and the *implicitly shared* ('Usness') which this gave to broadcasters in a range of genres immediately extended beyond those of radio. Although there was much awkwardness in developing an appropriately broad domestic register to start with, the success of *Tonight* indicates how powerfully television could employ its immediacy and intimacy to construct the terms of a new *sociability*. Within this, the modalities of the authoritative, the expert, or even just the informative, could no longer be voiced as they had been within the established conventions of sound broadcasting. The emergence of the TV 'personality' testifies more broadly to the stronger personalisms of the newer medium's

12

conventions, which nevertheless remain anchored in the ongoing flow of mundane realities in a manner which contrasts with cinematic 'stardom'. Television's newly familiar mediations were still predominantly male and middle class however, and though certain programme genres (and advertising too) had developed distinctive and new styles of gendered address, daytime transmission schedules did not yet have the space to court, and in part to construct, a 'housewife' audience in the way that had become central to radio.

Schedule and Genre

The terms Schedule and Genre indicate key, interconnected determinants of television form. The institutional strategy of scheduling identifies particular times of the day and particular sequences of programming in order to obtain either specific kinds of audience or the broadest possible audience and to obtain the best audience responses. It locates particular programme elements and ideas within a broader plan of competitive provision, published well in advance and then perhaps reinforced verbally by early evening continuity announcers in terms of an invited look at 'what's in store tonight'.[36] During the period covered by the articles collected here, the scheduling of television not only became a principal strategic component of the battle for ratings, but it also became more rigid, anchored around fixed slots in which regular programmes (notably here, domestic drama serials) could be found. The case of *Tonight* is once again instructive. Wyndham Goldie comments on the nature of the thinking that lay behind this way of filling the gap left by the ending of the 'toddler's truce,' mentioned earlier:

> Any such project would have to be related to our assessment of what viewers would be likely to be doing between 6 pm and 7 pm. We made inquiries. They would be coming and going: women getting meals for teenagers who were going out and preparing supper for husbands who were coming in; men in the North would be having their tea; Commuters in the South would be arriving home.[37]

The schedule set up a nightly and weekly framework of expectations, and within this outer framework the conventions of genre exerted a more specific shaping pressure. A primary factor in the formation of generic styles was the search for the distinctively 'televisual', which perhaps worked from cinematic, theatrical, radio, newspaper or music-hall precedents, but which then reshaped the material in ways which used the medium to best possible advantage. The following essays refer to examples of this quest (in some measure a shift from an early emphasis on television as a relay *device* to television as a separate *cultural form*) in respect of drama, sport, documentary and 'light entertainment', including situation comedy. Generic development involved the application of a distinctive televisual aesthetics, with consequent, prescriptive ideas about types of shot (the close-up, for instance, becoming a standard shot across a whole range of output), about studio/location combinations, about appropriate kinds of editing and about the use of speech and music.

Many of these conventions (and the experiments which sometimes flouted them with great success) can be related back directly to *technological* possibilities. Much television, including drama, was necessarily transmitted and edited live until the end of the 50s, with telerecording transfer to film used occasionally to preserve an item.[38] Of course, 'liveness', though in many respects a *limitation* on representational range and style, was also a grounding feature of the medium's whole social ethos – connecting with the values of immediacy and spontaneity and also serving to sustain that congenial co-temporality between institution and audience which I have referred to earlier. Much news and documentary material was necessarily shot on film of course, even if placed within a 'live' format, though unfortunately for media historians that does not guarantee its subsequent survival. Not until the early 60s did videotape, with the pre-recording and the new editing possibilities it brought with it, start radically to extend the options for studio-based work. The introduction of much lighter (16mm) film cameras into television at around the same time, if not a little earlier, ushered in a similar opening-up of generic potential for documentary and news teams.

Value and Popularity

As I suggested earlier in this introduction, television's move to national centrality during its first dozen years or so of post-war broadcasting is largely the result of its role as the principal agency of a reconstructed, commercially-driven popular culture and as the mediator, exemplar and dramatiser of a new welfarist egalitarianism.[39] As both an industry and as a purveyor of arts old and new – offering a dispersed, casual *confirmation* of a collective culture, while addressing viewers in their relaxed, individualised domesticity – it could not help but bring fundamental tensions and contradictions within the established cultural system into high visibility. After the war, BBC sound broadcasting had tiered its channels into the Home Service, the Light Programme and the Third Programme. This measure (controversial within the BBC and, it might be noted, opposed by Reith, now retired) was not designed simply to 'stream out' listeners, since it was assumed that many members of the audience would certainly switch between 'Home' and 'Light', if not the 'Third', during the course of the listening week. Indeed the Director-General at the time, Sir William Haley, in keeping with his belief in the Corporation's continuing cultural mission, hoped the system would 'lead the listener on to more serious things' and a 'move up the cultural scale'.[40]

Nevertheless, this was a shift away from the committed mixed-programming policy which Reith had seen as an essential part of broadcasting's project of *improvement*. In giving 'high culture' its own channel, it reduced scheduling tensions and 'taste' crossfire from listeners in a way that TV, technologically and economically, if not also for reasons of principle, could not do. With its requirements for audience maximisation, even ITV had problems negotiating the class-taste minefield on those occasions when, if only because it was under requirement to do so, it broadcast concerts and classic drama in 'majority' slots. Peter Black[41] records that when Halle concerts were networked in the late 50s, the BBC picked up a *further* 42 per cent of the viewers. He also notes the occasion when Associated Rediffusion networked *Hamlet* at eight in the evening and

14

ended up with 10 per cent of the viewers by 8.20 pm. These viewers were not terribly well served, as it happens, since the production overran and eventually had to be faded out to allow space for the commercials!

In 1956, as I have indicated earlier, there were severe cash-flow problems for some ITV companies after the capital costs of the launch. This brought a reduction in anything other than audience-building output.[42] Sections of the press dubbed the reductions a 'Retreat From Culture'. In response both to financial difficulties and criticism of the modified output, Roland Gillet, the Controller of Programmes at Associated Rediffusion, produced something of a *locus classicus* on television's view of public taste:

> Let's face it once and for all. The public likes girls, wrestling, bright musicals, quiz shows and real-life drama. We gave them the Halle orchestra, Foreign Press Club, floodlit football and visits to the local fire station. Well, we've learned. From now on, what the public wants, it's going to get.[43]

ITV could not, within the commercial logics then underpinning it, go too far beyond material having a ready appeal to a large audience, though it is important to note that this still included a number of programmes which received widespread critical acclaim as well as high ratings. In the sphere of TV journalism, the 'quality/popular' split was far less of a problem. Given the very late and uncertain development of BBC television news services, ITN was able very quickly to gain a wide-spectrum audience,[44] while current affairs and documentary programmes from the companies were able to develop in an atmosphere relatively free of the taste conventions troubling discussion of drama and entertainment.

Anxiety that emerging trends in television fare might somehow lull or divert the audience into acquiescence, as pliable members of the 'admass', carried speculative plausibility only if certain programmes (for instance game shows) were taken to be 'typical' television and their influence over viewers' attitudes assumed to be virtually total. A ritual denigration of television culture – 'goggle box', 'idiot's lantern', even perhaps the affectionate diminutive 'telly' – carried anxiety through into popular cultural speech, though here perhaps it is television's dangers as a time-waster rather than as a cultural debaser which are implicitly criticised.[45] Certainly, the commanding economics of ITV and of competition were those of Tory 'Enterprise', and though there were no *simple* consequences for the cultural character of the output, the overall accent on the viewer's consumptional aspirations and the direct connection with commodity transaction, were undeniably a long way from the terms in which the post-war socialist project had been cast. Unargued prejudices of taste and a comprehensive dislike of the 'vulgar' and the 'commercial' nevertheless often got in the way of clear critical analysis[46] and the suggestion of alternatives, leaving objectors ducking and weaving their way around charges of élitist paternalism, while those responsible for the bright new turn in television output claimed to be the harbingers of true cultural democracy.

In criticisms of the newer style of programming, there was often an inflexible use of high art values, emphasising the cognitively challenging or the morally exploratory in ways which completely ignored the class-grounded, experiential realities of *work*, in relation to which most of the population were likely to respond to opportunities for relaxation and leisure. The gap between the middle-class, professional culture in which most arguments about 'manipulation' were produced and the one in which many viewers lived gave many pronouncements about exploitation an insecure foundation. It also played into the hands of those who, in bad faith or otherwise, could speak more straightforwardly of pleasure.

Studies in Programme Culture

The studies which follow interconnect within the broad, emerging framework of British television culture as I have described it above. At points, of course, the writers place different and sometimes conflicting emphases in interpreting the shape and direction of programming and of cultural change. The idea of the book was, as far as possible, to avoid too broad an overview perspective in the chapters and, instead, to encourage a focus on specific programmes or series. This, it was hoped, would bring out not only something of the textuality and address of early television, but also the detail of interconnection between the industry, its generically-defined products and the shifts and contradictions at work in the broader culture.

The first six chapters offer case-studies in the early stages of TV's generic development as a popular medium. John Caughie explores the emerging terms of TV and drama, plotting its earliest cultural positioning in relation to the theatre, and also to cinema. This involves a concern with technological factors and their influence on the emergence of a television aesthetics, within whose terms 'liveness' became central. Caughie looks back at pre-war television in his tracing of the formation of TV drama and, like other contributors, he also connects outwards from generic form to questions of scheduling and the conditions of domestic viewing. As well as much else, in looking at the formation of TV as a commodity form (with the shift towards a pre-recorded and marketable product), his account offers an engaging agenda of issues for further research into both institutional and aesthetic history.

I have attempted to follow through some interrelationships between the technological and the cultural in my account of dominant strands in early documentary television. Here, I have used interviews with prominent documentary directors of the 1950s to develop an analytic commentary which is particularly concerned with the variety of ways in which the recorded voice was used both in journalistic and more freely impressionistic styles of film-making. This involves consideration both of the function which documentaries were given within the television system and the opening up of aesthetic range which technological advances and the requirement to address new kinds of audience brought with them.

Andy Medhurst places the focus on television as a culturally transformative new medium of home entertainment in his study of Gilbert Harding – one of the first British TV celebrities as a result of his appearances on *What's My Line?*, beginning in 1951. Medhurst explores why key aspects of Harding's persona projected so positively into contemporary popular sensibility (in particular, his style of rudeness). He also examines how Harding finally became a victim, not only of his own fame, but of the pressures and hostile inquisitiveness that were a dominant response to his homosexuality.

Peter Goddard's study of Tony Hancock connects at several points with Medhurst's discussion. Goddard is concerned not only to bring out elements of the distinctive Hancock 'character' in their formation within narrative and performance style, but also to note the extent to which a number of major shifts in production method were introduced during the run of Hancock's TV show from 1956. Among these was the use of videotape and, as a consequence, the emergence of a wholly new approach to the structure and scripting of situation comedy.

John Hill's essay looks at the importance of television for the projection of popular music as a key aspect of youth culture from the mid-50s. These early forms of music television were often planned to form a bridge between the broader family audience and the younger fan, often leading to uncertainty of treatment. Across detailed references to the more significant of the shows (such as *Six-Five Special* (1957), *Oh Boy* (1958) and *Juke Box Jury* (1959)), Hill shows how presentational forms and terms of address rapidly developed, as television became central to the industry and culture of British pop.

Joy Leman also takes classic examples of popular television, the three *Quatermass* series (1953, 1955 and 1958) and *A for Andromeda* (1961), in a study which inquires into the relations between gender and genre (in this case, science-fiction), and also offers a cultural comparison across the mid-50s and the early 60s. Her discussion of the *Quatermass* programmes brings out very interestingly the gendered nature of their discourse on 'intuition' and 'emotions', while her treatment of the *Andromeda* series provides a fascinating analysis of its highly innovative but often contradictory projections of 'new womanhood'.

The next two studies look at two highly important series of the early 60s, each in their very different ways having a controversial character projected in surrounding publicity and debate. Stuart Laing develops a detailed account of the emergence and development of *Z cars* (starting in 1962), as a series with a new kind of (documentary) realism and a new representation both of policemen and of policework. Drawing on comments from those involved in the project, he traces the tension between the initial nature of the series as documentary-drama (comparison here with *Coronation Street*, starting a year or so earlier, is interesting) and its developing profile as a kind of workplace 'soap'. In this generic swing, the characterisation of the police, and then of the surrounding community, underwent a shift which significantly modified the terms of the programme's projection of social realities.

Andrew Crisell examines the case of *That Was The Week that Was* (also starting in 1962) and links its remarkable success in providing popular television satire not only to shifts in general social attitude, but also to literary and theatrical developments. Crisell is sceptical about some of the grander claims made for satire as an effective tool of political and social criticism, but his account illustrates well the degree of social, as well as stylistic, thinking which went into the

17

planning of the programme. The quite radical reworking of modes of address which this programme crystallised, in terms of its relationship both with the wider sphere of broadcasting and with its audiences, is well brought out.

The three final studies also ground their analyses in the developments of the first decade of popular television, but have a broader thematic sweep which sometimes connects with more recent history.

Tim O'Sullivan's study of television audience memories is a very useful complement to that current strand of media research which seeks to investigate the domestic character of television viewing in ethnographic detail. O'Sullivan draws attention not only to the way in which television altered the physical space of the home, but also to its function in organising mundane time (the day, the weekly cycle, the weekend) around its schedules. Using an agenda partly drawing on some of the more recent audience studies, O'Sullivan is able to connect back with formative moments in those World/Home and Genre/Schedule relationships to which I referred earlier.

Garry Whannel offers a wide-ranging account of television's treatment of sport, referring particularly to the BBC's *Sportsview* (starting in 1954) and *Grandstand* (starting in 1958). He shows how competition brought with it a search for new formats and how the continuing need to appeal both to the sports fan and to the family audience (here echoing the double appeal required by pop music programmes) shaped these formats. Whannel sets his discussions of programme form within the framework of his research on the kinds of contractual relationship which developed between broadcasting institutions and sporting bodies in their search for mutual benefits.

Finally, Ed Buscombe looks at the early mutual hostility between television and the cinema industry, going on to analyse how feature films achieved their present dominance in the schedules. He compares the situation in Britain to that in the United States, where a different relationship between the two industries prevailed. The implications of these industrial tensions, indeed of open economic conflict, for the development of a distinctive television aesthetics are examined, thus connecting back to several earlier studies in the volume which explore the grounds of televisual specificity – both institutionally and formally.

It will be obvious that this is not an attempt at some comprehensive account of programmes during the period. Within a general editorial sense of 'fair spread', contributors have written on topics which they have found particularly engaging and which in many cases relate to their previous research interests. There are many gaps. Some of these are in areas which have already received a little attention in other publications (for example, the development of television 'soaps' and the centrality here of *Coronation Street*, broadcast from 1960; the drama-documentary debate and the controversies around *Cathy Come Home* (1966) and the banning of *The War Game*).[47] Other topics, those for instance to do with the development of news programmes, of talk shows, of childrens' television and of variety formats, would reward the pioneer researcher. It is to be hoped that access to the primary materials for such study will become easier in the next few years. And if this book helps to promote a wider critical interest in the cultural history of broadcasting, thereby increasing the pressure for the greater availability of archive material in teaching and research, the contributors will be well satisfied.

Notes

1. John Hill, *Sex Class and Realism: British Cinema 1956–63* (London: BFI, 1986), p. 5. The citation is from Pinto-Duschinsky 'Bread and Circuses? The Conservatives in Office, 1951–64', in Bogdanor and Skidelsky (eds.), *The Age of Affluence: 1951–1964* (London: Macmillan, 1970), p. 7. Hill's introductory chapter, 'British Society 1956–63' offers a very useful cultural survey. See also Arthur Marwick, *British Society since 1945* (Harmondsworth: Penguin, 1982) for a more general examination of social and cultural change. Stuart Laing's *Representations of Working Class Life 1957–1964* (London: Macmillan, 1986) is another, more focused, discussion of key themes in post-war culture which, as well as having an excellent preliminary chapter, 'This New England', also concerns itself with developments in television.

2. An exception here is Paddy Scannell's and David Cardiff's work on the cultural history of radio. See, for instance, their pioneering work on wartime British radio in the published units for Open University Course U203, Popular Culture, (Milton Keynes: Open University Press, 1981).

3. The Broadcasting Bill, 1989. At the time of writing, this bill is still in committee and the future of many of its measures remains uncertain due, among other things, to the anxieties expressed by MPs from both sides of the house about the implications for 'quality' of the proposed systems of funding and regulation.

4. These figures are taken from Asa Briggs, *The History of Broadcasting in the United Kingdom, Volume 4: Sound and Vision* (Oxford: Oxford University Press, 1979), p. 245.

5. See H. H. Wilson, *Pressure Group: The Campaign for Commercial Television* (London: Secker and Warburg, 1961), p. 109 on the circulation of this document among Conservative MPs at a later stage in the Parliamentary debate over the introduction of ITV.

6. Asa Briggs, *The BBC: The First Fifty Years* (Oxford: Oxford University Press, 1985), p. 241. Until the publication of Volume Five of Briggs' *History of Broadcasting in the United Kingdom*, this one-volume study remains the most useful source for the period with which I am concerned here, and I have therefore preferred to make it the primary reference for this introduction, even where the material is also to be found in the later chapters of his *Sound and Vision*.

7. See the diagram in Briggs, *The BBC*, p. 167.

8. Briggs, *The BBC*, p. 275.

9. A very useful discussion of these measures is to be found in Peter Black, *The Mirror In the Corner* (London: Hutchinson, 1972), pp. 45–47. This is in many respects an invaluable analysis of the transition from monopoly to competition in British television. On the nature of the 'compromise' involved here, see also H. H. Wilson, *Pressure Group*, pp. 188–90.

10. Briggs, *The BBC*, p. 286.

11. An example of this is Christopher Mayhew's pamphlet *Dear Viewer* (London: Lincolns Prager, 1953). It offers examples of the problems which follow from advertisers' direct involvement in programme-making.

12. *Report of the Broadcasting Committee 1949* (Cmnd 8116), (London: HMSO, 1951), Appendix H, p. 364. This Committee produced the 'Beveridge Report' on broadcasting in January 1951, a report which concluded that there was no good reason to break

the BBC monopoly. However, there were delays in implementing its recommendations for reform of BBC operations and the Conservative General Election victory in October changed the whole agenda for the discussion of broadcasting's future. See H. H. Wilson, *Pressure Group*, chs. III and IV for a clear and detailed account.

13. *House of Lords Debates*, 176: 1297 (22 May 1952).

14. This was one of the expressed aims of the Popular Television Association, formed in July 1953 as a campaigning group for commercial television. See Wilson, *Pressure Group*, pp. 170–71.

15. *Report of the Broadcasting Committee 1949*. Minority Report submitted by Selwyn Lloyd, p. 205.

16. See Black, *Mirror*, p. 74 on this and also the full account in B. Sendall, *Independent Television in Britain Volume I: Origin and Foundation 1946–62* (London: Macmillan 1982), pp. 303–16.

17. See B. Sendall, *Independent Television Volume I*, pp. 326–29 for the nature of this and company responses to it in terms of revised programming.

18. Black, *Mirror*, p. 108. However, see James Curran and Jean Seaton, *Power Without Responsibility* (London: Routledge, Third Edition, 1988), pp. 178–179 for an account of why cited figures are often unreliable due to the BBC and ITV adopting different methods of counting the audience. The result of this is an exaggeration of BBC 'losses' to ITV.

19. Grace Wyndham Goldie, *Facing the Nation: Broadcasting and Politics 1936–76* (London: Bodley Head, 1977) offers a useful account of how this 'trap' was perceived by her BBC colleagues. See, particularly, pp. 110–11.

20. Goldie, *Facing the Nation*, p. 111.

21. Briggs, *The BBC*, p. 302.

22. Briggs, *The BBC*, p. 302.

23. Much of the data on *Tonight* presented here is taken from the excellent Gordon Watkins (ed.), *BFI Dossier 15: Tonight* (London: BFI, 1982) and particularly from the substantial study within it, '*Tonight*: a Short History' by Diedre Macdonald.

24. Watkins, *Tonight*, p. 18.

25. Watkins, *Tonight*, p. 29.

26. Goldie, *Facing the Nation*, p. 217.

27. See John Caughie, 'Broadcasting and Cinema: 1: Converging Histories' in Charles Barr (ed.), *All Our Yesterdays* (London: BFI 1986), p. 196 for comments on this in relation to the broader question of British 'public service' broadcasting.

28. See the discussion of this in Black, *Mirror*, Chapter 11 as well as in Briggs, *The BBC*, pp. 320–30. Sendall, *Independent Television Volume 2: Expansion and Change* (London: Macmillan, 1983) offers a useful account of the Report's main findings in Part II 'Grand Remonstrance', pp. 85–133. See also the brief, critical survey in Chapter 12 of James Curran and Jean Seaton, *Power Without Responsibility*, pp. 185–92.

29. *Report of the Committee on Broadcasting 1960* (Cmnd 1753) (London: HMSO, 1962), para. 209, p. 68.

30. All newspaper quotations are taken from the selection given in Stuart Hall and Paddy Whannel, *The Popular Arts* (London: Hutchinson, 1964), pp. 428–29.

31. Laing brings out the educational context of anxiety about commercial television, an anxiety which informed the Pilkington Committee's thinking, in Laing, *Representations*, Chapter 7.

32. See Michael Tracey, *A Variety of Lives* (London: Bodley Head, 1983) for a detailed account of Greene's broadcasting career, including his response to Pilkington and his direction of television's development in the 1960s.

33. For a well-documented and thoughtful treatment of Reithian philosophy see Paddy Scannell and David Cardiff, 'Serving the Nation: Public Service Broadcasting Before the War' in B. Waites, T. Bennett and G. Martin (eds.), *Popular Culture: Past and Present* (London: Croome Helm, 1982).

34. See, for instance, Raymond Williams, *Television, Technology and Cultural Form* (London: Fontana, 1974), p. 26.

35. Editorial in the *Radio Times*, 16 September 1955.

36. For an excellent discussion of scheduling as an institutional practice which is determined by a number of social variables see Richard Paterson, 'Planning the Family: The Art of the Television Schedule', in *Screen Education* no. 35, 1980.

37. Goldie, *Facing the Nation*, p. 210.

38. See Denis Norden, Sybil Harper and Norma Gilbert, *Coming To You Live*, (London: Methuen, 1985) for a informative, if celebratory, account of the production of 'live' television during this period. Steve Bryant, *The Television Heritage* (London: BFI, 1989) provides a useful survey of technological factors affecting live and recorded television in the course of examining the reasons for television's cultural ephemerality, and as part of the case he puts forward for a national television archive. Many of the essays which follow in this collection refer to the live/recorded distinction and its implications for TV aesthetics and working practices.

39. Raymond Williams' widely-cited comments about the way in which television has helped to bring about a 'dramatized society' are pertinent here. See Raymond Williams, 'Drama in a Dramatised Society' in Alan O'Connor (ed.), *Raymond Williams on Television* (London: Routledge, 1989), pp. 3–13.

40. See Briggs, *The BBC*, p. 244.

41. Peter Black, *Mirror*, p. 109. Another useful account of the 'culture of competition' to put alongside Black's is Milton Shulman, *The Least Worst Television in the World* (London: Barrie and Jenkins, 1973). Shulman, like Black, was a TV columnist with a degree of 'insider' knowledge of the industry and his account substantially overlaps with that of Black, while nevertheless having complementary points of focus and an interest in developments through to the 'Franchise Politics' of the late 1960s.

42. On this period of financial uncertainty, referred to earlier, see Sendall, *Independent Television Volume 1*, pp. 326–29. Full accounts of the financial problems as they affected each company are given in pp. 183–200.

43. Quoted in Sendall, *Independent Television Volume 1*, p. 328. Garry Whannel relates this sentiment to sports programming policy in one of the articles in this present volume, '*Grandstand*, the Sports Fan and the Family Audience'.

44. See Briggs, *The BBC*, pp. 306–7, and Black, *Mirror*, pp. 116–18.

45. The values and assumptions at work in cultural disparagement of television were sometimes given expression in the popular cinema. See Charles Barr, 'Broadcasting and Cinema: 2: Screens within Screen' in Barr (ed.), *All our Yesterdays*, pp. 206–25.

46. See Anthony Crosland, 'The Mass Media' in *Encounter*, November 1962 for a perceptive and polemical analysis of the political and cultural character of television, prompted by a reading of the Pilkington Report. In particular, Crosland's address to the problems of 'taste' in relation to democracy and to the whole question of media power seem, for the period, uncharacteristically direct and self-questioning.

47. See, for instance, the excellent essays in Richard Dyer *et al*, *Television Monograph 13: Coronation Street* (London: British Film Institute, 1981) and those on drama-documentary developments in Andrew Goodwin and Paul Kerr (eds.), *BFI Dossier 19: Drama Documentary* (London: British Film Institute, 1983).

Before the Golden Age
Early Television Drama

JOHN CAUGHIE

The first regularly scheduled television programme service from the London Television Station of the BBC began on 2 November 1936. To viewers within an approximate radius of twenty-five miles from its production centre in Alexandra Palace, it offered broadcasts six days a week (excluding Sundays) for one hour in the afternoon (3–4 pm) and one hour in the evening (9–10 pm). Many of the items in the evening schedule were live repeats of the same item in the afternoon: thus *The Golden Hind*, transmitted 3.25–3.40 pm on 3 November 1936 – 'A model of Drake's famous ship made by L. A. Stock, a bus driver, who will describe its construction' – was repeated live at 9.25–9.40 pm the same evening, when L. A. Stock returned to the studio and described the model's construction again. On 5 November, a twenty-five minute afternoon performance by Marie Rambert's Mercury Ballet was performed again in the evening. But on 6 November, *From the London Theatre*, a twenty-five minute item in the afternoon schedule featuring Sophie Stewart in scenes from the Royalty Theatre production of *Marigold*, 'A Scottish comedy by Allen Harker and F. R. Pryor', was not repeated in the evening, presumably because Sophie Stewart was performing at the time in the Royalty Theatre.

It is worth beginning from these beginnings, partly to establish the pattern of live performances and live repeats which was to be central to the early formation of television drama, but partly also to compensate for the very short recall of television in which history tends to begin with recorded programmes.

For the week beginning 23 October 1936, the *Radio Times* published a 'Special Television Issue', featuring an article by Gerald Cock, the first Director of Television, with the title, 'Looking Forward: a personal forecast of the future of television'. In this article, Cock ruminates on the questions which he had asked himself when offered the job, and admits to doubts about 'the chances of "selling" the idea of television to a public already satiated with entertainment'. In projecting the future (it is not clear by how far), he suggests:

> We are entitled to imagine that programme hours would still be few – perhaps four a day – and that they would be confined to events of outstanding interest and entertainment value, for television will, I think, mean the end of 'background listening'. (p.6).

For television drama he foresees extracts rather than the single play, not as a temporary technological constraint, but as the essential and logical form for a medium which was more concerned with the dissemination of information than with the dissemination of narrative entertainment or the production of art:

> ... for, in my view, television is from its very nature, more suitable for the dissemination of all kinds of information than for entertainment as such, since it can scarcely be expected to compete successfully with films in that respect. Nevertheless, the lighter forms of entertainment will certainly have their place. (p.7).

And he takes this view to its logical conclusions:

> ... I believe viewers would rather see an actual scene of a rush hour at Oxford Circus directly transmitted to them than the latest in film musicals costing £100,000 – though I do not expect to escape unscathed with such an opinion. (p.7)

The view of television which emerges from Cock's predictions can be approached, not as a naively primitive misunderstanding of the medium, but as exemplary of a number of assumptions and uncertainties about the function of television which were formative in the early decades. Part of the argument of this essay is that these uncertainties cast residual shadows, stretching into the present, within the discourses which still surround television drama.

Most apparent, right at the moment at which television first appears, is the assertion of immediacy, liveness and the direct transmission of live action as both an essential characteristic and an aesthetic virtue of the medium rather than as mere technological necessity. The concept of immediacy is of continuing importance to television theory, and the 'immediacy-effect' (the process by which it moves from essentialism to effect will be one of the topics of this essay) is widely regarded as a defining characteristic of British television. Certainly, the term and its derivatives are continuous within the professional discourses which describe television drama. The effect of immediacy, of a directness which signifies authenticity, is one of the characteristics which gives British television drama its specific form – still, at the beginning of the 90s, distinguishing it from cinema or from the American telefilm.

Also significant within Cock's casual prognostication is an uncertainty around the competing claims of the 'dissemination of all kinds of information', 'entertainment as such', and 'the lighter forms of entertainment'. For the postwar period in which the BBC promoted itself as an instrument (if not *the* instrument) of national cultural reconstruction, the competing claims of entertainment and information within public service account for some of the suspicion with which television was regarded by BBC management. Television, it seems to have been felt, might err a little on the side of entertainment. Notably, however (and, in the 90s, somewhat ironically), information is privileged by Cock, not out of a

Reithian reverence, but out of a recognition of the greater popular appeal of cinema.

Cock recognizes, too, anticipating future theoretical debates, a form of attention specific to television, distinct from both film and radio, which, for him, imposes limits on the number of hours which properly should be available for scheduling, and the kinds of event appropriate to the schedules (though it is hard to square his insistence on programmes of 'outstanding interest and entertainment value' with the early love of demonstration items such as *The Handy Man*, in which 'J.T. Baily will demonstrate how to repair a broken window.')

Strikingly, many of the early uncertainties about the function of television echo uncertainties which had been experienced forty years before by cinema. The pioneers of cinema, too, had debated whether the new invention was to be merely a fairground attraction or an item of vaudeville entertainment, and the same doubts were expressed about the capacity of moving pictures to captivate an audience whose desire for entertainment was already satiated by a still popular live theatre. Was the new medium to be for the dissemination of information or for entertainment as such? Was it to record scenes and events from the real world or to tell stories? The early history of cinema, and the historiography of early cinema, record the various resolutions of these uncertainties.

Though they are clearly labelled as 'personal', then, Cock's assumptions and uncertainties point to questions not simply about the history of early television, but about the way the history of television is to be written. What I want to suggest is that the danger of starting the history too late, with, say, the beginnings of the regular recording of programmes, is that we miss the formative stages in which the practices of language and form are still unstable, in which institutional practices are experimental rather than routine, in which 'good television' still has to learn to be 'good', and in which that particular 'goodness' is only one of a number of possibilities. Much of the most productive recent work in cinema history, with important repercussions within film theory, has been informed by tracing the paths by which cinema moved through the 'primitive' towards what Noel Burch calls the 'Institutional Mode of Representation' or what Bordwell, Staiger and Thompson call the 'Classical Hollywood Cinema'.[1] While television belongs to a very different set of histories and practices (which call into question, for instance, whether something like a 'classical' television could exist), nevertheless the historical method which seeks to piece together the steps by which practices become routines seems to offer a way of understanding some of the working assumptions which persist long after the conditions which legitimated them have withered away.

I am interested, then, in a quite preliminary way, in the period before the more publicised and recoverable Golden Age, because it seems to me to be there that we can see some of the indecisions and decisions which came to define what television was, how it should look, and, crucially, how it should circulate.

Clearly, there is a difficulty. While cinema historians have a continuous, though incomplete, history of films from the 1890s, television has a pre-history in which programmes themselves do not exist in recorded form. Transcription, or recording television on film, was not developed till 1947, and recording on tape was technologically possible first in the US in 1953, and was probably not readily available in Britain till around 1958. Neither was in routine use till the 60s, and even when recording was possible there is a long chain of missing links which have been wiped from the record either to reuse the tapes or to save storage space (one-inch Ampex took up a lot of room). This makes the recovery of the early history of television form and style an archaeological, rather than a strictly historical procedure.

This, however, is not simply an historiographic problem, or an academic alibi: theatre scholars have, after all, a fair idea of what Shakespeare's Globe looked like, or what the conventions of acting were in nineteenth-century melodrama. What I will be using here to try to fill in this gap will be the fragments and potshards which can easily be recovered from accessible contemporary television magazines and journals: *Radio Times*, TV *Times*, BBC *Quarterly*, and later *Contrast*. These are not used to prove arguments, but rather to identify some of the discourses which were circulating within the early discussion and promotion of television . (I will also be extrapolating to some extent from a viewing of the few early television dramas which are held in the National Film Archive.) But for television itself, rather than for simply the writing of its history, the gap in the record and the problem over recording point very clearly to one of the crucial transformative moments in defining what television was to be. It seems to me to be at that technological moment when television ceases to be *necessarily* ephemeral that its commodity form, and with it its aesthetics and its function, begins to be decided. My interest in this essay is in identifying some of the discourses and practices which were in circulation at that moment.

Television drama was a central component of the early schedules, both pre-war, in the period up to September 1939 when the service was terminated for the duration of the war, and immediately post-war, when the service was reopened in June 1946. In the week beginning 25 December 1938, for instance, of the 22 hours 30 minutes transmitted, 14 hours 10 minutes were given over to drama (including some repeats). Allowance, of course, has to be made for the fact of Christmas week. Nevertheless, it is at least worth recording that the single play in the 1930s, and, later, in the 40s and 50s, seems to have offered some of the special attractions that films have for Christmas viewing now. The productions included *Hay Fever, Richard of Bordeaux, The Moon in the Yellow River, Charley's Aunt*, and *The Knight of the Burning Pestle*. In the immediate post-war period, drama usually occupied eight to ten hours of a very slightly expanded schedule.

Perhaps even more significant than the total weekly time allotted to drama, was the place it occupied within the evening schedule. In the pre-war years, by late 1937, week day schedules ran, roughly, 3–5 pm and 8–10 pm, with a Sunday schedule, 9–10.30 pm, being added in 1938. In the post-war years the schedules were expanded slightly to include a Children's Hour, but a so-called 'toddler's truce' between 6 and 8 pm was not breached until 1954, and then only partially, when a half-hour news programme was added at 7.30 pm. Scheduling, therefore, mainly consisted of two to three hour blocks.

On perhaps four out of seven evenings the programme would resemble the magazine format of later television; but on any evening when a full-length drama was shown, it dominated the evening schedule, relegating any other programming to supporting shorts. It is important to recall this when thinking about the place of the single play within the economy of viewing of early television. The single play was not simply a part of the flow of programming, but constituted a kind of anchor-point within the evening (and perhaps within the week), which structured viewing in a different way, and invited a different form of attention.

BBC audience research did not begin in any systematic way until the 50s, but a popularity poll conducted in 1939 placed drama in front of sport and only slightly behind variety. This, of course, may say more about the 20,000 London subscribers with joint radio/television licences than it does about the drama. Even by 1959, however, in a year when the Queen's Christmas message had an audience of 20 million from BBC and ITV combined, a BBC World Theatre production of *The Government Inspector* could get an audience of 9.5 million (beating the 9 million of the very popular *What's My Line?*).

In any case, more important within the Reithian and post-Reithian ethic than audience popularity was the fact, particularly important in the post-war period, that drama lent prestige to a public service television whose cultural credentials were sometimes in doubt. Director-General Haley's cultural mission to use broadcasting as an institution of national improvement seems always to have had a slightly edgy relationship with television, preferring the known territory of radio to the *terra incognito* of television with its slightly heady entertainment potential. Asa Briggs points out that 'key figures in the BBC itself were more interested in 1946 in the starting of the Third Programme than in the resumption of television'[2], and it was not until 1950 that television was promoted from the status of Department to that of Service: the same status, that is, that the Third Programme had enjoyed since it was opened.[3]

Of particular concern was the fact that television, with its demand for concentrated attention, seemed to threaten the stabilities of a family life which had learned to accommodate the less compulsive distractions of radio. Whereas radio seemed compatible with the rhythms of domestic life, television threatened to cut time out of the everyday flow of domestic ritual. In an article in the *Radio Times* for the week beginning 7 March 1952, celebrating the opening of the television service in Scotland, Melville Dinwiddie, the Controller of Scottish Broadcasting, is ambivalent about the pleasures of television in relation to the pleasures of the hearth:

> The advent of television is like the opening of a great window in the home. Those who have sets can 'view' in comfort events as they take place near and far, see news items from all over the world, and, in addition, find home entertainment of a most varied kind. This invasion of our homes must cause something of an upset in family life. Sound broadcasting as such is upsetting enough when reading and school lessons and other home tasks have to be done, but here is a more intensely absorbing demand on our leisure hours, and families in mid-Scotland will have to make a decision both about getting a receiver and about using it. At the start viewing will take up much time

26

because of its novelty, but discrimination is essential so that not every evening is spent in a darkened room, the chores of the house and other occupations neglected. We can get too much even of a good thing. (p.5)

Where else but in the BBC, before the days of competition, would one find a broadcaster warning the viewer against too much viewing? Dinwiddie's caution, replete with the authentic tones of a public service monopoly protected from ratings competition, points to a wonderfully BBC-ish, predictably paternalist kind of anxiety about the family and the home.

For an understanding of how television in its early years actually fitted into the domestic everyday it is important to recall that with only 4.5 million holders of the combined radio and television licence by 1955, it was probably more common for most people in the first decades to have their first experience of television in someone else's house. Up until the sharp increase in television ownership in the mid- to late-1950s, people went out to see television instead of staying in. It was common to be invited to 'come over and watch television'. The technology was not yet fully domesticated, and, consequently, the characteristic experience was not yet private or exclusive. Ivor Brown, in the BBC *Yearbook* of 1951, claims, 'In the suburbs, television is plainly acting as a cohesive force'[4]; and there is a nostalgically quaint letter in a 1953 *Radio Times* (24 July 1953) from a viewer who had been troubled by interference in his picture from hair-dryers in a neighbouring girls' college until he invited the girls over to view with him: he refers to his television set as a 'friend-collector'.

For many of us who had our first experience of television in the early 50s, there was no essential connection between television and the private sphere. Quite commonly, the early experience of television, even when it was quite extensive, did not coincide with ownership; it was not, as radio was, a ritual of home and family; and it was not continuous. It was acquired in glimpses as a special occasion, and as a social, even communal, activity.

Within this special occasion, drama figured strongly, a distinct event cut out of the everyday flow of television. The Sunday Night play and the serial offered the possibility of a collective viewing as part of a social gathering, and the letters pages of the *Radio Times* in the 1960s contain a number of complaints when the plays are no longer considered fit and proper for communal viewing.

It was an additional attraction if the drama came with critical or popular guarantees. The vast majority of the single plays and serials produced by the BBC until the 1960s were adaptations, coming to the viewer with a prior seal of approval from the West End theatre, the classics, or the best-seller lists. Most of the theatrical classics had been adapted, frequently in very abbreviated forms, together with some of the modernist plays of the contemporary stage: Fry and Eliot were regulars, but there were also productions of Capek's *R.U.R.* and Auden and Isherwood's *The Ascent of F6*, both in 1938. The institution of the classic serial began in 1955 with *Jane Eyre*, and by 1959 the list included *Villette, Nicholas Nickleby, Pride and Prejudice, David Copperfield, Vanity Fair, Kenilworth*, and *Precious Bane*. Best seller adaptations, such as Mazo de la Roche's *The*

Whiteoak Chronicles (1954), answered a demand for good, satisfying narrative fiction – the television equivalent of a 'good read' – when movies on television were restricted to a few European films or a few very old and tired films escaping the commercial cinema's embargo on its very threatening rival. Single plays and adaptations which worked particularly well were given a number of productions. *Richard of Bordeaux*, for instance, a 1930s West End success written by Gordon Daviot, was produced five times before 1950, and *Mourning Becomes Electra* was produced at least three times by 1955. For the record, and to show that it was possible, very exceptionally, to move the other way, it is worth establishing the career of *Dial M for Murder*: written first as a television play (23 March 1952), it moved first to the West End theatre, to be picked up subsequently by Hollywood and Hitchcock.

Drama, then, had double benefits for the BBC, bringing prestige and quality as well as entertainment to the institution of public service broadcasting, and offering special occasions to the public it served. This goes some way towards explaining why it should survive within public service broadcasting long after it has disappeared elsewhere. It also goes some way to explaining the place which it now occupies within discussions of 'quality' when public service is seen to be under threat.

Despite television drama's importance for the BBC, however, there was some uncertainty about what exactly it was, or what it was for. In 1947, Val Gielgud, BBC Director of drama, admittedly a committed 'radio man', was able to write in *BBC Quarterly*:

> It is probably true that once the television-receiver is as common a house-hold furnishing as the present-day loud-speaker, the play broadcast in a single dimension will have as little chance of survival as the silent film, once the strains of 'Sonny Boy' had echoed round the world. But apart from the practical difficulties of supply and demand and economics, and subject to indignant correction from Alexandra Palace, I am not yet convinced that television drama is sure of its target. Does it aim to be more than a photo-graphed stage play? Does it dream of competition with film? Or should its principal aim be that of *illustrating broadcasting*? For the practice and prac-titioners of televised drama there can be nothing but undiluted admiration. But looking forward into the future, it is perhaps not out of place to suggest that as far as any genuine theory of television is concerned, a question-mark is still the most appropriate symbol.[5]

Aesthetically and practically, the defining characteristic of early television drama was live transmission. Repeats, which were routine for major single plays (Sunday Night plays were routinely repeated on Thursdays), involved calling the cast and crew back for a second performance. Plays were transmitted live from the studio in real time, using a number of sets and sometimes more than one studio, with intervals to allow for regrouping or set changes which could not be accommodated within the flow of the action. Unplanned intervals to allow for a camera which had 'gone down' were not unusual. Film inserts into studio productions were possible – even as early as the 1937 adaptation of R.C. Sheriff's *Journey's End* (a one-hour adaptation cut for continuity from the two and a half hour stage play: 'the first time that an entire evening's programme has been filled by a single play' (*Radio Times*, 11 November 1937), in which scenes from Pabst's *West Front 18* were cut into the live drama – but they were functional rather than definitive for the aesthetic of live studio performance. Early television drama was a continual attempt to resolve the overwhelming contradiction between a rather cumbersome technology of mediation (however 'immediate') and an aesthetic of live performance. Some of the uncertainty of aim detected by Gielgud lay in the assumption that the technology was there simply to serve the aesthetic rather than to produce it.

Live outside broadcast transmissions direct from a current West End success were common before the war, and continued into the 1950s. In November 1938, the *Radio Times* claimed a first for a Basil Dean stage production of J.B. Priestley's *When We Are Married*:

> For the first time in the history of the theatre, a play with its West End cast, and given before an audience, will be televised direct from a theatre stage. By permission of Basil Dean, J. B. Priestley and the theatre lessees, viewers will see the entire performance direct from the St Martin's Theatre, London (*Radio Times*, 16 November 1938)

Pre-war Television Drama: *Journey's End* being broadcast live from Alexandra Palace in December 1937.

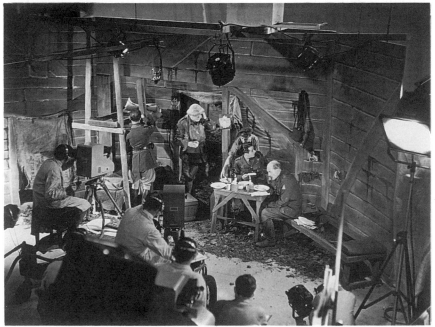

The programme ran from 8.30 till 10.40 pm.

More common were outside broadcasts of scenes or a first act from a live performance. These were usually designed more to relay the occasion, and presumably advertise the stage play, and less to capture the drama:

7.45–8.20 pm: *Under Your Hat*. First night scenes direct from the Palace Theatre, London. By permission of Lee Ephraim, viewers will meet first-night celebrities in the foyer, will see Cicely Courtneidge and Jack Hulbert in their dressing rooms, and will witness the first act of the show. (*Radio Times*, 24 November 1938)

These outside broadcasts crystallise the uncertainty of 'target' and the problem for 'a genuine theory of television'. Was it the function of television simply to relay theatre as live action into the home? Was this what television did best? Was its public service role to serve other forms, bringing them to a wider public, rather than establishing an independent aesthetic of its own? For television drama, the relay function characteristic of the outside broadcast converted easily into an aesthetics of adaptation for television drama, and live outside broadcasts of bits of stage plays are only symptomatic of a powerful current of dependency which ran between television and 'real' theatre.

This was reinforced by the institutional fragility of television within the BBC. For much of the immediate post-war years, television's aesthetic horizons were pegged by institutional thinking and institutional authority to the achievements of radio. In cultural, social and artistic terms, the Sunday night play on television was conceived as a continuation – with pictures – of the popular and successful Saturday night play on radio, or the more 'artistic' experiments of the Third Programme.

Writing in BBC *Quarterly* in 1948, Cecil Madden, very much more a 'television man' than Gielgud, nevertheless picks up some of the same doubts:

Some people ask where television drama is going, whether it aims to be a photographed stage play, a competitor to the film, or an illustrated broadcast. The truth probably belongs somewhere between them all.[6]

Television's live transmission was celebrated from the very beginning as direct, spontaneous, authentic reality, and, in drama, its place in the showbiz (and somewhat macho) nostalgia of television is assured still by the perpetuation of the legendary 'disasters' of broken cameras, trembling sets, tangled cables, and actors dropping dead on the set while the show – as shows must – went on. But the insistence on liveness as an essentialism of television, and the function of relay which went with it, made for a dependency on other forms, giving it a functional, service aesthetic with very little space for television drama to develop its own 'genuine theory'.

Adaptation and relay, then, were, for early drama and for most of early television, more than simply a necessity in the search for material: they defined the horizons of aesthetic ambition. This is not to deny the practical experimentation and the heated debates which went on, but to place them within a more or less accepted dependency on an original reality – of event or performance – which went on elsewhere, but was not produced by television. And for television drama it was theatre, rather than cinema, which provided that reality.

It is worth dwelling a little on this lack of connection between British television drama and cinema, since it may be one of the specific features of British television. By the early 1950s, the close relationship between the rising television industry and the declining film industry was already established in the USA. Much of the programming was shot on film, and even the much celebrated live drama of the mid-50s seemed like a preparatory school for emerging stars on the route west from Strasberg's New York Method school of acting to the big screen of Hollywood on which ultimate success would be judged: James Dean, Steve McQueen, Kim Hunter, Rod Steiger, all appeared on NBC's Goodyear Television Playhouse or Kraft Television Theatre, or CBS's Studio One. In France, John Swift tells us in his very useful survey of the first twenty-five years of television, *Adventures in Vision*, that the Paris service had established good relations with the French film industry and relied for around 50 per cent of its programming on films, occasionally brand new films, and sometimes shown on television before their cinema release.[7] In Britain, on the other hand, though a number of foreign and/or 'old' films were shown on television – Swift lists *Panique*, *Open City* (sic), *Un Carnet de Bal*, *Les Enfants du paradis*, *Dr Caligari*, *Blue Angel* and *Birth of a Nation* – they tended to be shown as unprogrammed stop-gaps, and in appalling versions. A 1951 review in *The Listener* complains of the butchery of *Paisa*: 'heavy cutting, undecipherable captions and commentary help so feeble that often it could not be heard' (5 July 1951).

Swift goes into some details on the use of film on television, and limits its usefulness to fairly specific conditions:

> ... the transmission of action recorded on film is not television in its true meaning. But it has three main uses:
> (a) as a stop-gap between 'live' studio programmes, or as a substitute for programmes unexpectedly postponed or cancelled. Examples: Rain may stop play at the Oval or Lords. The sudden illness of a leading artist may cause postponement of a play or other programme. In such cases the commercial cinema film is generally used.
> (b) as a 'convenience', such as continuity shots to link action (if necessary) between studio scenes. Also to establish scenes other than those in the studio ...
> (c) to bring to the screen something that can only be shown by film, including news – news of events, that is, taking place outside the range of the O.B. units, or where it is inconvenient for the O.B. cameras to operate.[8]

British television's resistance to cinema film is clearly attributable to some extent to cinema's hostility to television. Recent English language films were simply not made available to a television which was increasingly seen as a competitor, and the practice of dumping unwanted films in unwatchable prints onto television was one of the reasons why such material would only be used to patch up unprogrammed gaps in the schedules. But it is important to recognise also that there were aesthetic reservations about cinematic style, and about the appropriateness of film to the conditions of reception and forms of attention particular to television. John Swift again articulates these clearly:

> It is doubtful if there exists a cinema film of any appreciable length that is ideally suited to the television screen. In the first place, the commercial film is made essentially for a mass audience, not a group in the sitting room. Secondly, because it is for a mass audience its tempo is much faster, with a quick-cutting technique that can be disturbing when viewed at home. Thirdly, there are certain differences, not appreciated by the layman, between television and film lighting, and what is suitable for the cinema screen is not always so for the television screen.[9]

Cinema, then, did not simply represent the technologically or institutionally unattainable for television, but also the aesthetically undesirable. The suspicion directed against film was a quite conscious preference not only for immediacy as an essential quality, but also for a televisual style appropriate to the conditions of television viewing.

Theatre, and to a lesser extent, radio, seemed to offer the possibility of such a style for television drama. The most obvious effect of this preference for theatre and radio over cinema is that British television drama, as opposed, say, to American television drama, tended towards the literate rather than towards the visual. The privileging of the word and verbal exchange over the image and visual style has been frequently remarked, and forms the basis for much of the attack on so-called 'naturalism' initiated by Troy Kennedy Martin in 1964.[10] Significantly, Kennedy Martin calls for a television drama which owes more to the formally inventive cinema of the French *nouvelle vague*, particularly the films of Resnais, than it does to the established – and 'Establishment' – theatre of the West End.

It is worth repeating that the adaptation of theatre was not simply a question of reworking scripts, but rather of capturing on television something of the nature of theatre performance. Television, in its immediacy and liveness, relayed performance. The absence of expressive *mise en scène* and editing – the absence, in other words, of 'style' – which comes to be confused with 'boring naturalism', was not simply a limitation borne out of technological constraint or imaginative failure; it was rather the logical aesthetic of a technology whose essence was conceived in terms of immediacy, relay and the 'live':

> The primary function of television is to transmit pictures as they are being made . . . The *basic* attraction of the new medium is not so much the subject matter that it presents but the realization that whatever is happening *is happening at the time*.[11]

Such a technology was less concerned to make art than to serve an art which was produced elsewhere. Whereas cinema, in its classical form, as David Bordwell describes it[12], subordinates the codes of time and space to narrative causation, television drama, in its formative stage, subordinated time and space to performance. The time, in particular, of early television is the real time of live performance; the construction of space is that necessary to follow the continuous performance. Whereas cinema constructs a narrative space and time by ellipsis and fragmentation, live television drama was not simply constrained by continuous recording to play in real time, it actually aspired to continuity as a relay of a 'real' (rather than constructed) performance. This specific relationship between time, space and performance, in which performance – rather than narrative causation – is the dominant, is the specific characteristic of early British television drama, marking it off from cinema and aligning it with theatre. The residual forms of this relationship seem to me still to characterize the single play, even when shot on, and labelled as, film.

The values of live drama become clear in a 1964 article in *Contrast* by Don Taylor:

Pictorially, we are limited by the demands of continuous or near-continuous performance, but we still have a fairly large degree of freedom to select what our audience shall see. I emphasize the question of continuous performance because it seems to me to be television's key advantage over film. The small screen, the small audience, the semi-darkness, all encourage a drama of high emotional and poetic intensity. The discontinuous film performance, even by the cleverest film actor, always suffers by comparison with a TV performance that really clicks. This seems too obvious to need amplification. In the emotion of a performance growing from scene to scene, new things are discovered about a part in the act of playing it.[13]

Admittedly, Taylor, writing at a point at which (and in a journal in which) the question of a new kind of drama was on the agenda, goes on to bemoan the lack of a visual language of television, and to berate 'directors who put their actors in a box set, stick their cameras ten feet away, one in the middle and one on each side, and swing their lenses or zoom in when the actors says the shocking bit'.[14] Nevertheless, the values that he attributes to television are still the values of a captured performance, a reality constructed in front of television rather than by television. The visual language which he seeks is one which will best serve the performance:

Our medium can communicate through word and image and sound, by using an intellectual argument, a poetic cinema, a pictorial composition, a lighting effect, a piece of music, or a mixture of all these things. The one thing that should be nailed over the desk of every writer and director in television is the statement that these things are servants, not masters. They are the tools of communication, not what is to be communicated.[15]

33

The instrumentalism of Taylor's approach to form is characteristic of much writing about television (both early and late), and seems to me to be directly tied to a functional approach to television aesthetics in which the function of form is to relay content rather than to be content.

For early television, then, I would argue that, characteristically, the artistic values were those of the theatrical event or the studio performance, and the values of form and style were the functional values of relay: how well, or with how much immediacy and liveness, the technology and the technique communicated the original event.

Beyond this, it is difficult to generalise. Indeed, one of the characteristics of early television drama is that there is no standard, no classical system against which norms and differences can be measured. Like theatre productions, single plays were interpretations of an original – an original which could be reinterpreted by successive generations of producers and directors. There were debates – between those, for instance, who wanted to expand the limits of the studio by bringing in film inserts, and the purists, who wanted to push towards greater depth by use of close-ups; between the 'one-camera-technique' and 'the big head method'. And there was scope for stylistic experiment, such as a 1939 attempt, in a play called *Condemned to be Shot*, to shoot entirely in a first person subjective point of view. But each of these debates and experiments seems to have hinged around how best to communicate the original, the literary classic, or, more centrally, the theatrically conceived performance, rather than around how best to produce original television drama with its own specific values.

Given the centrality of time to the relay of continuous performance, editing style is of particular significance. In it can be seen some of the mediations of the immediate. As one would expect of continuous recording, editing is slow in tempo. Victor Menzies' 1955 production of *Richard of Bordeaux* has an Average Shot Length (ASL) of something around thirty-five seconds. It is admittedly at an extreme of theatricality, with long council discussions shot frontally in long shot, and very sparsely cut into with close-ups. More typical is Rudolph Cartier's famous 1954 production of *1984*: imaginative in its construction of space and setting, and liberally interspersed with exterior film sequences, its cutting rate still ends up with an Average Shot Length of just under seventeen seconds. (This compares with an ASL of around ten seconds for cinema film, and, by my calculation, of around twelve seconds for 1960s television drama.) Interestingly, a Rediffusion production of *A Month in the Country*, directed in 1955 by the Ealing film director, Robert Hamer, has an Average Shot Length of twenty-seven seconds, and is shot with very few close-ups, concentrating instead on a kind of theatrical stage grouping. Even an established film director like Hamer is lured into theatricality by the exigencies of television.

Clearly, there are technical constraints operating, and there are technological advances which allow shifts in style. Michael Barry, BBC Head of Television Drama, writes in BBC *Quarterly* in 1954 of the arrival in 1952 of the variable lens camera:

The variable lenses on these camera broke through the shallow field of focus.

They allowed the camera-man to compose in depth instead of restricting his clear vision to a narrow alley running at right angles before his lens. He was enabled also to reach in to observe detail without thrusting a bulky vehicle across the foreground of the other apparatus on the floor.[16]

Obviously the ability to pull focus and to shoot in depth might well have the effect of encouraging a more leisurely editing style. But the shifts in style cannot be explained simply by technological constraint and innovation. Each belongs within an aesthetic of television drama which privileged the live performance; each finds its place comfortably within the logic of communicating and servicing the 'original' performance event.

Where, then, did change come from? The most obvious answer is from competition. The arrival of Independent Television in 1955 did indeed shift the BBC in a number of very material ways. At a less material level, too, it shook up the gentlemanly aesthetic and the cultural discourse of the patrician public service institution. The shift in the 'tone' of the *Radio Times* is remarkable, and the first issue of the *TV Times* (22 September 1955) bursts onto the scene ringing with the very same mixture of populism and aggressive entrepreneurialism which becomes familiar once again with the promotion of satellite television by Rupert Murdoch and his press:

> Television is at last given the real freedom of the air. The event is comparable with the abolition of the law that kept motor-cars chugging sedately behind a man carrying a red flag.
> Now it's the 'go' signal, the green light for TV, too – with no brake on enterprise and imagination.
> So far, television in this country has been a monopoly restricted by limited finance, and often, or so it has seemed, restricted by a lofty attitude towards the wishes of viewers by those in control.
> That situation now undergoes a great and dramatic change. Viewers will no longer have to accept what has been deemed best for them. They will be able to pick and choose.
> And the new Independent TV programme planners aim at giving viewers what viewers want – at the time viewers want it.

As well as competition, then, Independent Television brought with it a change of class address, and although the class composition of the audience had changed dramatically even in the decade before ITV arrived (Briggs records a decline in Class 1 television ownership between 1947 and 1954 from 48 per cent to 25 per cent, and a rise in Class 111 ownership from 16 per cent to 59 per cent[17]), it was ITV which first addressed this new television public in the terms which it deemed appropriate. This in itself changed the nature of the discourse in which television drama was promoted and supported.

In this new competitive context, drama could no longer maintain its secure place as an automatically self-justifying cultural good, but had to be seen also as a way of reaching and attracting an audience. The BBC had to respond very directly, in a way which Reith and his successors had resisted, to the demands of public taste as they found it, rather than as they thought it ought to be. Though it was the BBC which eventually reached its Golden Age in the 60s, it was ITV which scared them into it. It was commercial television which initiated the original, live and *popular* Armchair Theatre series at the end of the 50s, a series of live dramas written specially for television, which not only introduced the first 'school' of original television drama in Britain, but also attracted huge ratings by scheduling it on Sunday nights immediately after the ratings 'chart-topper' *Sunday Night at the London Palladium*. It was from ABC that the BBC had to poach the producer, Sydney Newman, who was to lead them into the Golden Age.

But it is worth noting that when ITV opened in 1955, it continued rather than closed the privilege of theatre. Excerpts from *The Importance of Being Earnest* were shown on ITV's opening night, and though they brought the viewers *I Love Lucy* and *Dragnet*, they also brought a regular schedule of classic theatre. Under the heading 'Classics Needn't Be Gloomy', the TV *Times* of 7 October 1955 published an interview with the theatre director, John Clements, introducing an International Theatre series: 'I believe that we can televise the kind of drama that appeals to an intelligent public', says Clements, 'a really highly educated public in the theatrical sense.' By the beginning of 1956, Clements, now billed as drama adviser to Associated Rediffusion, was announcing a series of classics at the Saville Theatre to run throughout the year: 'Each is scheduled to run for roughly eight weeks in the theatre and, soon after, will be shown on ITV – with the same cast.' (TV *Times*, 13 January 1956). The first play of the Saville Theatre series was Ibsen's *The Wild Duck*, to be followed eight weeks later by Sheridan's *The Rivals*. At the same time, for a more popular theatre, the Granville Melodramas, a fortnightly series, was resurrecting popular stage melodramas of the nineteenth century such as *East Lynne* and *The Poor of New York*. The early ITV conceded little to the BBC in its love of theatre.

Every bit as significant as the arrival of Independent Television was the arrival of new technology. The 50s witnessed a series of technological shifts which changed the way in which television, and in particular television drama, was conceived, moving it out of the essentialism of immediacy.

In 1948, technicians at Alexandra Palace effectively solved the synchronising problems of recording television signals on 16 mm or 35 mm film. In an article in BBC *Quarterly* the following year, H. W. Baker and W. D. Kemp explained the system and the uses to which it might be put. It might be used, they believed, in four important ways: a) to repeat important outside broadcasts; b) to repeat drama productions, saving the time and expense of bringing actors back for a second performance; c) to conduct 'post-mortems' on productions, allowing more informed discussion of where they succeeded and where they failed; and d) to meet the 'demand for complete recorded television programmes of good technical quality and programme value in the

Dominions, in the USA, and possibly in other countries where English is understood'.[18]

In December 1953, a feature in *The Listener* reports that General David Sarnoff was about to release a television picture-on-tape recorder, introducing reusable tape:

> General Sarnoff proposed two years ago that his scientists and research men should try to give him three presents to mark his fiftieth anniversary in the electronic business: he suggested that one should be a television picture-on-tape recorder; another should be an electronic air-conditioner without moving parts; and the third should be a true amplifier of light.
>
> The first present is apparently ready ...[19]

What these inventions did was more than simply to add to the resources of television, but to change its essential nature. They brought to an end its essential ephemerality, and transformed immediacy and liveness from technological necessities into residual aesthetic aims. Throughout the 1950s, recording was possible even if it was still restricted, and even if there were, in the BBC, a strictly limited number of recording channels. The change was slow to take effect, and it was not until the 60s that recording became routine practice, leaving the 50s as a transitional phase with all the interesting tensions which such a phase usually displays.

The most apparent reason for the delay was the resistance of the unions. In an article on 'The Labour Situation', written in *Contrast* in 1963, Peter Jenkins reports:

> All means by which a man's work can be mechanically reproduced appear to the unions as means, if improperly used, of undermining the livelihoods of their members. Equity's policy on this is 'It is no longer reasonable, if ever it was, for artists to be paid a single sum for recorded work, leaving freedom to the employer to use that recording exactly as he pleases and frequently not only to the detriment of the employment of his colleagues in other media.'[20]

The ACTT took a similar line.

Since the 1930s, it had been common practice to repeat Sunday night's play later in the same week. Under the conditions of live transmission, such a repeat involved reassembling cast and crew for a second performance. With the introduction of transcription, and, particularly, of tape, the second performance, and therefore the second fee, were no longer necessary. Understandably, Equity viewed this loss of earnings with concern, and both Equity and the craft unions saw the prospect also of a loss of employment for its members, exacerbating a situation in which the post-war rise of television was seen, in any case, to threaten employment in live and public forms of entertainment: 'The closing of theatres and cinemas became a familiar feature of the fifties: it was estimated that the acquisition of a television set reduced family theatre going by twenty per cent and cinema going by thirty per cent.'[21]

Union resistance, however, only provides a visible explanation for the relatively slow and patchy take-up of recording technology. More invisible, though no less material, was the attitude which can be traced all the way back to Cock in 1936: the belief in what an editorial article in *Contrast* in 1961 called the 'magic of see-it-now':

> Television grew out of the magic of see-it-now. It was only natural that the idea of immediacy became all-powerful. That a passing event could be held seemed to contradict the magic, and was thought undesirable if not positively impossible. And to see-it-now became extended to mean see-it-now-or-never.[22]

The article complains that even programmes such as the celebrated and popular plays of Armchair Theatre which, by the end of the 50s, were recorded, were still not repeated. For a decade or so after the development of recording technology, television seemed to prefer to think of itself as ephemeral, preserving liveness as an aesthetic long after it existed as a technological constraint.

Against this, however, a more material, institutional interest was pulling in the opposite direction. Even before recording on tape was possible, Hugh Carleton Greene, then Assistant Controller, Overseas Services, later to be the Director-General of the BBC during the 'Golden Age,' wrote an article in BBC *Quarterly* in 1952/3 titled 'Television Transcription: the economic possibilities'. This article introduced to official BBC discourse the terms of an international television market:

> Television transcriptions, whether kinescopes or specially produced films, are, for a variety of reasons, extremely costly. Only by breaking into the United States market could a television transcription service hope to make both ends meet. The potential earnings from the rest of the world will not, for some time to come, approach what, with the right sort of programmes, can be obtained from the United States alone.[23]

Interestingly, in his concluding paragraph Carleton Greene backs off from the language of the market and adopts the more traditional national, cultural, moral (and imperial) discourse of the BBC:

> In television transcription this country has a potential means of enormous power for spreading knowledge of its way of life through the most intimate and immediate of the senses, through the eyes of viewers in all parts of the world. If the opportunity is not grasped by this country it certainly will be by others, particularly by the United States, and in Asia, by Japan. Things are moving quickly in the television world, and the change, if missed, may be gone for ever.[24]

As well as introducing a more populist discourse to television, the arrival of an entrepreneurial independent commercial television in 1955 marked a new interest in the international trade in programmes. Early ITV companies not only bought in US programmes and formats, but also sold them. Their most successful item in the early years was probably *The Adventures of Robin Hood*, shot on film, starring Richard Greene, produced by Sapphire Films for the ITPC, and sold to the US as a series before ITV began transmission. A blatant public relations feature article in the *TV Times* of December 1955 revels in ITV's dollar-earning capacity:

> If you think that ITV is laying out large sums of money and drawing a revenue only from English advertisers, the news of the dollar-earning capacity of the shows will surprise you.
>
> *The Adventures of Robin Hood*, which has been sold to the United States, has brought to England a million and a quarter dollars – nearly half a million pounds.
>
> If that were the sum total of ITV's success in the tough American markets, it would still be a wonderful contribution. But there's more to hear yet. And even more to come later.
>
> *The Count of Monte Christo* is not yet completed. But it has been pre-sold to America for a large guaranteed sum. Then I hear that 'Theatre Royal' is also being syndicated over dozens of stations on the other side of the Atlantic.
>
> The actual return from these three shows is not known. But I would not be surprised to hear it was around a million pounds – all in much-sought dollars. (9 December 1955)

The terms now seem very familiar, but it is still surprising to see how far back they stretch. It is also somewhat surprising to see how much more successful British television was in breaking into syndicated US television then than it is now.

By 1961, the BBC, loathe to commit itself to the high-cost, high-risk strategy of shooting series on film for the uncertainties of foreign taste, had come up with an answer by recording *Maigret* simultaneously on Ampex tape, 16 mm and 35 mm, using the cheaper techniques of drama production for the production of a crime series for the international market. The significance of the development of recording technology cannot simply be measured in terms of practical advantages, commercial benefits, or formal effects. What recording did was to lift television out of ephemerality and give it a commodity form. The shift from direct transmission to recording turned television from use value to exchange value, re-forming even public service television as not only a cultural good but also a tradeable good. Previously there had been some exchange of films of important events, but now what was conceived as cultural production entered the market place as commodity. Much of the subsequent development of British television drama – the drift over the next three decades or so towards an International Style drama, the rise of the classic serial, the shift to film technology and film aesthetics – can be dated from the moment at which drama becomes expensive, marketable and recordable.

Alongside the identifiable material effects in the mid-50s, there is a shift in the cultural place of television drama, and the attitudes that supported it. In 1963, a hint of a pervasive BBC attitude of the 40s and 50s is given by none other than John Grierson:

> ... the cheapness of television's methods – the sometimes appalling and appallingly unnecessary cheapness of television's methods – drives it inevitably to what we can only in visual terms describe as amateur theatricals. But there are other factors involved. The medium itself is in some ways predisposed, and properly predisposed, to the amateur.[25]

Like Ealing of the same period, television in the immediate pre-war years was still driven by the enthusiasm of the amateur inherited from the pre-war pioneers. The whole discourse of production, the celebration of disaster, the informal working relations, the try-outs, carried something of the 'wizard prang' about it, an extension of church hall dramatics. In many ways, this period parallels the experimentalism and lack of standardisation characteristic of 'primitive' cinema as described by Bordwell and Burch. The significance of the 50s, with the arrival of competition and the technology of recording, was to install professionalism in the place of the enthusiastic amateur, and to begin the process of the institutionalisation of the mode of production of television drama, similar, but in no way identical, to the process which Burch describes in early cinema. The transition which the 50s began, however, has not yet been completed. Competition and commodification did not finally eliminate the 'old' values of ephemerality and the amateur, they simply placed them into contradiction with other values. More than that, as a cultural public service, the BBC in particular, found in television drama a relatively protected place for the 'old' values. The development of drama through the 60s and 70s was defined by the often contradictory relationship of the 'free' and unruly creative individual and the needs of the institution.

Within the cultural and creative privileges of a public service television which valued originality and venerated the uniqueness of the writer, television drama could never become a completed classical form. It lacked the industrial streamlining and the clearly demarcated divisions of labour which could standardise its production system and its practices within 'classical' rules. With the institutionalisation of those contradictions between creativity and commodity, between national culture and international market, it could, however, from the late 50s, begin the historical development which would lead, in the late 80s, to the virtual convergence of a British art cinema and a British art television.

Notes

1. See Noël Burch, *Correction Please; or How We Got Into Pictures* (London: Arts Council, no date), and 'Porter, or ambivalence,' *Screen* vol.19 no.4, 1978/9, pp. 91–105; David Bordwell, Janet Staiger, and Kristin Thompson, *The Classical Hollywood*

Cinema: film style and mode of production to 1960 (London: Routledge and Kegan Paul, 1985).

2. Asa Briggs, *The History of British Broadcasting, Volume 4: Sound and Vision* (London and Oxford: Oxford University Press, 1979), p. 208.

3. Ibid., p. 132.

4. Ivor Brown, 'Television in the Englishman's castle', BBC *Yearbook 1951*, p. 17.

5. Val Gielgud, 'Policy and problems of broadcast drama', BBC *Quarterly* vol.2 no.1, 1947, p. 23.

6. Cecil Madden, 'Television: problems and possibilities', BBC *Quarterly* vol.2 no.4, 1948, p. 225.

7. John Swift, *Adventure in Vision: the first twenty-five years of televison* (London: John Lehman, 1950).

8. Ibid., p. 185.

9. Ibid., p. 186.

10. Troy Kennedy Martin, 'Nats Go Home: first statement of a new drama for television', *Encore*, no.48, 1964, pp. 21–33.

11. Swift, p. 11.

12. Bordwell, Staiger and Thompson, *The Classical Hollywood Cinema*; see particularly pp. 3–59.

13. Don Taylor, 'Style in Drama (I): the Gorbuduc stage', *Contrast* vol.3 no.3, 1964, p. 153.

14. Ibid., p. 206.

15. Ibid., p. 153.

16. Michael Barry, 'Shakespeare on television', BBC *Quarterly* vol.9 no.3, 1954, p. 144.

17. Briggs, *Sound and Vision*, p. 12.

18. H. W. Baker and W. D. Kemp, 'The recording of television programmes', BBC *Quarterly* vol.4 no.4, 1949–50, pp. 236–48.

19. *The Listener*, 3 December 1953.

20. Peter Jenkins. 'The labour situation', *Contrast* vol.2 no.3, 1963, pp. 166–7.

21. Ibid., p. 157.

22. 'Partialities', *Contrast* vol.1 no.2, 1961, p. 128.

23. Hugh Carleton Greene, 'Television transcription: the economic possibilities', BBC *Quarterly* vol.7 no.4, 1952–3, p. 217.

24. Ibid., p. 221.

25. John Grierson, 'Grierson on television', *Contrast* vol.2 no.4, 1963, p. 221.

Documentary Voices

JOHN CORNER

> (E)phemeral as a one-night stand television may be, but to counteract its sudden birth and death is its fantastic simultaneous access to a mass audience under conditions wholly different from the movie in the cinema . . . To those who still believe that documentary has a specific social job to do, this mass access to audiences and quick answer is of paramount importance. It is something new in the documentary experience.[1]

It was with this sense of purpose and of optimism that Paul Rotha, the BBC's newly appointed Head of Documentaries, addressed his colleagues in an internal memorandum of 1954. As television documentary defined its role, scope, and forms to become a staple genre of broadcasting during the 1950s, reference was often made back to the 'classic' British cinema work of the 1930s and wartime, when a poetic-realist imagination had combined with a distinctive sense of national identity and community to produce what seemed to some to be the defining terms of the 'documentary idea'.[2] But at the level of developing television's documentary practice, another medium and another established tradition of representational work was equally, if not more, influential. It was that of BBC Radio Features and particularly of the programming produced at the Manchester studios from the mid-1930s onwards. For the radio feature was, necessarily, an imaginative organisation of recorded voices, often speaking within the context of what was to become broadcasting's principal mode of talk – the interview.[3] It was in thinking through new conventions of speech style and of speech use, most importantly the 'accessed' speech of those not themselves professional broadcasters, that television documentary most clearly and immediately departed from the majority of its cinematic forerunners both in its forms and its social relations. Its often quite central inclusion of a 'regional' (usually Northern) rather than Metropolitan-London perspective is also significant and partly follows from the strength and influence of regional work in radio features. The 'domestication' of the documentary idea within the institutions and schedules of public service broadcasting required that the invitation to 'look' be accompanied by an equally strong and attractive invitation to 'listen'. The new terms of visual and verbal combination which followed, emerging in relation to a developing and increasingly flexible recording technology and to an increasingly differentiated sense of possible programme types, carried documentarists forward into fresh, and sometimes rather disparate, documenting activities.

In this essay I want to consider some key features of documentary developments during the 1950s, and specifically the emerging conventions for positioning the viewer as both an onlooker and an overhearer, as well as an addressee of
direct information.[4] I want to do this by selecting two bodies of work for particular scrutiny, using extensive quotation from the documentarists themselves, as
well as close analysis of the programmes, in order to develop some propositions
about the links between aesthetic form and social imagination during this formative period in documentary's emergence as a broadcast genre.

These bodies of work are, first of all, the BBC monthly series *Special Enquiry*,
which ran from 1952 to 1957 and which involved a considerable rethinking of
documentary as a form of *reporting* and, secondly, a selection of the 1950s work of
Denis Mitchell, the most distinguished maker of 'authored' documentaries
during the period and a pioneer of tape-recorder use. The two areas are connected, in a way which will be examined in some detail, by certain general
principles concerning TV documentary's function and also by close co-operative
links between the respective programme-makers. Both studies illustrate very well
not only different inflections given to documentarism as a key element within the
performance of television's newly-dominant 'public sphere' role, but also the
increasing centrality of non-professional talk to documentary's criteria of realism
and rhetorics of address. In a final section, I shall consider more generally a
broader range of developments during the period and pursue further a number of
questions to do with documentary language and the political and social conditions
of its use.

'Special Enquiry': Documentary as Reporting

> The aim is to forge a new style of television journalism. (*Radio Times*,
> September 1952)
> What was missing from television documentary before the mid-50s was,
> quite simply, people. (Norman Swallow)[5]

Norman Swallow, an ex-radio producer who had worked for some years after the
war in BBC Manchester's features department, was the producer of the *Special
Enquiry* series and the person chiefly responsible for its original design. In the
comment below he notes the chief influences bearing on the conception of the
programme and reflects on some of the characteristics of address and of tone
which made its representations different from those produced within the conventions then current:

> *Special Enquiry* was actually inspired by our head of programmes Cecil
> McGivern who himself had also been in features in radio, which I was. He'd
> carried that tradition along with him of course, and I think when he came
> into television he realised that perhaps there was one area which he knew
> well in radio which television, the BBC at that time, hadn't in fact got round
> to, which is a form of journalism, I suppose you could call it. And he
> suggested to me that I produce a series which was to some extent the

television equivalent of *Picture Post*. We were inspired by *Picture Post* and, in television terms, by the Ed Murrow and Fred Friendly series *See it Now*, from CBS New York. They were our two main influences, I think, together with the old British documentary tradition of course. I was a great admirer of the documentaries when I was at school in Manchester in the late 1930s. It's not coincidence that the first *Special Enquiry* was about housing in Glasgow, actually my favourite pre-war documentary was *Housing Problems* made in 1935 by Arthur Elton and Edgar Anstey. It was probably no coincidence that that was the first *Special* we had. However, what Cecil McGivern wanted was a series. . . . And the main thing really was up to that point he could see that television and to some extent radio treatment of what we call current affairs subjects had been a little pompous. It was mostly so-called experts, well so-called, they probably *were* experts, talking about things as experts in whatever kind of territory, and the thought was that we would do something in which our presenter would in fact be one of *us*, so the presentation would be from the point of view of the audience, of the public, not from the point of view of someone who knew everything about it or thought he did.[6]

Elsewhere, Swallow has described in more detail the kind of speech which the programme wanted from its presenters and reporters and the kinds of listening relationships which it sought with the audience. He notes of the reporter's job:

He never dominates the programme, for most of its length he is only a voice speaking words that are slightly more personal than those of a film commentator . . . He moves from place to place, using his film camera as a reporter might use his notebook and pencil. He asks the questions that a sensible layman would ask . . . He was the fixed point of the enquiry, the man through whose eyes and ears the viewer absorbed the story.[7]

Each edition of *Special Enquiry* was forty-five minutes long, of which a central section was a filmed location report. This was framed by an introduction from the studio presenter (in Lime Grove) and, at the end, by a return to the studio and a discussion with a studio guest which drew out some of the more general implications of the account. Significantly for later modalities of alignment between broadcasters and viewers in television, the presenter swung round to look at a screen at the start of the filmed report and swung away from it to address the viewers at the end. Not only, therefore, was the location reporter 'our' representative and 'our' eyes and ears, but the studio space itself was projected as a parallel space to the space of the domestic viewer, affirming both co-presence and co-temporality.

The studio material was, of course, delivered live and the resident presenter (as distinct from the location reporter who changed from programme to programme and who was often local) was Robert Reid, who had worked for BBC radio in Manchester and whose northern accent was felt to lend the programme an extra note of 'no-nonsense' integrity. Some idea of the emphatic directness of parasocial address with which Reid projected his introductions to the audience can be got from this example of the opening he gave to an edition of the programme on the United Nations International Children's Emergency Fund (UNICEF). After opening shots of diseased and hungry children had been shown, he picked up on the cry of a child heard on the soundtrack:

> That was the voice, the cries, of a child who is hungry, or living in some dark hovel; a child maybe diseased and racked with pain; or just – dying ... Not just one child but more than 400 million of the world's children who are condemned to live or die under conditions like those ... nearly half the children of the world. Now, horrifying though that statement is – and probably many of you will not believe me – these are hard facts, on record. Wars, ignorance, shortages, superstitions, backwardness, greed, neglect and the harshness of political doctrines and economic creeds – these things are responsible for this crime against the children of the world.[8]

Among the many topics which the series addressed were housing, education, youth, old age, race relations, food poisoning and care of the disabled. All the filmed material was shot on 35mm stock and optical sound (with reels lasting four minutes). A complete production unit was formed to work on the series, which got full co-operation from all the regions of BBC radio. One of the conventions used by many of the programmes, which links the series directly back to Anstey and Elton's *Housing Problems* of 1936, was extensive use of direct-address to camera by interviewed participants. In many instances, these interview sequences work as self-contained 'access' slots (rather similar in some respects to Channel Four's videobox), in which apparently unsolicited testimony and opinion is offered directly to the viewer, without the mediation of a professional broadcaster. In fact, this often required considerable scripting and rehearsal. A contemporary manual for television writers, using *Special Enquiry* as an example, notes of the reporter's dealings with his interviewee (here, referred to as his 'actuality'):

> He may have to see people a dozen times and get the story or opinion or secret out of them bit by bit and then hand it back to them in logical form. The questions by which the material was extracted have been cut out and the actuality has now what is called 'a straight piece' to say ... having been started off (he) will say his piece uninterrupted. The commentator (unseen) may break in once or twice, but the general effect is still that the actuality is talking straight rather than being interviewed.[9]

Swallow remembers the considerable impact which the series made, particularly the difficulty which some viewers had in believing the honesty of the first programme (broadcast on 3 October 1952) about the poor housing conditions in Glasgow's Gorbals district:

... we had many phone calls, even letters, from people who because they knew nothing about it, hadn't seen that sort of thing before, wouldn't believe it. They thought we were lying. That it was somehow fiction. So this was a television breakthrough.[10]

Press comment on this first edition of the programme was almost unanimous in its praise, using terms which point interestingly to some of the current expectations and conventions against which the series defined itself. The *Star* congratulated the programme for 'not using rose-tinted lenses on this job', the *Daily Mail* noted that there was 'no attempt to dramatise the sorrow and squalor', while the *Sunday Times* observed that 'it was made by adults for adults, with no taint of that glib, insulting superficiality that has ruined many a promising programme'. Nearly all the papers referred to the 'human' power of the reporting and the capacity of this style of programme to transform an 'intellectual awareness' into an 'urgent demand'.

However, as Paddy Scannell has observed, both in respect of this kind of programme and of features and current affairs more generally, the BBC's institutionalised separation of the 'political' from the 'social' serves (however broad a programme's brief may be) to narrow the terms within which a problem can effectively be handled.[11] Such a separation may, of course, be thought enabling rather than restrictive by producers. By thus limiting their terms of address (at least, their 'official' ones), producers are freed from the risks and potential delays consequent on their programme being caught up within the conventions and rituals of party political debate. Swallow himself places the emphasis even more narrowly:

I think it was a form of journalism which dealt more precisely with human beings as individuals and their problems as individuals rather than making political generalisations, which of course television did and still does to a great extent.[12]

Yet, despite this declared stress on individuals, the sphere of 'the social' in *Special Enquiry* (in respect, for instance, of the relationships of employment, authority, institution and citizenry) was a category within which a range of more structural factors, of power and inequality, could at least be identified if not confidently addressed *as* structural.

One of the most discussed programmes in this respect was the edition of 31 January 1955, 'Has Britain a Colour Bar?'. The filmed report on this occasion was given by René Cutforth and the programme was made in Birmingham. Immediacy was given to it by a reconstructed scene in which a black worker arrives in the city only to be turned away from a whole series of lodging houses and to be treated with suspicion and hostility in a pub. However, the main thread of the programme is carried through a sequence of interviews with both black and white residents of Birmingham and with a number of local government and union officials (as noted above, these are often of the 'direct testimony' type rather than 'question and answer', producing personal accounts of discrimination as well as some very blunt and fully developed statements of prejudice).

While giving a number of speakers opportunity to put their case *for* discrimination, among whom is a union leader at the local bus depot, Cutforth's narration and questioning do not adopt a framework or tone of 'impartiality'. The man in the arrival sequence is identified, in a marked way, as a 'British citizen' and prejudice rather than immigration is seen as the *primary* problem. Yet, despite this, the narration's concern with registering essential cultural *differences* ('they look different and they sound different and their tastes in matters of food are different') seems to set up a strongly skewed framework of primary perceptions. For instance, towards the end of the programme a black interviewee states his disappointment at finding the extent of the prejudice against him in Britain and remarks how this is grounded in assumptions and anxieties about a fundamental 'difference'. Yet Cutforth immediately follows this with a voiced-over comment which begins 'But let's face it, they *are* different', before going on further to *understand* in personal terms, if not at all to condone, the attitudes of discrimination which the programme has documented. The programme's uncomplicated address to white viewers concerning a grouping sharply differentiated from the terms of that address both visually and verbally (a self-evidently problematic 'they'), radically reduces its ability to push very far with questions either of cause or of possible solution.

However, the answer which the programme finally gives to its own basic question is clearly 'yes' and this provoked extensive discussion in the press on the following day. Some of the problems with its framing of the issues in the context of contemporary attitudes both to the topic and to television journalism are perhaps reflected in the *Daily Sketch*'s observation that 'with scrupulous fairness the BBC balanced each blow against the West Indians with a defence of them'(!). The *Daily Express* regarded it as 'one of the most outspoken programmes ever screened'. Some testimony to the way in which the social meanings generated by the programme were extensively determined by viewers' own existing attitudes may be got from the fact that, after it, Robert Reid received a terse postcard from one viewer with the message that 'You and your black friends ought to be put up against a wall and shot.'

From the point of view of subsequent developments in documentary, the most significant of the programmes in the series was perhaps 'Teenagers', broadcast first on 1 November 1955, with the filmed report being re-shown on its own as *On the Threshold* in 1957, winning an international prize the following year. This saw the first co-operation between Swallow and Denis Mitchell and the first application to television of Mitchell's experiments with sound recording. These involved constructing the core of the programme from an assemblage of speech recorded on tape, then using this as the soundtrack for a large part of the film. Swallow remembers the terms of their co-operation:

> So 'Teenagers' was Denis' first television work. He brought along his radio techniques and used them to produce off-screen voices, because we were shooting on 35mm stock and the film ran out after four minutes, just about

the time when someone you're talking to is getting really good, getting into his stride and saying something really important, you know, you have to cut. So to some extent we avoided that with Denis' sound tapes, which of course went on much longer.[13]

The chance to use a much more portable silent camera with a reduced crew also introduced the possibility of greater spontaneity in the visual depiction. Swallow, despite being an ex-radio producer himself, had initially been sceptical of so emphatic a sound-based approach with its consequent loss of synchronised speech (although the programme contained some of this too). However, when the programme was finished, he judged that it had got the viewer 'closer to the real hearts and minds of those teenagers than to any other people in any previous television programme.'[14]

There was a good deal of excitement generated around its completion and Swallow remembers Lindsey Anderson and Karel Reisz (both then active in the 'realist' campaigning of the Free Cinema group) coming to Lime Grove to see the rough cut. The freshness and directness of the off-screen voices, especially those of two Teddy Boys, once again won *Special Enquiry* praise among the newspapers' television critics and this time the praise registered the *technical* dimension of the accomplishment as well as the social force of what was said and shown. The *New Statesman* critic wrote:

> The justly praised programme on teenagers stands out as the finest piece of television I have yet seen; its experimental technique, its montage of film and sound-tape, were highly effective.

Peter Black, in the *Daily Mail*, looked to the implications for the development of documentary form:

> *Special Enquiry* brought off a shining success with its investigation of teenagers, a success of the kind that sets new standards for the judgment of television documentary techniques.

In its six years of operation, with six programmes transmitted in each yearly series, *Special Enquiry* significantly re-structured the discourses of British television journalism. It established the discursive mix of investigative, filmed reports 'anchored' from a studio base and 'accessing' a variety of non-official speakers. It carried the democratising *potential* of documentary representation further than either filmed or photo-journalistic depiction (for instance, that of *Picture Post*) had achieved, and it did this by drawing powerfully on radio as well as cinematic antecedents. As programme formats developed into an increasingly differentiated range of styles and specialisations, the sheer scope of its brief perhaps became out-of-line (in terms of the capacity to retain a clear series identity) with emerging convention. The originality of its own approach had often influenced, and become absorbed within, these conventions. Of its ending in 1957 (after which there were one or two relatively unsuccessful attempts at revival using similar titles and formats) Swallow notes:

> What happened was the political aspect of the thing went into *Panorama* and other current affairs programmes, and the social side of it went into documentaries like *Morning In the Streets*, etc.[15]

Following his success with 'Teenagers', and a subsequent return to the BBC in Manchester, Denis Mitchell began to develop his own distinctive sense of documentary possibilities through a series of films which, in many cases, departed quite radically from the *Special Enquiry* model. These provide the basis for a second brief case-study in documentary television's genealogy.

Denis Mitchell: Documentary and 'Social Impressionism'

This was the essence of what I was doing – I had no plan.[16]

During the late 50s and early 60s, Mitchell became perhaps the most important and influential documentarist working in television. At the centre of his programme ideas and working practices was a concern with the extensive use of popular speech as the route to a richer and deeper portrayal of popular experience and attitudes. His work is thus marked as 'subjective' in two interrelating ways. First of all, in its interest in the *consciousness* of the people whose talk he recorded (his approach was initially called the 'think-tape' method), and secondly in the way in which a clearly 'authored' aesthetic control is exerted across all the materials in the final programme. This took his work away from the framing conventions of the 'current-affairs' or 'social problem' documentary, towards a more relaxed and indirect investigatory style.

The foundations of his documentary concept lay (as noted in the discussion of *Special Enquiry*'s 'Teenagers' above) in the technology of the tape recorder. After War Service, Mitchell had become a radio producer with the South African Broadcasting Corporation. In the late 1940s he was invited by Geoffrey Bridson (then Head of Radio Features at the BBC) to join the features department at Manchester, a job made vacant by the departure of Norman Swallow to London. It was in South Africa that his interest in tape technology began and he transferred it to Manchester with quite revolutionary consequences:

> In South Africa, again by chance, and messing about with ex-US equipment, I had got interested in tape recorders and how they worked and I realised that this was really something new. And when I got back to this new job I discovered to my absolute surprise that nobody in the BBC even knew about tape. It was amazing. And they were still, for example, if they were doing *Down Your Way* they would go out and find, say, the local blacksmith and they would either record him on disc but usually take it down in shorthand, then transcribe it, then tidy up the bits, you know the hums and ahs, and then they would write it into a script and get *him*, the blacksmith, to actually

do it. It was incredible. And nobody had thought of using the actual person, unless they were set up and reading a script. It is true that at the time nobody listening to features ever heard real people *talking* – they were always actors or else reading from a script, which most people couldn't do anyway. This seemed to me to be ludicrous and so I started off on quite another tack. Something that really nobody was doing at all, and so that when I got launched with a series called *People Talking* it was an astonishing success mainly because for the first time ever they were listening to real people saying whatever came into their minds.[17]

Following his stint of secondment with *Special Enquiry*, the success of the 'Teenagers' film and further radio features work in Manchester, Mitchell teamed up with Roy Harris to make his second film, *In Prison* (BBC, 1957). This, in its formally distinctive approach to a subject previously unexplored on television, remains among his most impressive pieces. Mitchell's preference for getting talk into his programmes through the expansive and relaxed comments of tape-recorded 'wild track', rather than by setting up synch-sound interviews, was one which fitted in conveniently with the Prison Commissioners' requirement that all comment from prisoners be presented anonymously and without sight of their faces. Mitchell remembers the way in which the broader question of censorship was resolved:

I had an agreement with the Prison Commissioners. They were very keen on having a caption that said the thing was not censored in any way. So I devised the notion that I would take, record, endless lots of stuff and throw away a great deal of it, finishing up with say two hours of material. And I would go to them and play the whole two hours and if there was one thing in my selection that they pulled a face at, they couldn't have their non-censored caption. It worked. So I could use absolutely anything that I wanted to in the film.[18]

In Prison, extensively pre-researched by Mitchell (who had been given a cell at Strangeways), uses a full range of the documentary devices available at the time. Its basic narrative is organised around the prison 'cycle' of entry, process-ing, daily routines, parole board and release. The opening is a long, tracking shot which follows a woman and two children as they walk down backstreet pave-ments towards the prison gate and are permitted entry through the small door set within it. The soundtrack is that of a man's voice, telling of the first visit of his family. As the prison door shuts, this gives way to a few lines of song by Ewan McColl ('Time on my Hands') in the revived urban-realist style. Like the open-ing voice, the song serves to frame the programme's topic and the subsequent distanced exposition within the terms of an 'inner' structure of feeling, closing the imaginative distance between prisoners and viewers right from the start. Most of the subsequent stages, phases and times of day are depicted through narrated film of institutional activity. Within this structure, sequences of a more observa-tional kind occur, with overheard exchanges and conversation providing something close to a 'vérité'-style relationship with the action (though, given the equipment, this degree of naturalism would have required extensive directorial shaping). At points, dramatised reconstructions are used to sustain immediacy.

However, the dominant discursive element is undoubtedly that provided by the voices of the prisoners, used as voice-over across the scenes of (faceless) activity. These voices, male and female, talk of the reasons why the speakers are in prison and how they see their future, their attitudes to other prisoners, to prison life and to the warders. They sometimes contradict one another in their assessment, for instance, of prison food and hygiene or the use of violence by the warders. This sets up a dialogue, and sometimes an unresolved tension, not just within the edited flow of their reflections but also with the framings and assessments of the narrator. They are thus not used to constitute some unified 'voice of the prisoner', but to retain and project to a considerable degree a multiple, dialogical dynamic.

Their effect is both to place the prisoners centrally *in* the film, rather than their merely being people observed *by* it, and to bring the viewer into a much closer relationship with the 'inside' of prison life (as the film's title suggests), now essentialised in terms of the 'inside' of a prisoner's mind. This concern with the 'interior' experience as much as with the outward activity is the film's most powerful rhetorical characteristic and in several scenes it extends to the visual depiction as well as the soundtrack. Prisoners legs (cut off by the camera at knee height) circle the maze of the exercise yard in a sequence which moves out from its particular documentary referentiality to become more generally symbolic of the prisoners' entrapment in frustrating, repetitive routines, circling round inside a tightly limited physical and mental space. A sequence showing a newcomer being put into his cell after his passage through several locked gates and doors is accompanied by cacophonous sound effects, a musical crescendo and angled 'expressionist' camerawork, as the narrator draws attention to the destabilising pressures which the prison world of isolation and rumour often bring. Pushing yet further into the subjective, night scenes depict prisoners in their cell beds (here, in a clear break from actuality methods, actors in a studio set), restlessly reflecting on their lives or dreaming. Once again, the voices are provided by real prisoners on a taped soundtrack.

Towards the end of the film another, more conventional, kind of voice is heard – that of the prison governor who, seated behind his desk, gives a straight-to-camera account of his charges (they are fond of children, kind to animals and appreciative of the simple justice which has been handed out to them!). Placed 'across' the line of the documentary's own discourse in such a manner (he interestingly *puts* himself *outside* this by grounding his preliminary address to viewers in the observation that 'You've seen the film'), the *form* of his statement, and then what it has to say, develop a relationship of tension with what has gone before and what will follow in the closing 'release' sequence. This final sequence is, again, built around prisoners' voices. It shows an old offender being let out through the gates and walking slowly down the road, reflecting on his chances of not coming back. The contrast between the brisk, confident but superficial externality of the governor's perspective and the troubled 'interior' which Mitchell penetrates through to by his use of voices couldn't be more marked, or more indicative to viewers of the terms of understanding in which they should place *their* confidence.

Mitchell went on to make a number of other films with Roy Harris in which reflective talk, either as voice-over or as speech-to-camera (but rarely as question-and-answer interview) were central. Of these, *Night in the City* (BBC, 1957) and *Morning in the Streets* (BBC, 1959) are attempts at applying his ideas to a rather more diffuse topic than either 'Teenagers' or *In Prison*. Both films were shot on location, primarily in Salford and Liverpool, using the newly available 16mm cameras and, of the two, *Morning* is the more accomplished and consistent piece, winning the Prix Italia in the year of its transmission and becoming extensively screened and cited. It was, said programme notes:

> An attempt to capture an impression of life and opinion in the back streets of an industrial city, and to show the warmth, vitality and good humour to be found there . . .[19]

In it, Mitchell dispenses altogether with narration, since he has no *exposition* of a sufficiently particularistic kind to justify its use. The informational function is once more carried by recorded speech, used for the most part as voice-over. But this is now accompanied by a more stylistically expansive use of the camera, connecting the film back to rhetorical elements in the 'classic' work of the 1930s and particularly to the Humphrey Jennings of *Spare Time* (1939). The dominant mood of the piece is, despite Mitchell's own comments and a vigorously positive ending, that of the *sadness* of a resilience demanded by particular conditions and circumstances of living. This is generated by the interweaving of images and voices from various generations living on the 'streets' (a term closed down to mean the poorer working-class districts of the two cities, which are conflated into one by the account).

An ironic framing is established early on in the film when, following a measured, consciously aestheticised opening, moving in gracefully and silently from long shot to pursue a closer, tracking acquaintance with the (as yet deserted) terraces, a number of street nameplates are rapidly cut to and from – the references are to Hope, Paradise, Love, and Energy. As the opening music fades (wistful 'urban folk' harmonica), the first voice to speak is that of a woman remembering her visit to Shrewsbury with the Townswomen's Guild. She speaks of the astonishing greenness of the countryside ('I didn't know there were so many shades of green'), as the camera continues on its way along the pavements and past the rows of doors. Underneath the testimonies, observations, anecdotes and assessments of the voices, the film shows families waking up, children going off to school and various scenes of street activity, including some heavily directed and theatricalised shots of a sprightly tramp who contributes his own story to the soundtrack. The derelict nature of much of the housing is obvious, yet while registering this, the film pulls in voices which speak of harder times in the past and which scornfully reject the notion of 'the good old days', asserting that 'it's a better world than it was'.

The bleakness of the surroundings continues in the lives of many of the older people. An old man talks of his regular visits to the local library reading-room where he meets 'my cronies, the one-time Empire builders trying to live on less than three pounds a week.' This cynicism comes over as at least a part of the film's own attitude, further reflected in a Remembrance Day scene which counterposes a widow's own voiced-over account of her husband's departure for the war, and her subsequent receipt of the news of his death with the official, public language of the radio broadcast she is listening to, relayed from the Cenotaph ceremony. The next shot is of a rag-and-bone man's cart and the sound of his braying trumpet unsteadily mimics the tones of the 'Last Post', provocatively recovering them from conventionalised ritual and recharging them with meaning.

Towards the end, the film quickens pace with a gossip sequence, in which fragments of conversation are rapidly juxtaposed with one another to the punctuation of a child's trumpet blast. A sense of the social energy and the centrality of this aspect of 'street' life is projected. A lengthy, comic story is told in synch-sound, as an overheard conversation between neighbours.

The ending brings together conflicting evaluations and tones. A woman reflects on her sad and lonely life as a deserted wife, the tramp judges that 'it's a bit of a lousy life, taken all together from top to toe', while the woman who told the funny story reflects on 'happy days'. One of the speakers given to generalised reflection places a more ambitious abstraction into the montage of themes, telling his friend:

We're all part of a great mass. This mass is just split up into little bits, moving little bits. I'm part of you, you're part of me.

Throughout the film, the most positive images and voices are those of children, running to and from school, shouting, playing games and singing. At the end, the film returns to their songs and their play. Over a selection of shots of individual girls, smiling and singing in their 'solo' and 'chorus' roles, their song is suddenly taken up orchestrally. As it increases in volume, the deserted playground featured in the early morning opening sequence is suddenly filled by a rush of boys and girls. Underneath the music and in relation to its volume and buoyancy, the camera now picks them out and frames them individually in a mode not of observed particular action but of projected general significance. Their faces stand for the future. The comparison here with the ending of Jenning's wartime film *Listen to Britain* is striking. A musical theme and a mood located within the film become that of the film itself (Mitchell was a great admirer of Jennings' films, having been shown them first by Karel Reisz). Something of the intended implications can be got from Mitchell's own description of the children at the end, that 'their shouts and songs drown the voices of the old and resigned and defeated'.[20] Nevertheless, despite the rhetorical force of the ending, the combination of themes and of treatments in *Morning* – implicit social critique and hope, a sombre gravity and a celebratory lyricism – seem at times to be imperfectly integrated or otherwise placed into an overall relationship with one another.

The Listener's television critic commented on how the film's essential structure was 'a brilliant sound-radio script in the latest and purist style superimposed on to the pictures', but had some reservations about aspects of the visual portrayal, particularly the way in which this drew on a previous tradition. Noting, rather archly, how the opening sequence was done in the manner 'which the thirties had taught us to find significant', he went on to observe that 'the film, though never dull, seemed at times to belong to a style which is already beginning to date a little'.[21]

This, on the face of it, rather unusual registering both of 'latest' and 'dated' elements of style in the film is an interesting reflection of Mitchell's attempt here to run his voices over a far more ambitious and self-consciously 'poetic' visual evocation of place and of feeling than had hitherto been the case. The 'impressionistic' brief which the film works to fulfil means that the sense of particular and thwarted lives established on the soundtrack for most of its length is rather unsatisfactorily subsumed into a (perhaps too easily available) visual depiction of generalised cheerily-stoic victimhood, with its posing of human figures against their bleak and sharply localised environment. There is also a tendency towards recording behaviour marked as slightly odd or grotesque which, at times, disturbs both the framing of 'ordinary' life on the streets and also proper attention to the social and political relations upon which the terms of living are premised. These limitations aside (probably much more apparent now than then), the clarity and steadiness of its unhurried gaze at aspects of individual and collective life and its acute sharpness of ear are remarkable, and the film duly deserves its status as a TV documentary classic.

Mitchell's approach was consciously non-journalistic (he was later to be quite open in his hostility to the kind of urgent, heavily-narrated documentary form favoured by series like *World in Action*). In a comment on his general approach, he defines the directorial role in terms not dissimilar from those of John Grierson making the case for documentary cinema in the 1930s, though with more elaboration and awareness of difficulties. Explaining why such films are 'more than journalism', he notes that the documentarist gives:

> . . . a harmony to the people in his film by means of his vision of them and of the world they live in. He himself has something to say about them – must have something to say, otherwise he wouldn't have become interested in them in the first place. His task is to imply his own view of life (he can never openly state it by any form of editorialising) without distorting the truth that is the lives of the people he has chosen. What he manages to say, or rather what he and his selected people say together – for this is in a profound way a piece of mutual co-operation – is in my opinion much more significant than what is said in a current affairs programme with a spoken pseudo-objective comment.[22]

This view of documentary as an exercise in co-operative communication is revealing for its open playing-off of notions of fidelity and truth against that of the directorial 'view of life' and, despite the obvious obstacles to any real honouring

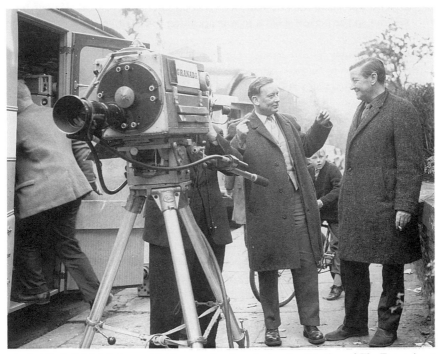

Denis Mitchell (right) chats with Norman Swallow during the shooting of *The Entertainers*, an early 60s experiment with videotaped documentary.

of mutuality in the actual process of film-making, its own particular formulation of balance is one which accords well with Mitchell's use of the medium as essentially the means for a form of popular ethnography.

Both Mitchell and Swallow were active innovators, directors and producers throughout the next decade. In the early 60s, Swallow joined Mitchell in Manchester; the latter had formed his own company there and had negotiated a contract with Granada which allowed Swallow and himself to work alternating stretches with Granada and with the company. In Manchester, they carried out the first experiments with using videotape on documentary projects, experiments which led to programmes like Mitchell's *The Entertainers* (Granada, 1964), about the life of club artistes in Manchester, and Swallow's *A Wedding on Saturday* (Granada, 1964), which was an in-depth, almost anthropological study of a mining community, conveyed around a central depiction of the preparations and celebrations of a village wedding. Both of them worked on the Granada series *This England*, in which components of the Mitchell philosophy were the working convention:

> The idea was we'd have no narration at all. Sometimes we allowed it at the beginning to set the scene, you know 'here we are . . . this is . . .' after about thirty seconds, end of voice and no voice at all whenever possible. And if

55

anyone was being interviewed there was no interviewer heard. He cut himself out so the person spoken to was speaking to me or you at home.[23]

Voicing the Social

Ours was, in a real sense, the 'Art of the Welfare State'.[24]

I have examined above two prominent examples of the way in which documentary television developed its principles and methods of social representations in the 1950s, in relation both to the existing cinematic tradition and to established and currently emerging work in radio features. *Special Enquiry* reorganises the terms of the 'documentary perspective' within the broader generic conventions of *journalism*, a journalism in which new and immediate relationships of public speaking and listening are constructed between the 'ordinary people' in the programme and the viewer. These relationships are regulated not just by interview and editing practices, but by the contextualisation of 'ordinary speech' within new forms of reportorial and presenter address. Denis Mitchell's concern with the primacy of taped voices as a route into people's everyday realities pulls him away from the topic-focused depictions of series journalism and into a more aesthetically-marked use of documentary for single studies in relaxed observation. Here, the occasion for the documentation is not so much legitimated as *professional duty* (routine surveillance of the pre-constructed territory of the 'social' and updating of information on 'problems' and 'issues') but as *artistic expression* (perceptions and comment grounded in qualities of authorial sensibility and technique).

This is so even though much of Mitchell's work can also be seen to operate as a kind of early version of 'access television'. In their rethinking of the relations of listening, both approaches require that 'ordinary', and usually anonymous, speech be removed from the specific dialogical contexts of its utterance or, indeed, any simulation of this, and re-projected to take its significance as one element in a programme's overall design. However, *Special Enquiry* does this to cross-connect accessed viewpoints around the professional mediation of an 'issue' (anchored in exposition and inquiry), whereas Mitchell's aim is to provide the listener with a more extensive and symbolically rich entry into 'other' experience, organised into significance around directorial impressions.

As early as the mid-50s, though, other modalities of documentary speech were being developed in which it was precisely the interactive and situated character of talk which became the primary object of projection to the viewer. In these modes, most often occurring in the lighter 'magazine'-style programmes which had been seen as a distinct sub-genre of documentary television from the early 1950s, the broadcasting possibilities of series formats, strongly personalised presentation and the use of the interview as a *dramatic* form of exposition were brought together.

One such series, broadcast in the first full year of ITV, was *Look in On London* (Associated Rediffusion, 1956). This was a development out of Associated Rediffusion's highly successful news magazine *This Week* and was probably influenced, too, by a number of earlier series in which a 'lively' look had been taken at the Capital (for instance the BBC's *London Town*, which ran from 1949 and featured Richard Dimbleby).

Here, a narrative structure for each edition is provided by the *excursions* made by the presenter into different realms of city life and his *encounters*, while 'out' there, with a variety of interesting people. These people are questioned both about the activities for which, in the programme, they stand as typical representatives and also about the more personal aspects of their lives. The visual framing and the direct and indirect speech of the programmes are designed, in a manner clearly different from that of the examples discussed earlier, to *perform* a replication and an extension of everyday sociability. The relationship between viewers and viewed is emphatically mediated in parasocial terms. The opening address of one of the programmes, on streetcleaners, shows the projection of this relationship at the start of an 'excursion':

(CU shots of broom sweeping gutter: presenter speech in VO)
Who wields this broom? Fred Robinson, Robbo to his friends. He keeps one and half miles of Maida Vale in a state in which you'd wish to find it – which is not the state you left it in.

The programme thus launches itself upon both a 'personal' and a 'civic' inquiry, addressing the viewer within the two modes simultaneously. That the programme offers the audience a more intimate rendering of the cleaner's identity is an indication of the bridge which, through its onlooking and overhearing practices, it wishes to construct between the world it is visiting and the world of its viewers.

Elsewhere,[25] I have attempted to discuss the manner in which the series connects 'public' to 'private', thus linking the more established concerns of documentary's topic-centred, social surveillance with a much more loosely-structured focus on the informative, interactive delights of question and answer. The role of the presenter, not primarily a reporter, but a genial guide who takes the audience on a journey (from studio/home out on location), places him much more centrally in the documentary frame than is the case with the programmes discussed above. The apparent happenstance and immediacy of his Mayhew-like social adventures in 'finding out' are as much part of the programme's appeal as *what* is found out, a naturalistic narrativisation of the inquiry itself which, given the limitations of equipment at the time, called for extensive scripting and rehearsal. Such a displacement of topic by personality and interaction can only occur within an overall lightening of tone of the documentary project, a shift from the 'social' towards the 'sociable'. In the edition on street-cleaners, this allows the programme to move between a relatively 'straight' account of refuse collection and disposal and a strongly personalised cameo of Robbo's own living conditions and way of life.

The terms in which the programme ends reinforce the sense that it is the (then novel) pleasure of meeting people via television, as much as the conveyance of any 'civic knowledge', which is the programme's aim:

(Presenter's VO; CU shot of broom sweeping gutter)
And tomorrow Robbo's old broom will be busy again. This time we shall know who it is we are passing the time of the day with (Presenter in street; passes Robbo at work, greets him and walks closer to camera for direct address):
One more of London's millions who's no longer a stranger.
(walks off, with a farewell wave to Robbo).

This re-inflection of the Griersonian perspective on public information, with its aesthetics of *community* – a re-inflection towards the generic imperatives of popular entertainment – was thus a further, formative strand in documentary's diversification and development during the period.

By taking the above examples of early TV documentary work, I hope to have indicated some of the main shaping factors at work in the development of documentary as a televisual form in Britain. Most of these were premised on a recognition of the primarily domestic character of television services and on the new relations, both of direct address and of onlooking and overhearing, which the social relationships of broadcasting could sustain. I have given particular emphasis to the use of speech in these developments, drawing on a continuity with kinds of pre-war radio work. It is important to note that beyond the first formative phase from which I have chosen my examples here, innovations in speech forms continue with new purpose and direction, most notably perhaps in the style of journalistic address and film-making associated with Granada's *World in Action* series from the early 60s onwards.

During the period I have examined, the socially exploratory project of documentary was, as in 1930s cinema, crosscut by a variety of impulses and ideas as to aims and methods.[26] Among these, there was an interplay between an investigative surveillance of the social world and its 'problems', sanctioned by broadcasting's public service role and the salience of journalism within this, and altogether more indirect and relaxed renderings of 'people' and 'life' within the new terms of post-war social democracy. Both aesthetically 'serious', impressionistic/symbolic exploration and also a more 'lighthearted' taking up of TV's potential for the projection of extended sociality were attempted, as I have shown. The new terms had inscribed within them, among other factors, changing attitudes to social class and its portrayal and changing forms of relationship between the official and the popular. It is also significant that it was at this time, too, that television programmes and series were themselves becoming key constituents in the formation of both national identity and the *dynamics* of social change.

Notes

1. Paul Rotha, 'Television and the Future of Documentary', unpublished internal memo (29 October 1954). Cited by Elaine Bell, 'The Origins of British Television Documen-

tary', in John Corner (ed.), *Documentary and the Mass Media* (London: Edward Arnold, 1986), p. 71.

2. Among the most useful accounts of the Documentary Film movement of the 1930s are Elizabeth Sussex, *The Rise and Fall of the British Documentary* (Berkeley: University of California Press, 1976), and Stuart Hood, 'John Grierson and the Documentary Film Movement', in James Curran and Vincent Porter (eds.), *British Cinema History* (London: Weidenfeld and Nicolson, 1983), pp. 99–112.

3. For an account of the emergence and development of radio features in the regions and London see Paddy Scannell, 'The Stuff of Radio', in John Corner (ed.), *Documentary and the Mass Media*, pp. 1–26.

4. Previous studies of this period include Paddy Scannell, 'The Social Eye of Television 1946–55', in *Media, Culture and Society* vol. 1. no. 1, 1979, pp. 97–106 and Stuart Laing, *Representations of Working-Class Life 1957–64* (London: Macmillan, 1986), ch. 6. See also Bell, 'Origins', in John Corner (ed.), *Documentary and the Mass Media*, pp. 65–80 for a valuable historical sketch of the institutional formation of the genre within the BBC.

5. Cited in Scannell, 'The Social Eye', p. 104.

6. Interview with author, 25 July 1989.

7. Norman Swallow, 'Documentary TV Journalism', in Paul Rotha (ed.), *Television in the Making* (London: Focal Press, 1956), p. 51.

8. Cited in Arthur Swinson, *Writing for Television* (London: Black, 1955; Second Edition 1960), p. 113.

9. Ibid., pp. 108–109.

10. Interview with author, 25 July 1989.

11. Scannell, 'The Social Eye', p. 97.

12. Interview with author, 25 July 1989.

13. Interview with author, 25 July 1989.

14. Norman Swallow, *Factual Television* (London: Focal Press, 1966), p. 195.

15. Interview with author, 25 July 1989.

16. Interview with author, 9 August 1989.

17. Interview with author, 9 August 1989.

18. Interview with author, 9 August 1989.

19. Cited in Norman Swallow, 'Denis Mitchell', in *The Listener*, 24 April 1975, p. 551.

20. Cited in Swallow, 'Denis Mitchell'.

21. K. W. Gransden, 'Critic on the Hearth', *The Listener*, April 2 1959. I became aware of this review through references in Laing, *Representations*.

22. Swallow, *Factual Television*, p. 178.

23. Interview with author, 9 August 1989.

24. Norman Swallow, unpublished notes on documentary television in the period.

25. John Corner, 'Interview as "Social Encounter" in early TV Documentary', in Paddy Scannell (ed.), *Broadcast Talk* (London: Sage, forthcoming).

26. Very useful accounts of the changing conditions of British cultural and social life during this period can be found in Laing, *Representations* and J. Hill, *Sex, Class and Realism: British Cinema 1956–63* (London: British Film Institute, 1986).

I would like to thank Norman Swallow and the late Denis Mitchell for being so generous with their time in helping me prepare this account, and also Julian Henriques (then working for the BBC) for his help with technical and archival information.

Every Wart and Pustule
Gilbert Harding and Television Stardom

ANDY MEDHURST

I just behave as I am and talk as I think, which for some reason appears to be remarkably novel.

Gilbert Harding

He was fat, he was ugly and he was headline news. GILBERT HARDING HAS BRONCHITIS. GILBERT HARDING ORDERED OUT. CLASH OVER SAUCE A LA HARDING. GILBERT HARDING IN GREAT RAIL DELAY. ANOTHER HARDING RUMPUS. HARDING APOLOGISES AS 3,000,000 WATCH. STOP HARDING'S RUDENESS: THE JOKE IS OVER. He turned on the Blackpool Illuminations, he made a record the BBC banned as obscene, he was offered stage roles as both Toad of Toad Hall and Hamlet, he advertised cigarettes and indigestion remedies, he tried his hand at being an investigative journalist and a disc jockey, he cooked with Fanny Craddock and he acted with Cliff Richard. For nine years he was one of the most famous people in Britain, but who exactly was he and why did he matter so much to so many people?

Today we suffer from a surfeit of stars. It doesn't take much to earn a back-page pin-up in *Smash Hits* or to have your favourite recipes outlined in TV *Times*, but there was a time when television was a novelty and when the television star was a new and unfamiliar phenomenon. Gilbert Harding was the single most emblematic figure of that era – in the popular imagination he *was* television. For in the first half of the 1950s, television meant, above all, *What's My Line* and *What's My Line* meant Gilbert Harding.

It has to be one of the unlikeliest success stories in the history of British popular culture, but it's also an exemplary narrative, a cautionary tale that reveals a lot about how television was constructed, perceived and understood in the 1950s. I want to try to use the career of Gilbert Harding as a way of unravelling some of those discourses, because it fell to poor Gilbert to be Britain's first major television personality. He was the test-case for definitions of televisual stardom, for the placing of the dividing line between 'star' and 'personality', for the working out of the acceptable limits of public curiosity and press intrusion. Before him there was no yardstick, so the particular and tragic fascination of his

60

career is that it enables us to see what has become an archetypal trajectory acted out for the very first time.

Gilbert Harding: A Career Outline

Although this essay is concerned with a far wider area than the merely biographical, clearly it's necessary to have some sense of the man at the centre of it all. He was born in 1907, in Hereford, in a workhouse. Not as a child of one of its inmates, however, but the child of its Master and Matron. His father died while Gilbert was very young. He went to school in Wolverhampton and studied History and Modern Languages at Queens' College, Cambridge. He became a Catholic and in the 1930s worked as a teacher, a police constable and a journalist. His ambition to become a lawyer was thwarted by the outbreak of the Second World War, and in December 1939, being found medically unfit for the armed forces, Harding joined the BBC's Monitoring Service as a sub-editor. He subsequently moved to the Outside Broadcasting Department and here made his first radio broadcasts. In 1944 he went to Canada for three years, working at the BBC's Toronto office. On returning to London, he became Question Master in a new radio panel game called *Round Britain Quiz*, though in doing so he left the BBC staff (at whose insistence, his or theirs, remains unclear) and worked on a freelance basis. This programme was his first bite at a regular broadcast slot, though his function was limited to introducing the panellists and asking the questions. There was little scope for individuality.

Panel games and quizzes were a central part of BBC output at that time, both on radio and television. They were relatively cheap to produce, had the appeal of regularity and familiarity within tightly circumscribed guidelines, and blended entertainment with education in a way that adhered securely to the prevailing Reithian ideology of broadcasting. Harding also introduced *The Brains Trust* and *Twenty Questions*, though his pretensions to intellectual seriousness ensured that he greatly preferred the former, in which academics and philosophers chewed over weighty metaphysical issues, to the latter, in which variety performers and radio comedians strove to identify a mystery object. This tension between intellectual capability and the supposed soft option of light entertainment is one that runs throughout his career.

Television, at this stage, was still very much the junior partner to radio. It could only be received in a small area around London, and transmissions only lasted for a few hours per day. The BBC *Yearbooks* of this period clearly indicate, by the number of pages and detail of information allotted, the relative standing of the two media. Television was a tricksy upstart, radio was where the serious broadcasting went on. Harding's early ventures into TV, then, were seen by him as an adjunct to his proper work. Nonetheless, it was on television that he first achieved some public impact, when, on a panel game called *We Beg To Differ*, in which a male and a female team debated whether men and women viewed issues differently (a touching indication of the innocence of early post-war television), he told one of the opposing side to 'mind your own business'. This incident was the first sighting of the quality on which Harding's stardom was based – his legendary rudeness.

Early 50s Television and 'What's My Line'

What's My Line, which originated on American television, was a simple game in which four panellists sought to guess the occupations of members of the public. There is no indication at all that anyone in the BBC saw it as substantially different from the other panel games then being broadcast. It was cheap, inoffensive entertainment; nothing as brash as large prizes were on offer – if a contestant succeeded in baffling the panel she or he went away with nothing more than a commemorative scroll. That was the official prize, perhaps, but like any game or quiz show the real trophy on offer was a brief taste of fame, a few minutes *on television*. And, as the series progressed, a few minutes on television *with Gilbert Harding*.

Harding at first thought he would be suitable as the question master, but, after his one attempt was wrecked thanks to backstage mistakes, that job went to Eamonn Andrews. Harding reappeared as a panellist on the fifth programme, broadcast on 13 August 1951. The series rolled along on its mild, bland, early 50s way for another few weeks, but then something happened. Harding took a vehement dislike to a particularly evasive contestant and, losing all patience, snapped at him, 'I am tired of looking at you'. Now it was, perhaps, not one of the great savage put-downs of all time, but this was 1952, the era of Sylvia Peters and Muffin the Mule, when the world of BBC television was a world of almost inconceivable niceness. Everyone on screen behaved with deep-frozen cocktail party politeness, in the midst of which Harding's offhand sourness came across like Kenneth Tynan saying 'fuck' some years later.

Complaints poured in ('I felt like walking out of my own drawing room', wrote one viewer[1]) and the incident was widely reported in the national press – and this, remember, at a time when most of the country could not yet receive television. What had happened was that Harding had become a talking point, last night's TV became what you discussed next morning on the train, or at school, or over the garden fence. If, that is, you owned a television set. Harding and *What's My Line* became central to the process whereby those without television increasingly perceived themselves as socially disadvantaged, left behind. That first outburst should not be given unique credit for any of this; Harding's manner on the programme had always been somewhat tougher than his colleagues', since to be the 'hard man' was his function in the text, but his impatient attacks now increased in frequency and punctured the balloon of blandness in which the BBC had hitherto cocooned itself.

Rudeness-by-Harding became *What's My Line*'s secret weapon, the Ingredient X that marked it out from other panel games, and here we reach another of the key tensions in the Harding persona. The 'rudeness' began to be seen by an enthralled public as Harding's 'act': it was what he *did*. But for Harding it was not an adopted device, a behavioural catchphrase, but his genuine personality – it was what he *was*. This tension between role and real is crucial, and I'll come back to it when discussing the precise contours of the notion of the 'personality' on television.

Harding's inherent tendency towards short-temperedness was only increased by his fondness for alcohol. He often appeared on *What's My Line* mildly (or less mildly) drunk. The looser his tongue became, the more the audience approved – frequently, of course, concealing that approval behind a thin cloak of affronted outrage. He told one contestant she was 'too elegant to come from Rugby', and in response to Eamonn Andrews' attempt to defend that town added, 'Have you ever been there?' When the mystery celebrity contestant was the hairdresser 'Teasy-Weasy' Raymonde, Harding spat 'you call yourself some peculiar name which I am determined not to remember'. Television viewers were not used to this bitchy abuse, and Harding's elevation to stardom rocketed on the back of his crushing one-liners.

Better yet, his behaviour off-screen was scarcely different – in fact Harding's whole argument, repeated *ad infinitum* in interview after interview, was that there was no difference at all. He was the way he was, on television or off, and if people were shocked by his actions and outbursts then they had no reason to be. They had seen him on TV, they ought to know what he was like. On what was probably the most celebrated occasion, he arrived rather drunk at an annual dinner for Hounslow magistrates and denounced it as 'third-rate . . . just another suburban do'. The headlines screamed, the public clucked, Hounslow never recovered.

This was not, after all, the way BBC employees were expected to behave. Harding's only possible rival for the title of television personified was Richard Dimbleby, and the contrast between the two men is stark enough to bring out the full flavour and significance of Harding's transgressive appeal. Dimbleby was measured, calm, solemn, reliable, authoritative, a man of sonorous marble – Harding inverted all those adjectives: he was a bluff, reckless bottle of scotch on the loose.

This is not to say he relished his notoriety. On the contrary, he was frequently and publicly contrite (remember HARDING APOLOGISES AS 3,000,000 WATCH? – which may well have been the first newspaper headline to cite an audience figure for television), pleading in mitigation that the rudeness was not affectation but simply the way he was made. What he failed to appreciate, though, was how much the rudeness was central to his popularity. This persona (which he always denied was anything other than his true self) was far too adored to allow any modifications – the circus audience had acquired its very own dancing bear, and all he was permitted to do was dance.

The Harding Industry
The real Harding boom occupied the first half of the 50s, the period before the arrival of commercial television. Harding was front-page news because if he was on TV, nothing else was – literally. There was only one channel, and *What's My Line* epitomised that era of BBC monopoly, with its Festival of Britain graphics and its fuss over necklines. ITV introduced big-money quizzes like *Double Your Money* and *Take Your Pick*, which offered far more than scrolls. *What's My Line* maintained its success, but increasingly it couldn't help looking dated. No longer did it encapsulate the televisual *zeitgeist*. So where could Harding, its unquestioned star, go next? The problem was that he was so overwhelmingly associated with that one programme that it was difficult to find convincing alternative slots. His popularity was so huge that the sheer force of his personality carried some

limp programme ideas like *Harding Finds Out*, a stab at investigative reporting, and *I Know What I Like*, in which audiences were treated to Gilbert's defiantly middlebrow tastes in poetry, music and painting. There was even a fifteen-minute slot shown late at night (or what passed for late in those days of early bedtimes), in which he simply sat and pontificated on issues of the day.

This role as national oracle seems hard to imagine from today's perspectives. Why did people take so seriously the views of a quiz panellist? It's as if, in terms of 1990's division of televisual labour, there was no difference between Jeremy Beadle and Michael Ignatieff. What seems to have been behind Harding's elevation into guru status was his reputation for 'speaking his mind'. He wrote various newspaper columns, most prominently in the *People*, where he took on cases of bureaucratic injustice rather in the way later adopted by *That's Life*. Perhaps it was the crusty schoolteacher exterior, perhaps it was a naive belief that he 'wouldn't take any nonsense', but readers trusted him with all manner of problems. He was seen as a superhuman ombudsman.

Then there were the books. His autobiography (ghost-written, like all the publications that came out under his name) was serialised in magazines and on radio, bought by a major book club, and reprinted a number of times. This was followed by, among others, *Gilbert Harding's Book of Manners*, the gag/tag being, fairly obviously, that here was the man dubbed 'Britain's rudest' giving his version of correct societal interaction (a phrase he would have loathed). *Master of None* was a collection of anecdotes loosely related to work and occupations, the association with *What's My Line* thus still strongly maintained. Harding even formed a company to take care of this burgeoning industry. It was called, with touching self-deprecation, Gilbert Harding (Exploitation) Ltd. The array of media outings and opportunities I list in this chapter's first paragraph were only some of the more notable of his high-earning achievements. He had become this country's first unequivocal media personality. He was famous for being famous.[2]

The underlying paradox of all this success was that Harding the man was lonely and dreadfully unhappy. There's a way of reading this which slips it neatly into the 'tragic star' stereotype, particularly as his personal unhappiness was directly linked to his homosexuality (the register shifts slightly to 'tragic queer' in this case[3]). The fact of his sexuality *is* relevant, and I'll return to it later. But it's relevant in a way that most accounts of Harding seem either blind to or unwilling to grasp. Firstly, though, it's important to look at the exact moment when the rude-Harding paradigm is overtaken by the unhappy-Harding persona.

The 'Face to Face' Interview

Face To Face was a series of interviews with prominent people in which John Freeman attempted to penetrate more deeply than the standard conventions of televisual conversation allowed. The studio was dark, the camera kept fixed on the person being interviewed (either in painfully tight close-up for the especially tortured moments, or a more reticent medium shot), while Freeman was only seen from behind. Its ambience now reminds one inevitably of *Mastermind*, but the victims' specialised subject was always the same: themselves. According to at least one of Harding's biographers[4], Freeman had had Gilbert in his sights for some time. The reason was not made clear at the time, but when in 1988 a batch of *Face To Face*s were shown again, a letter to *The Listener* from a former executive involved with the series let this fascinating and rather chilling cat out of the bag:

> In the Harding interview, John Freeman had been intending to bring the conversation around to the fact that Gilbert was homosexual – then a virtually unmentionable subject.[5]

The Harding *Face To Face* has always had a legendary status as an exceptionally tough, relentless piece of interviewing. Armed with the above information, it takes on another, more sinister, connotation entirely.

It is an extraordinary piece of television, even today. There is nowhere to look except at the great mournful landscape of Harding's face as Freeman drills away, almost all his questions being variations on a theme of pain and discipline. The interview has inescapably taken on an obituary flavour, since it was broadcast only a few weeks before Harding's sudden death in December 1960. What makes it so grisly and gripping is the victim's complicity in carving his own headstone – it's an *autobiographical* obituary, and as such it serves as a convenient summary of all the conflicts and tensions created by the success of this most unlikely of stars.

The *What's My Line* team in September 1958. L. to r.: Isobel Barnett, Ted Moult, Sara Leighton and Gilbert Harding.

Thus we get the idea that Harding has sold short his intelligence (his 'first-class mind', as Freeman puts it) by participating in light entertainment. Then there is the pivotal issue of the role of 'Harding' versus the real Harding. The exchange runs like this:

> Freeman: Are you ever conscious of cultivating the mannerisms of Harding the public figure?
> Harding: I've never had any mannerisms.
> Freeman: Well, you know, you have, but you're not conscious of them.
> Harding: I've never cultivated my mannerisms. I have never pretended. If I knew how to pretend, I would. But I don't know how – so I don't.

This, encapsulated with a kind of tragic inarticulacy, is the absolute core of the Harding dilemma, a dilemma which has been played out so many times since by later personalities – when you are only known and liked for certain characteristics, do you risk alienating the public by changing, or do you suppress your own need for change and conform by playing out the same, tired tropes?

Freeman strides on, and Harding admits to profound unhappiness with almost every response – 'Nothing has ever happened that's given me any sort of a sense of achievement or satisfaction' – until the (in)famous moment when Harding's reserve cracks and he cries on recalling the death of his mother. This is the incident that burned itself into the memories of those watching, precisely because it is a rare moment of unmediated emotion, a glimpse of profound and untreated grief that has no place on a medium as committed to sparkling insincerity as television. It is, in many ways, the logical conclusion of the whole Harding trajectory; the man who made his name by rejecting the toning-downs, the evasive gloss of television, achieves here the most direct, naked communication possible.

Freeman clearly subscribed to that school of thought which traced male homosexuality back to a 'dominant mother', so he seized Harding's grief as another way of trying to get at his sexuality. The question is painstakingly, exquisitely polite:

> Is there any truth in the notion I have in the back of my mind that it is this particularly deep relation you obviously had with your mother which has made it impossible so far for you to marry?

(Note, especially, the feline inclusion of 'so far'), but its meaning is plain enough. Harding was being invited to declare his queerness, but he refused to deliver the 'confession' that Freeman was so assiduously pursuing; instead he does something even more remarkable: he sketches the sexual predicament of an entire culture:

> My sister didn't marry, and I didn't marry and my mother was a widow when she was just thirty, and so when we came to live together we put up a sort of cloud of sexual frustration that was enough to blot out the sun.

There's a terrible eloquence in this, a revelation of the pain and fear engendered by living in a society committed to the repression of all but the most conventional sexual options. It's the kind of statement, I'd argue, that has a particular relevance and poignancy coming from a homosexual man on the brink of the 1960s.

Harding and Homosexuality

The importance of Harding's sexuality has a far wider relevance than as the subtext of the Freeman crucifixion. His anxiety about maintaining privacy was particularly acute given the possibilities of blackmail at a time when homosexual acts between men were still illegal. The 1950s had seen an unprecedented level of public debate around this subject (a fact that makes nonsense of Leonard Miall's claim, in his letter about *Face To Face*, that it was 'virtually unmentionable').

Whether in vindictive tabloid articles called 'Evil Men' or purportedly balanced analyses called *They Stand Apart*[6], that debate was invariably couched in terms of homosexuality as otherness, and was undertaken primarily by heterosexuals, but at least the subject was being aired. Harding is an intriguing figure in this context, since, if he embodied television in the history of the 50s, he also embodies the 50s in the history of television – that is to say he was a key cultural figure of the decade in which, thanks to the Burgess/Maclean scandal, the Lord Montagu trial and the Wolfenden Report, homosexuality was centrally on the social agenda.

Some of the images of Harding, seen today, are almost comic in their conformity to known stereotypes of homosexuality. He lived in *Brighton*, doting on a *Pekinese*, a big fan of *Marlene Dietrich* and so on. Clearly such signals were available for interpretation to the homosexual cognoscenti at the time, but it's interesting to speculate what the mass heterosexual audience made of them. Alison Hennegan, recalling her 50s childhood with lesbian hindsight, comments on Harding's much-publicised relationship with another gay television personality:

> At twelve . . . I wasn't clear who I was yet, but I had inklings. I knew that the figure of Nancy Spain, with her uncoiffeured hair, well-cut hacking jacket, open-necked shirt and rakish cravat, gave me a warm glow . . . And I knew that . . . her . . . cross-talk act with Gilbert Harding . . . gave me the same comforted pleasure, but I couldn't explain it. Now, of course, I know that they were having a whale of a time playing at being a flirtatious heterosexual couple, enacting an outrageously camp open secret. It was fun, it was flagrant, and utterly unperceived by the bulk of their audience.[7]

The Spain/Harding relationship was one of the odder gossip column items from the mid-50s, and what is attractive about Hennegan's reading of it is how enjoyable she makes it sound. The prevailing construction of Harding as poor, unhappy homosexual would clearly have to be modified to accommodate the idea of Gilbert playing an extended camp trick on the great British public.

That, though, does seem to have been the case, particularly with reference to press speculations about a Spain/Harding marriage. Nancy Spain's contribution to *Gilbert Harding By His Friends* (a collection of reminiscences published the year after his death, the very existence of which amply demonstrates the level of public interest in the man), declares that:

> we talked it over one lunchtime at Antoine's in Charlotte Street. 'It would be a very good idea,' Gilbert finally summed it all up, large myopic eyes glazing over like two lightly-boiled plovers' eggs. 'But I should want *all* the serial rights!'[8]

This is the kind of camp one-liner that would have a special resonance to those in the know. Other contributions to this tribute volume hint at Harding's sexuality, though they tend to shore up the tragic-and-unhappy side. Robin Maugham, another resident of Brighton's 1950s gay community, recalls an evening when Harding confided his entire life story:

> Even now, I cannot bear to think of the story he told me that night ... without going into any details by revealing anything I shouldn't, I think I can say this. If ever a man had difficulties of character and temperament to contend with, it was Gilbert. The trouble was that he was fastidiously honest with himself and his standards were extremely high. The result was that he disliked various aspects of his own nature ...[9]

These 'difficulties' could be taken to mean the irascibility, the fondness for drink, the standard Harding complaints, and no doubt they're relevant up to a point, but I trust my own gay judgement to decode this as a comment about sexuality, more specifically about homosexual self-oppression.

Self-oppression sounds like a loaded term, perhaps, but what I mean by it here is the variety of ways in which homosexuals were persuaded to collude in the negative constructions of homosexuality circulated by certain strands of heterosexual opinion. The comparatively widespread and public discussion of homosexuality in the 50s included all manner of proposed 'solutions' to the 'problem'. The idea that it was possible to be happy and homosexual was strenuously discouraged, one psychiatrist going so far as to state:

> Possibly the greatest importance of homosexuality is that it causes so much unhappiness. If happiness is of any value ... then homosexuality should be eliminated by every means in our power.[10]

It was that kind of breathtakingly arrogant illogicality (if homosexuals are 'unhappy', it is because of the heterosexual misrepresentation and bigotry that surrounds them), which led otherwise intelligent men like Gilbert Harding to seek a way out of their 'condition'. He affixed himself to two of the more tenacious heterosexual disciplines, Roman Catholicism and Freudian psychoanalysis, as part of this saddening search.[11]

It's a relatively unbroken line from Harding to Russell Harty, in terms of press treatment of homosexual celebrities. After Harding's death, a pack of journalists descended on Brighton trying to unearth some scandal, much as the ghoulish hacks of the late 80s flocked to the dying Harty's hospital in an attempt to generate some seedy copy. Happily, in both cases, they failed. Once again, though, the point is that Harding set the precedent for later traditions of journalistic interest in the private lives of the famous. An 'exposé' of Harding's sexual tastes would have been the scoop of the 50s. His fear of this, and of blackmail, coupled with a more general feeling of guilt and failure pumped into him by priests and psychiatrists, conspired to leave him sexually unfulfilled; the first, but not the last, homosexual television personality to be imprisoned by fame.

Harding, Television and Cinema

One of the best ways of understanding just how central Harding was in embodying the *televisual* in the 1950s is by looking at the feature films in which he appeared. It's odd that while many of the biographical pieces and reminiscences mention Harding's aspirations to acting, none of them refer to these films. This is a notable oversight, but in a way it's curiously appropriate, because in those roles he is not so much acting in any conventional sense, but *signifying*, and what he signifies is television.

Feature films of this period have an ambivalent attitude towards the younger, threatening medium.[12] To begin with, in the days of the BBC monopoly and its concomitant addiction to blandness, a 1949 film like *Train of Events* can treat TV with ridicule. One scene in a television studio begins with two penguins walking out of shot, while a very BBC voice says: 'Well, Charlie and Mabel, a remarkable exhibition of ballroom dancing. I'm sure Victor Sylvester has nothing to teach you'. This shrewd jibe at the novelty-at-all-costs magazine programme is followed by a swipe at the Corporation's tendency to foist high culture on to its audience – the next item 'televised' is a pretentious discussion about classical music. Clearly, at this stage, the cinema wasn't troubled by competition from quickstepping penguins.

That confidence wavered, inevitably, as the popularity of TV grew. Performers who had made their names on the small screen were turned into film stars, most notably Norman Wisdom. Harding did not have the performing talents to carry a whole film, but he was a name – in television terms the biggest name – and his potential as a box-office draw proved an irresistible temptation. With the exception of *The Gentle Gunman*, a deeply confused drama about the IRA that uses Harding, in scenes outside the main narrative, as a symbol of stubborn Englishness,[13] it's notable that the films he appeared in are all comedies. It is as if film was trying to use him as a joke about television.

The Oracle, for example, skits Harding's bizarre reputation as social commentator, his voice used as a supernatural predictive force that rises up from the bottom of a well (perhaps a joke about the small, dim picture produced by 1950s TV technology). More significantly still, three films released in 1955 were part of the Rank Organisation's conscious attempt to woo audiences away from TV by offering big-budget colour spectacle. *An Alligator Named Daisy* and *As Long As They're Happy* are, as their titles indicate, ferociously winsome concoctions, and they each simply wheel on Harding for one scene and one joke. *Daisy* climaxes at a large fête-cum-alligator-show (it's a weird film), in which a number of personalities from radio and television are present. They include Frankie Howerd, Jimmy Edwards, the flamboyant racing tipster Prince Monolulu, and Harding. All he is required to do is walk around and be 'rude' in response to a couple of questions. In *Happy* he is incongruously included in an audience for a visiting American pop singer (the film centres on a parody of Johnny Ray). An elderly fan of the singer asks Harding if he 'digs' the singer. 'I'd bury him', scowls Harding in response. 'Oh you rude man', she replies. Again, it is the easy, obvious deployment of Harding-equals-rudeness. (By the singer's third song, Harding is sobbing along with the rest of the audience – with hindsight this slight gag becomes a teasing foretaste of the tears at the Freeman interview).

The third and by far the best of these Rank films is *Simon and Laura*. Based on a hit stage play, it tells of two actors who are offered a daily television serial. Simon, played by Peter Finch, is at his gentleman's club when he meets a fellow member, Harding. Seeking his advice about the wisdom of regular television work, he gets this reply:

Do you know what happens to you when you allow yourself to be regularly exhibited in that glass rectangle? You become public property. Your face, electronically distorted, is huddled round and gawped at by three-quarters of the population of the United Kingdom, and within a month every wrinkle, every wart and pustule, has become part of our British way of life. Start speaking your mind, they'll say you're rude. Stop speaking your mind, they'll say you're namby-pamby and you're slipping. Mind you, I'm not saying that the British public isn't warm-hearted and generous. They are. Terrifyingly so. You have but to clear your throat and the next day you'll be inundated with linctuses, pastilles, pills and potions . . .

That, in a nutshell, is the Harding philosophy. What's so noteworthy about this appearance of it is that it's part of a fiction film, but with the obvious double-bluff assumption that the film's audience is supposed to recognise it as an authentic Harding tirade. By this stage of the 50s, even those without televisions would have read Harding pieces or interviews in the press. In the film's next scene, Laura (Kay Kendall) meets Isobel Barnett, another *What's My Line* fixture, at the hairdresser's and asks her advice. She gets some words of wisdom on earrings and necklines, these two points of fashion also by this time part of general folklore about television.

Four years later, in 1959, the satirical musical-comedy *Expresso Bongo* includes, as part of its attack on pop music, a scene where the TV documentary series *Cosmorama* (no prizes for guessing the real series parodied here) visits a Soho coffee bar to film the new teenage craze. *Cosmorama* is fronted by Gilbert Harding, who makes bluffly disparaging comments about 'teenage rebellion' and 'plastic palm trees'. In a later 'studio discussion', Harding has the show stolen from him by the unscrupulous manager of the pop singer at the centre of the plot. *Expresso Bongo* was released less than a year before Harding died, and brief as his appearance in it is, it does raise questions about what might have happened to Harding's career if he had lived.

Putting it bluntly, wouldn't he have seemed embarrassingly out of place? In a television culture dominated by *Z-Cars* and *That Was The Week That Was*, Jimmy Tarbuck and *Steptoe and Son*, Harding would have been stranded, an unlikely rebel from the generation before last, his claims to once-upon-a-time innovation going unheard, as boys in Beatles suits laughed at his elderly colonel appearance. What *Expresso Bongo* does is to expose Harding as old hat, an emblem of a superseded cultural moment, the sad sight of a subversive voice co-opted beyond redemption into the establishment he had once (however unintentionally) scandalised. The cruellest blow of all: by having him front *Cosmorama*, *Expresso Bongo* turns him into Richard Dimbleby.

TV Star or TV Personality?

To conclude, then, Harding, as well as being a fascinating character in his own right, draws together in an exemplary way all the key discourses about television in the 1950s. He was not the only hugely popular television performer of that era, but it would not be possible to write an essay such as this centred on Jeanne Heal or Mary Malcolm or Philip Harben. They lack the extra layers of meaning, the added clusters of contextual relevance, that make Harding so absolutely central.

Is it possible to sum up what it was that made him so monstrously, freakishly popular? Which public nerves did he touch with such electrifying accuracy that he became the Elephant Man of British television? It could be that he matched closely one of the cultural archetypes the British have liked to see as peculiar to their national identity – the brusque, dyspeptic, plain-speaking, short-fused, common-sense archetype that led many of Harding's contemporaries to compare him to Dr Johnson. (It speaks volumes, I think, that such a literary comparison was felt appropriate; few, if any, of today's television favourites would merit such an accolade.) The *Gilbert Harding By His Friends* collection was explicitly conceived to fill the gap left by a Johnson with no Boswell to pen the official record.[14] More recently, in a tour de force of cultural-historical analysis, Raphael Samuel has constructed a typology of British archetypes, in which he too places Harding in the Johnsonian camp.[15]

If we accept that it was 'rudeness' that was the key to Harding's success, it was highly fortunate that he was offered a place on *What's My Line*. After all, if a man has delusions of intellectual grandeur, nothing is more liable to trigger a fountain of frustrated spleen than being asked to identify correctly a Theatre Fireman's Night Companion, a Pepper-Pot Perforator or a Wuzzer.[16] It was, undoubtedly, a trivial way to earn a living, and the sense of wasted time was clearly what lay behind Harding's irresistible volcano of pique. He belonged to the generation of broadcasters who saw documentary reporting as the highest possible calling. He might be an exact inversion of Richard Dimbleby, but deep down it's more than likely that Dimbleby was exactly who he wanted to be.

If the exasperation at ending up in light entertainment was one of the sources of the Great Rudeness, then the other was the way the public, inexplicably but wholly in love with this cantankerous man, laid claim to his time and his person.

Every time we hear a soap star today lament the fact that they can't go shopping in peace, they are but an echo of Harding, and at least they know they have to expect it. He didn't – it was all new, unexpected and thus immeasurably less welcome:

> Lowering the car window to ask a simple question can either cause obstruction, so great is the crowd of only-too-willing but inarticulate helpers, or provoke immediate insults . . . 'Gilbert!' they mutter convulsively and somewhat familiarly, clutching their tie. 'It's Gilbert!' It is, and all I want to know is where the ill-lit, badly signposted road to some confounded parish hall is.[17]

The bitterest irony of all was that the angrier he got with this kind of public response, the more they loved him for it: getting more angry meant getting more *Gilberty*. It was a bonus, a double helping, an encore. He really couldn't win. Which is why he could never convince anyone that it wasn't all an act. If he tried and was disbelieved, his temper would boil over and there was the 'act' all over again. Long before the novel was published, Harding was forced to live out a Catch-22.

There remains the question of the distinction between a television star and a television personality. Using John Ellis' basic definition of a star as 'a performer in a particular medium whose figure enters into subsidiary forms of circulation, and then feeds back into future performances',[18] Harding would seem to qualify. All those headlines were subsidiary forms of circulation, while one newspaper ran a *daily* column called 'Gilbert Harding – Day By Day', such was the insatiable appetite at one time for Hardingiana. Then there were all the books: many TV performers have written autobiographies, occasionally members of their family will add a second volume (such as Mabel Pickles' irresistibly-titled *Married To Wilfred*), but the Harding collection would fill a small shelf. Add to this all the extra radio, stage, film and public appearances, all the journalism and the records and the advertising, and Harding looks like a classic star. Besides, all the things I have attributed to his career as firsts were only firsts in terms of TV – the journalistic prying and public hysteria were nothing new to film stars.

And yet . . . something still pulls me back from calling him a star. I think it's something to do with the fact that most film stars have an aura of mystery, of otherworldliness, of sexual desirability, that is enhanced by the size of the screen and the darkness of the cinema. To visit a cinema in the golden decades of Hollywood was to enter a palace, a temple, a sacred site of surrender and completion. To watch television is to enter the living room. Television performers are too available, they're on too often. If in the 1950s you wanted to see Marilyn Monroe's new film or gasp again at the beauty of James Dean, you had to wait months. Gilbert was yours at the flick of a switch every Sunday night. No mystery. Not a lot of sexual desirability either, though he did apparently have one or two exceptionally devoted female fans.[19]

Gilbert Harding, then, was the first paradigmatic television personality. He wasn't, after all, enacting a fictional role, but trading on an aspect (however heightened) of his own personal attributes. He unwittingly inaugurated a tradition which has included Patrick Moore, Barbara Woodhouse and Keith Floyd (Harding and Floyd might, I'd like to think, have enjoyed the odd glass or two together). They, even at their best, aren't much more than flavour-of-the-month eccentrics, but Harding meant more than that. He occupied the historically pivotal role of undergoing the first-ever public baptism of small-screen adulation. He was typecast as himself, a part he could scarcely unlearn.

On a more personal level, he fascinates and means a lot to me because those tensions between private and public lives overlap with a larger struggle over definitions of sexuality. The 1960s, as I have said above, would not have suited Gilbert, and I suspect he'd have regarded gay politics as unduly exhibitionistic. He'd have been wrong, of course, but that wrongness would be due to the lies about his own sexuality that he was coerced into internalising. Still, fortunately, there are enough alternative images of Harding to combat that trapped, goaded, sweating man on *Face To Face*. I like to think of him shaking with laughter, three whiskies down the road to oblivion, plotting and bitching with Nancy Spain.

Notes

1. Quoted in Dicky Leeman, *What's My Line: The Story of a Phenomenon* (London: Allan Wingate, 1955), p. 127. The sheer existence of this book, with its detailed account of the minutiae of every programme in the series, testifies to how central to 50s television *What's My Line* was.
2. See Gilbert Harding, *Along My Line* (London: Putnam, 1956); *Gilbert Harding's Book of Manners* (London: Putnam, 1956), *Master of None* (London: Putnam, 1958). Also, there are two biographies of Harding that I have used in researching this account: Roger Storey's *Gilbert Harding* (London: Barrie and Rockcliff, 1961), a memoir written by Harding's private secretary; and Wallace Reyburn's *Gilbert Harding: A Candid Portrayal* (London: Angus and Robertson, 1978). This latter, as its subtitle suggests, is a muck-raking, warts-and-all biography, the prurient tone of which is especially gratuitous in its offensive, misinformed chapter about Harding's homosexuality. At one point, for example, Reyburn uses the phrase 'alcoholics, neurotics, murderers, homosexuals and so on' (p. 104).
3. I ought to say that, being gay myself, I'm using the term 'queer' not to endorse it, but because it is the term most in use at the time concerned. As Simon Shepherd suggests in *Because We're Queers: The Life and Crimes of Kenneth Halliwell and Joe Orton* (London: GMP, 1989) the word 'queer' can be used to 'denote, historically, a pre-gay homosexual identity and culture, p. 9.
4. See the final chapter of Storey, *Gilbert Harding*.
5. Leonard Miall, letter to *The Listener*, 3 November 1988.
6. 'Evil Men' was published in the *Sunday Pictorial* in 1952. *They Stand Apart* was published by Heinemann in 1955. For the best overview of this period, see Jeffrey Weeks, *Coming Out* (London: Quartet, 1979).
7. Alison Hennegan, 'On Becoming a Lesbian Reader', in Susannah Radstone (ed.), *Sweet Dreams: Sexuality, Gender and Popular Fiction* (London: Lawrence and Wishart, 1988), pp. 167–8.
8. Nancy Spain, 'Gilbert and Women', in Stephen Grenfall (ed.), *Gilbert Harding By His Friends* (London: André Deutsch, 1961), p. 162.

9. Robin Maugham, 'Final Release', in Grenfall (ed.), *Gilbert Harding*, p. 206.
10. Clifford Allen, *Homosexuality: Its Nature, Causation and Treatment* (London: Unwin, 1958), p. 34.
11. See Reyburn, *Gilbert Harding*, ch. 12 (taking care to filter out Reyburn's homophobic interpretations). John Freeman obviously knew about Harding's experiences with psychoanalysis, hence certain questions on *Face To Face* – another part of the project to unmask Harding's queerness.
12. See Charles Barr, 'Broadcasting and Cinema: Screens within Screens', in Barr (ed.), *All Our Yesterdays: Ninety Years of British Cinema* (London: BFI, 1986) for the definitive survey of films that addressed television.
13. For a full analysis of this film see John Hill, 'Images of Violence', in Kevin Rockett, Luke Gibbons, John Hill, *Cinema and Ireland* (London: Croom Helm, 1987).
14. See Grenfall (ed.), *Gilbert Harding*. Fanny Craddock's contribution is specifically titled 'The Johnson Who Lacked a Boswell'. In the BBC tribute programme, broadcast a few days after Harding's death, Sir Compton Mackenzie had employed the Johnson comparison.
15. Raphael Samuel, 'Introduction: The Figures of National Myth', in Samuel (ed.), *Patriotism: The Making and Unmaking of British National Identity, Volume Three: National Fictions* (London: Routledge, 1989). Samuel also, intriguingly, links Harding with another crucial 50s TV figure, Tony Hancock. There's more work to be done here, especially given Hancock's treatment on *Face To Face* (he stated there that he thought happiness was impossible – a very Hardingesque sentiment).
16. A Wuzzer, according to Dicky Leeman, *What's My Line*, worked in a Yorkshire woollen mill and described his job thus: 'you gets t'wool and you wuzzes it'.
17. Harding, *Master of None*, p. 174.
18. John Ellis, *Visible Fictions* (London: Routledge and Kegan Paul, 1982), p. 91.
19. Both Storey and Reyburn document examples of this.

'Hancock's Half-Hour'
A Watershed in British Television Comedy

PETER GODDARD

In the early 1950s, the principal forms of popular entertainment in Britain were radio, the cinema and the variety-theatre. Since the beginning of the 1960s, the dominance of television has been almost unchallengeable. In the intervening period, television comedy became established as a recognisable entity in its own right, differentiated in form and content from its predecessors. The development of a distinctive television comedy can be seen as an adaptation of 'the comic' to the particular qualities of television as a medium of representation and to the production processes of television as an industry. It also reflected changing social attitudes as Britain moved from post-war austerity to a time of relative prosperity and full employment.

Television comedy took a number of forms in the early 1960s, as it does today. Spectacular entertainment shows featured comedians such as Ken Dodd and Morecambe and Wise in sketches, routines and production numbers, often using conventions of performance reminiscent of the variety-theatre. Various series featured satirical sketches of different types, including the broad (*The Arthur Haynes Show* (ATV, 1956–66)), the zany (Michael Bentine's *It's A Square World* (BBC, 1960–64)) and the literate (*That Was The Week That Was* (BBC, 1962–63)). But the dominant form of early 1960s television comedy was the situation comedy series, based on a readily replicable but infinitely variable formula well adapted to the representative strengths and production requirements of television; in other words, a televisual form for the presentation of comedy.

British television situation comedy had its sources in radio's production routines and formats, in the sketches and comic performers of the variety-theatre and the NAAFI and in the characterisation and cultural representations associated with British cinema. But television needed to develop its own comic forms rather than to recycle material from other sources. During the 1950s, a number of formal, stylistic and technical breakthroughs helped to develop situation comedy as a televisual form. Remarkably almost all of these were associated with one series – *Hancock's Half-Hour* (BBC, 1956–60).

Background: British Television Comedy to 1956

Before the appointment in 1952 of a more sympathetic Director-General, Ian Jacob, senior BBC figures saw television as 'an extension of sound'[1] whose chief strength was actuality, leaving little incentive for the development of specifically televisual forms of programming. Studio-based entertainment was given a low priority and still lower budgets, even after the BBC acquired the physical space in which to make it after moving to Lime Grove in 1950. The total budget for the opening show at Lime Grove was £300, less than a single star performer could earn for one show at the London Palladium.[2]

At this time, most television Light Entertainment consisted of nothing more adventurous than the presentation of variety and musical comedy artists before cameras. Most Saturdays and some Wednesdays saw some sort of Light Entertainment show and occasional series were produced as vehicles for artists such as Bobby Howes and Terry-Thomas, where budgets allowed. As early as 1949, Norman Collins, then Controller (Television), sought to increase the proportion and quality of Light Entertainment, singling out the scripted series as an area for development.[3] But little had been achieved by 1951, the year in which Ronnie Waldman, recently appointed as Head of Television Light Entertainment, took stock of the situation in an article in *Radio Times*.[4] He wrote of the difficulties involved in producing Light Entertainment for a television audience, noting that established material designed for a collective theatre audience would not necessarily appeal to individual viewers at home. He believed that the solution depended upon the Light Entertainment producer developing entertainment forms especially suited to television: 'He must create something that had never existed before the invention of television – something that we call Television Light Entertainment.' He warned that this could not be achieved immediately ('it took sound broadcasting about fifteen years to reach the first real and pure radio comedy programme [*Band Waggon*]', but singled out the Terry-Thomas series *How Do You View* (BBC, 1950–53) as an 'encouraging sign'. This series, he said, was 'doing something that could not be done in any other medium. In other words it is television'.

How Do You View did indeed have several of the hallmarks of a televisual comedy. Much was made of its 'intimacy' in comparison with stage shows but, despite a rudimentary location (Thomas' apartment), it bore a much closer resemblance to the self-reflexive wise-cracking then common in radio comedy than to the naturalism and character comedy which later proved to work so well in television sitcom.[5] *Radio Times* described it as consisting of 'frantic impersonations of celebrities and nonentities, subtle sketches, crazy interviews with Leslie Mitchell'.[6] When it ceased in 1953, *How Do You View* had no natural successor and did not of itself offer the solution to Waldman's problem.

Despite further experiments, advances towards the production of televisual forms of comic programming had been few by the time competition was introduced in September 1955. Generally, the television service had borrowed radio's stars and formats and tried to graft a visual element. Topical satire was quite successful in *The Eric Barker Half-Hour* (BBC, 1951–53). Rudimentary (and highly predictable) domestic comedy was tried, putting well-known couples in a thinly fictional setting, with Bernard Braden and Barbara Kelly in *An Evening At Home* (BBC, 1951), and later in a television version of *Life With The Lyons* (BBC, 1955–56). The former was deemed successful enough to warrant a second series but, in a telling example of the low importance placed on television entertainment by the BBC hierarchy, this was vetoed by the radio service, who had Braden under contract.[7] The four short series of wholly fictional domestic comedies which were made during this period were no more innovative. Of these, Peter Black recalls *Friends and Neighbours* (BBC, 1954) and *Dear Dotty* (BBC, 1954) as the best: 'they were terrible, but an improvement on the ghastly'.[8] Only Arthur Askey's *Before Your Very Eyes* (BBC, 1952–55), little more than televised concert-party, could be considered anything like a hit. Like *Life With The Lyons*, it transferred to ITV shortly after competition began.

Competition put extra pressure on the BBC to create successful forms of television comedy. It was forced to court viewers' preferences in order to compete with the new ITV companies for a share of the audience. From the start, ITV showed well over twice as much Light Entertainment and dominated the London top ten with American imports and British variety shows such as *Val Parnell's Sunday Night at the London Palladium*.[9]

Imported pre-filmed American comedy series were used by both BBC and ITV as weapons in the struggle for audience share. Their technical superiority amply demonstrated the inferior production standards of their ('live') British counter-parts and led to expectations of perfection among British viewers. Although only the wholly inappropriate *Amos 'N' Andy*, a slice of American racism already cancelled amid protests in the USA (and hence available cheaply), was screened before competition was introduced, in September 1955 the BBC introduced two more American comedy series, while ITV began showing the seminal (and highly televisual) *I Love Lucy* with enormous success. By the end of 1956, the BBC and the principal ITV regions had shown no fewer than twelve different American comedy series.[10] British television could produce nothing to approach them for style or suitability to television, despite a sudden abundance of home-produced comedy shows. Of these, only the Goon-inspired *Idiot Weekly Price Twopence* (Associated-Rediffusion, 1956) represented a significant departure from previous low standards. It is against this background that the importance of *Hancock's Half-Hour* must be evaluated.

'Hancock's Half-Hour' and 'Reality'

The television *Hancock's Half-Hour* began on 6 July 1956 with Hancock and Sidney James as the only regular characters. Over the next four years, six series were shown, containing a total of fifty-seven half-hour episodes. For the seventh and final series, in 1961, Hancock left Sid and moved to an Earl's Court bedsitter for six twenty-five minute episodes simply entitled *Hancock*.[11] All sixty-three shows were written by Ray Galton and Alan Simpson and produced by Duncan Wood.

Hancock's Half-Hour was already established as a radio vehicle for Hancock by the time the television version began. Tony Hancock's growing radio success in the early 1950s included regular appearances in *Educating Archie* for one season (1951–52) and in the *Star Bill* variety series (1953–54), in which he began working regularly with Galton and Simpson as his scriptwriters. The radio *Hancock's Half-Hour* (BBC, 1954–59) was innovative from the start. The use of a situation comedy format with episode-length narratives helped Hancock to move

77

beyond the variety show but, in the naturalism of their characterisation and dialogue, Galton and Simpson also intended to break away from the cosiness of radio domestic comedies such as *Meet The Huggetts* and *Life With The Lyons*.

In most of the radio and television comedies of the early 1950s characterisation tended to echo the larger-than-life performance qualities associated with the variety-theatre. Scripts seemed all too frequently to be a series of gags strung together by dialogue which was merely a means of getting from one to the next. As Alan Simpson put it: 'comedy sketches were five minutes of puns and parodies and funny voices'.[12] From the beginning, the radio *Hancock's Half-Hour* was conceived as 'non-domestic with no jokes and no funny voices, just relying on caricature and situation humour'.[13] Galton and Simpson were not immediately successful in this – Kenneth Williams' funny voices became a major feature of the radio series, for example – but, as the series developed in radio and television, the injection of more 'reality' became a preoccupation of the production team.

Galton and Simpson's idea of 'reality' – a naturalism of language, characterisation and location allowing for almost-believable story lines and audience identification – is crucial to understanding the impact of *Hancock's Half-Hour*. The first two years of the radio series saw the gradual evolution of the setting in which this 'reality' was to flourish. 23 Railway Cuttings became established as the location of most episodes, plots became less far-fetched as the writers gained experience, and the cast's delivery began to relax from the frenetic pace then common in radio comedy. Characterisation was allowed to deepen in surroundings in which gags were eschewed for comedy of character. Hancock, Sid James and Bill Kerr were funny because they behaved in familiar ways in situations with which their audience could identify. The character for which Hancock became so well-known – the seedy misfit with intellectual pretensions, sure he was missing out while those around him had never had it so good – was also beginning to develop. At the same time the popularity of the programme was growing and by 1955 its appreciation index already stood at 69.[14]

But it was as a prescription for television comedy that Galton and Simpson's 'reality' was to become particularly significant, because of its suitability to the representational qualities of television itself. In radio, locations and the consistency of comic situations depend only upon listeners' imaginations, which can be used not only to create the illusion of naturalism but to stimulate the flights of comic fancy and surreal formal disruption common in radio comedy from *Band Waggon* to *The Goon Show*. In contrast, the visual nature of television demands that locations must not merely be suggested but shown, with detail remaining consistent. *Hancock's Half-Hour*'s apparent 'reality' of language, characterisation and location, therefore, was ideally suited to and reinforced by the nature of television as a visual medium.

In transferring *Hancock's Half-Hour* from radio, Galton and Simpson made few of the overt concessions to the visual nature of television which were felt to be important at the time:

> Everybody told us that we must change because television *is* visual and actors had to be *seen* to be moving about. They were all obsessed by moving

about. But most of our scripts were dialogue anyway, so instead of saying 'pick up that bucket', we'd say 'pick that up'. That was our concession to television.[15]

But although *Hancock's Half-Hour*, unlike *I Love Lucy* for example, remained a discursive rather than a visual comedy, the addition of a visible consistency of location and character acted as a further indicator of 'reality'. Galton and Simpson were able to simplify plots by eliminating supporting characters (except Sid James) and audible devices such as catch-phrases, and to rely increasingly on credible speech and believable story lines, with truth to character being the all-important consideration: 'anything that seemed like a joke, on its own grounds, was left out – whether or not we hooted at it – because unless it was true to the story and the character it was turned out'.[16]

As a result, by the beginning of the third television series (September 1957), *Hancock's Half-Hour* had become something which none of its predecessors had been – a comedy of observation with which viewers were invited to identify and to find believable, rather than merely to be entertained by. Galton and Simpson were conscious of the importance of putting Hancock in situations with which his audience could identify:

> Perhaps one reason for the success of the Hancock shows is that they stay close to life as known by their audiences, finding humour in popular newspapers and double-feature film programmes or putting Hancock in the sort of situation where we all feel ineffectual.[17]

In so doing, they were helping to recast the comedy scriptwriter as comic dramatist rather than 'comedian's labourer'. *Hancock's Half-Hour* was a critical as well as a popular success. 'Hancock, with or without Sid James, reconciles critics and Ad-mass', wrote Ken Hoare in 1961.[18] 'The writers are quite the best in the land. Their success derives from establishing a believable world and peopling it with believable characters.'

The believability and consistency of *Hancock's Half-Hour* – its 'reality' – became a model for many of its successors and led by the early 1960s to this kind of 'sitcom naturalism' becoming almost a defining characteristic of the situation comedy form. It has remained so. But reading situation comedy is no simple process and the notion of sitcom naturalism requires investigation.

Jim Cook has suggested that situation comedy must be read on two levels – naturally (so that the narrative makes sense) and structurally (so that we recognise the intention to produce laughter).[19] As a result, it cannot approach the sort of non-comic naturalism that many drama series attempt to create. After all, the non-naturalistic intention to produce comedy must detract from the apparent naturalism of setting from which it often seems to spring. But although intrusive devices such as comic timing, audience laughter and 'playing for laughs' mark out sitcom naturalism from that of the naturalistic drama series, it is equally differentiated by situation comedy's intentionally life-like settings and apparently natural relations of cause and effect from the explicit non-naturalism of formal disruption, in which the conventions of drama and/or television are made visible. Recent examples of this 'comic non-naturalism' include *The Young Ones* (BBC, 1982–84) and John Godber's *The Ritz* (BBC, 1987).

As Mick Eaton[20] notes, drawing on the work of Freud, jokes turn on the recognition of the familiar and the disruption of conventional norms and expectations. The narrative concerns of situation comedy tend to be domestic and individualised, encouraging viewers to find them familiar and providing conventional norms against which to measure comic excess. This aspect of situation comedy can be equated with Cook's 'natural' level of reading – the narrative 'makes sense' not least because it connects with commonly-held impressions of the nature of 'the real world' and 'the typical'. But against this must be set the structural elements of situation comedy within which pleasure and comedy are found or enhanced – exaggerated aspects of plotting and performance, the intrusive laugh-track, the use of stereotypes for comic effect and so on. These depend for their effect on their atypicality – their zaniness – and their transgression of expectations. Often they challenge for comic ends the very norms of naturalistic behaviour upon which sitcom naturalism is founded.

So sitcom naturalism must depend upon reading texts on both of these levels and on suspending disbelief in return for pleasure. If the pleasure of situation comedy comes from the disruption of conventional norms, it must also present those norms themselves to be disrupted. It seems that viewers do indeed read situation comedy in this way. Dorothy Hobson, researching the manner in which viewers 'made sense' of *Butterflies* (BBC, 1978–80), concluded that: 'situations and settings were perceived in terms of their verisimilitude, but dramatic licence was allowed in relation to the comedy elements'.[21]

Another innovation of great importance to the development of situation comedy also grew from the *Hancock's Half-Hour* team's search for greater 'reality'. As early as 1957, Hancock discussed with Wood the possibility of replacing comedians or comic actors with straight actors in the casting of minor roles.[22] Not only were comic actors accustomed to 'playing for laughs' – many had moved to television from the variety-theatre – but it was more difficult for them to be believable in supporting roles because audiences identified them as comic and expected them to be funny. Although the divide between television comedy acting and 'legitimate' theatre was greater then than now, the quality and success of *Hancock's Half-Hour* was enough to break down the inhibitions of some, such as Raymond Huntley, Jack Hawkins and Patrick Cargill. John Le Mesurier remembers that he was approached by Hancock in 1957 to be part of a 'repertory' of supporting actors to be drawn on when necessary. The 'repertory' also included actors such as Hugh Lloyd, Sylvia Sims, Barbara Murray and Hugh Fraser.[23] The better the supporting cast, it was found, the better Hancock worked and the more taboos among actors about television comedy were broken down.

The use of actors very soon became common in more naturalistic sitcoms. Comedians in situation comedy had largely been replaced by actors by the beginning of the 1960s. In 1961, when Galton and Simpson's *Comedy Playhouse* (BBC) series began, it was a matter of course that the ten half-hour comedies were cast purely on the demands of character. Although the casts contained some well-known comedians, actors such as Joan Hickson, Tony Britton and Terence Alexander were involved, as well as Wilfrid Brambell and Harry H. Corbett in the original version of *Steptoe and Son*. Galton and Simpson discovered that they could write better for actors: 'Actors don't argue – they don't reject scripts as unsuitable – they just get on and read the lines'.[24]

'Hancock's Half-Hour' and the Development of Production Techniques for Television Comedy

The contribution of the *Hancock's Half-Hour* team to the emergence of British television situation comedy was not confined to the development of new approaches to naturalism and new styles of performance and writing. At the same time, breakthroughs in production techniques were being made which enabled the series to use these developments to maximum effect. As the series progressed, Duncan Wood and the team created a production style which made use of the particular strengths of television representation and gave situation comedy many of the qualities which were to make it so successful in the 1960s and beyond.

Television is a particularly intimate medium in comparison with film or the variety-theatre. Television cameras were found to be well-adapted for shooting small groups and close-ups in which facial expressions and reactions could be used to great effect. *Hancock's Half-Hour* exploited this feature of television to create comic effects which were both more successful and more suited to television than those used by any of its predecessors. Tony Hancock's extraordinary talent for facial comedy was used to create an intimate comic style ideal for television, in which many of the funniest moments come from reactions or facial expressions rather than from dialogue.

The value of the reaction shot to television comedy seems to have been understood in the USA, where situation comedy was already being produced, by the beginning of the 1950s. When *The Burns and Allen Show* began in 1950, it used two cameras – one on the character making the joke, the other to catch the reaction.[25] This mirrored the relationship which Burns and Allen had built up as a husband-and-wife act in years of vaudeville and radio, in which Gracie's bizarre logic would get a laugh and George's perplexed reaction to it would yield a second. *I Love Lucy*, which began in 1951, used three cameras. One of these normally stayed on Lucille Ball at all times to pick up her reactions.[26]

The suitability to television of the close-up was being recognised in Britain as well. In 1952, Jan Bussell was advising television playwrights of the need to take account of the size and detail of the television image: 'Scenes between twos and threes are what television wants: quiet intimate stuff which the camera can get right into'.[27] Meanwhile, in Light Entertainment, Terry-Thomas claimed to use 'a very close close-up technique' in *How Do You View*: 'The home-screen offers scope for subtle expression, fine-grain comedy that can be touched off by the flicker of an eyebrow, the roll of the eyes, a twitch of the mouth'.[28] Despite this, *How Do You View* was not the breakthrough which television comedy needed and the comic potential of television's facility for close-ups and reaction shots was not fully understood, even five years later, by many performers.

Almost completely inexperienced in television comedy, Galton, Simpson, Wood and Hancock probably did not set out to create a comic style based on facial and reaction comedy, but all of them recognised its potential very soon. It seemed to grow naturally from the verbal nature of the scripts and from Hancock's extraordinary personal talent. His understanding of the technique of the reaction shot came apparently from Sid James' wide experience of film acting.[29] Hancock persuaded Duncan Wood to make use of close-ups for reaction shots in planning camera routines and, as a result, Wood developed more precise plotting, cutting and camera techniques than had hitherto been necessary in British television comedy:

> I was having to break sentences down into half, so that Tony would say a line in close-up, half the sentence, then cut to Sid for a reaction, then back to Tony for the remainder of the sentence, and then back to Sid for the reaction. Of course, the net result was to double the camera rate – that whereas you used to shoot situation comedy on 150 shots in half-an-hour, you were now taking 250 to do the same amount of dialogue. Suddenly you were having to work at twice the capacity on camera routines, and this put pressure on the crews, and on everyone. It was one of the great revolutions, I think, reaction as against action.[30]

By 1959, Galton and Simpson were writing for Hancock on the assumption that 'the basis of television is the close-up, which allows the audience to see facial expressions in detail'.[31] 'Hancock has such an expressive face', they explained, 'that though much of the humour is verbal there is always the fascination of watching him react to it'.[32] Hancock, in turn, was responding weekly with performances in which he was able to use the subtlest changes of expression to tremendous comic effect, maximising the comic potential of every line by his reaction to it. Many of the funniest and most memorable sequences from his later BBC shows arose when Galton and Simpson created situations in which Hancock was required to communicate a wide range of emotions and uncertainties using little more than his face. In 'The Missing Page' (tx. 11 March 1960), Hancock mimes the entire plot of a thriller to a crowd of bemused browsers in a library. In 'The Reunion Party' (tx. 25 March 1960), confusion, uncertainty, exasperation, desperation, inspiration and embarrassment chase each other across Hancock's features as he tries to remember a name. By the time of the final BBC series (*Hancock*, 1961), the team had refined the technique to such an extent that Hancock was able to perform entirely solo for a complete half-hour (in 'The Bedsitter', tx. 26 May 1961), doing little more than reacting to his surroundings. It was one of his most successful shows ever. Hancock himself was later to claim: 'the biggest battle I ever won was to do comedy in close-up'.[33]

By the early 1960s, the situation comedies which were being produced followed Wood's model closely, using three cameras for most scenes. Establishing shots were used to set scenes, but close-ups and two-shots were common, as was precise cutting for reaction shots. Vision-mixing and camerawork were found to be central to the creation of a seamless shooting style capable of drawing out every nuance from what were often very economically written scripts.

As important as Wood's shooting style to the subsequent development of British television comedy were the series of events which led to the introduction of discontinuous recording in television situation comedy. Following the success of *I Love Lucy*, shooting scene by scene on film had become the normal method of situation comedy production in the USA by about 1954. In Britain, however, almost all forms of television comedy remained live. Budgets for television remained tight even after ITV began in 1955 and film was felt to be prohibitively expensive.[34] Telerecording (off the tube) on film, though used very occasionally for repeats in Light Entertainment, was not thought to produce an image of sufficient quality for everyday transmission.

'Liveness' was not necessarily seen as a limitation on British television. Many arguments were advanced at the time in its favour: it was a positive distinguishing feature of television, differentiating it from both film and theatre; the adrenalin flow of live performance brought out the best work from artists; audience knowledge that television performances were live led to a qualitatively different viewing experience. Beneficial though these qualities may have been, pre-recording enabled better programmes to be made more cheaply at only a small cost to television's immediacy.

Pre-recording was attractive to the television industry because it enabled a more efficient use of resources. Programmes could be recorded when artists, crew, studios and equipment were available. Recording had the effect of creating a tangible product which could easily be repeated, sold abroad or accumulated for future transmission. Pre-recording improved the quality of programmes because it gave producers and artists the opportunity to dissect their work, allowed retakes to eliminate mistakes and enabled television to use a wider range of artists because recordings could be timed to suit their commitments. As pre-filmed American imports increased after 1955, British programmes began to look slow and unprofessional in comparison.

Hancock's Half-Hour provided several graphic illustrations of the pressures involved in producing live television. The first two series of six episodes were live, as was the third (Autumn 1957), planned for thirteen episodes. The strain on Hancock of learning and performing thirteen consecutive shows was considerable and the eighth had to be postponed and replaced by a telerecorded repeat when he contracted Asian 'flu. Duncan Wood believed that Hancock might not have been able to complete the series without this week's rest. He expressed his concern in a memo requesting that he be allowed to pre-record four shows from the next series to relieve the strain on Hancock.[35]

Another incident in the third series provided further evidence of the value of pre-recording. The eleventh episode, 'There's an Airfield at the Bottom of my Garden' (tx. 16 December 1957), contained a set which was due to collapse spectacularly at the climax of a scene. Eight pages too early in the script it began to fall apart, forcing Hancock to spend the remainder of the scene propping up a table while he and the rest of the cast improvised wildly in front of millions of bemused viewers.[36] Hancock, never comfortable when forced to ad-lib, was determined not to repeat the experience.

The Ampex system of videotape recording became available in 1958 and the BBC purchased their first machine in October. Wood's request was granted and he was allowed to use it to pre-record four shows for the fourth series in November and December 1958, an indication of the prestige which *Hancock's Half-Hour* had gained by then. This was not wholly successful, as the pre-recorded episodes were shown at the beginning of the series and were followed by a run of ten successive live episodes. Again the strain took its toll on Hancock, who was forced to miss the sixth of the live shows. It was replaced by a repeat of one of the pre-recorded episodes.

Although videotape recording allowed shows to be stockpiled, at this stage it was not thought possible to edit videotape. Mistakes could only be eliminated by re-recording a whole show – practicable in cases of complete disaster such as the 'Airfield' episode, but no use to cover small errors or to enable the series to be made with the pace and slickness of American imports. This worried not only Wood and Hancock but Cecil McGivern, Deputy Director of Television, who was concerned to extract the maximum in content and audience size from what was by now a very costly series by the BBC's standards. Commenting on the fourth series in a BBC memo, he wrote:

> In my opinion the production (as opposed to the content) is far too slow. I know the producer Duncan Wood would retort with the inevitable slowness of television as opposed to film, the changing of the clothes and set, the necessity to hang on to captions, bridging shots and all the rest of it. Nevertheless, despite that, the production must be quickened up and the writers should be told this. Live television need not be *so* far behind the speed of *Bilko*.[37]

Meanwhile, Wood was working to challenge the notion that videotape could not be edited. He spent a day cutting up a recording of *On The Bright Side*, a song and sketch show featuring Betty Marsden and Stanley Baxter, and found that it was possible to make cuts without disturbing the synchronising pulses which stopped the picture rolling. From a forty-five minute show he made a twenty-five minute collection of continuous sketches which retained the picture quality of the original.[38] He used the tape to demonstrate that *Hancock's Half-Hour* could be made in five to eight minute segments with breaks between scenes to move cameras and change costumes. In the event of a mistake, only a single segment would need to be re-recorded.

With videotapes costing £100 each and tapes not reusable when cut, the BBC considered Wood's system of recording to be 'costly and unprecedented', but Hancock forced the issue by refusing to sign a contract for another series unless it was recorded in this way.[39] All of Hancock's subsequent BBC series were recorded scene by scene and by 1961 it was a common method for recording other shows, especially at the BBC.[40]

Discontinuous recording considerably increased the scope of situation com-

Classic Hancock: Playing opposite June Whitfield in 'The Blood Donor', 1961.

edy. The pace indeed quickened as bridging dialogue to cover costume changes and camera movements between scenes could now be omitted and principals could spend more time on screen. As cameras no longer needed to move in mid-scene to be in position to cover the opening of a subsequent scene, more cameras and hence more close-ups could now be used. In the first episode of *Hancock's Half-Hour* in which he used this technique ('The Economy Drive', tx. 25 September 1959), Wood edited together two takes of one sequence in order to use six camera positions without any cameras appearing in shot.[41] In-vision edits remained extremely difficult however and were (and still are) only used rarely in situation comedy.

'Hancock's Half-Hour': Context, Conclusions and Consequences

The success of *Hancock's Half-Hour* was unprecedented. The show was already attracting a 23 per cent audience by 1957, when Light Entertainment shows were averaging 11 per cent and the proportion of viewers watching ITV was at its highest. As writing and production techniques for the series developed, its audience share grew still more: to 27 per cent for the fifth series, 28 per cent for the sixth series and 30 per cent for the *Hancock* series in 1961.[42] Most of the episodes from these series have been shown at least four times, most recently in 1986, and are available on videotape. 'The Blood Donor' (tx. 23 June 1961) has been shown six times, a remarkable number for a comedy show in black-and-white.

Hancock's Half-Hour was a watershed in the development of British television comedy, popularising and 'fixing' situation comedy as its dominant form. It enlarged the scope of the situation comedy, taking it beyond its previous role as a dramatised television 'vehicle' for an established comedian, despite the fact that this was clearly part of the original conception of the series. Although, like Jack Benny and Burns and Allen in the USA and the Lyons family and Terry-Thomas in the UK, Hancock purported to play 'himself', he did so not as a well-known vaudeville comedian in a fictional scenario, but rather as a character in an internally consistent and apparently naturalistic world closely connected to that of his audience. *Hancock's Half-Hour* enabled the creation of a form of comedy for television which shrugged off the traditional qualities of comic performance inherited from the variety-stage and abandoned both jokes and comedians in favour of characterisation and acting. In its style and method of shooting, it enabled home-produced shows to compete for the first time on an almost equal footing with American imports.

The indirect influence of *Hancock's Half-Hour* can be traced in almost every subsequent television comedy series, but its most direct successor was *Steptoe and Son* (BBC, 1962–74). Again written by Galton and Simpson and produced by Duncan Wood, it dominated British television comedy throughout the 1960s. There are strong parallels between Hancock's character and that of Harry H. Corbett's Harold Steptoe in their tatty intellectualism and desire for self-betterment, as well as in their performance styles. Galton and Simpson again clung firmly to the notion of 'reality', reinforced with the casting of straight actors in the leading roles, to the extent that *The Times*' television correspondent could write in 1962: '*Steptoe and Son* virtually obliterates the division between drama and comedy'.[43]

Many other series also followed the Hancock model closely. In the early 1960s, *Citizen James* (BBC, 1960–62) with Sidney James, *Here's Harry* (BBC, 1960–65) with Harry Worth and *Hugh and I* (BBC, 1962–67) with Terry Scott and Hugh Lloyd were all concerned with the struggles of their otherwise mundane and ordinary leading characters to overcome their bafflement with a disingenuous and bureaucratic world. Later, *Till Death Us Do Part* (BBC, 1966–75) offered a similar role to a less sympathetic leading character. *Shelley* (Thames, 1979–) is one of various more recent developments on a similar theme. Even Dougal in Eric Thompson's *The Magic Roundabout* (BBC, 1965–1976) seems to share Hancock's laconic bewilderment with the world which he inhabits.

Of course, the rise of the situation comedy cannot be attributed entirely to the success of *Hancock's Half-Hour*. However influential, the series was part of a wider process in the broadcasting industry and in British culture as a whole. In its naturalistic style and narrative consistency, *Hancock's Half-Hour* became the standard-bearer of a fashion for social comedy which had been growing in broadcast comedy throughout the 1950s. The radio comedy of the 40s had been characterised by the self-consciously zany and surreal worlds of shows like ITMA (BBC Sound, 1939–49). But from the beginning of the 50s, comedians, scriptwriters and the BBC Variety Department began to talk increasingly of creating 'comic situations' and 'comedy of character'.[44] By 1958, even Frankie Howerd, traditionally a stand-up comic, was saying: 'I now prefer being funny in a situation, rather than just telling jokes. That, after all, isn't fashionable any longer'.[45]

ITMA drew much of its inspiration from a grotesque extension of common public attitudes to the petty officialdom, wholesale upheaval and sense of communal unity against a shared enemy engendered by the war. If the product of the uncertainty of the war, in comic terms, was a comedy of the outrageous, there are equally good historical reasons why the comedy of the 1950s should generally have been a comedy of the mundane. By this time the social attitudes of wartime were beginning to be replaced by an emerging sense of affluence and stability whose popular symbols were economic prosperity, full employment and the idea of 'the new Elizabethan age'.[46] Whereas the outrageous offered the chance to escape and criticise safely an unpalatable present, *Hancock's Half-Hour* and its successors were set in a more acceptable world, where comedy could be found in personal relations, in the thwarting of aspirations and in the mundanity of everyday life. In their own way, each kind of show offered a social critique and reflected the preoccupations of their time. By the late 1950s, however, this critique could take place on a domestic rather than a global scale.

In its underlying critique of 50s affluence, its obsession with 'reality' and its dramatisation of the mundane, intended by its writers to 'reflect life as known by their audiences', *Hancock's Half-Hour* bears comparison with contemporaneous works in fiction, cinema and theatre which have come to be associated with social realism. Indeed, there are close comparisons, as Eric Midwinter points out, between 'the windy verbose monologues about the trivialities of their circumstances' declaimed by Hancock and by Jimmy Porter in *Look Back In Anger*.[47] Although Hancock's tribulations were principally comic, lacking the cutting edge of radical drama, his appeal was much wider and the form of comedy fostered by his series was at the forefront of television's own popular articulation of social realism. Harry H. Corbett, for example, was prepared to abandon the radical atmosphere of Theatre Workshop for television situation comedy because he believed that the comedy of people like Hancock, Eric Sykes and Michael Bentine offered the only 'good social comment' available on television at the time.[48]

Notes

1. Sir William Haley, 1949, quoted in Asa Briggs, *The History of Broadcasting in the United Kingdom, Volume 4: Sound and Vision* (London: Oxford University Press, 1979), pp. 2, 235.
2. Hunter Davies, *The Grades: The First Family of British Entertainment* (London: Weidenfeld and Nicolson, 1981), pp. 139–40.
3. Quoted in Briggs, *Sound and Vision*, p. 287.
4. *Radio Times*, 23 February 1951, p. 46.
5. For a discussion of self-reflexiveness in BBC comedy see David Cardiff, 'Mass middlebrow laughter: The origins of BBC comedy', *Media, Culture and Society* vol. 10 no. 1, January 1988.
6. 14 September 1951, p. 47.
7. Peter Black, *The Biggest Aspidistra in the World* (London: BBC, 1972), p. 163.

8. Ibid., pp. 195–6.

9. Burton Paulu, *British Broadcasting: Radio and Television in the United Kingdom* (Minneapolis: University of Minnesota Press, 1956), p. 283.

10. As well as *Amos 'N' Andy* and *I Love Lucy*, these were *The Burns and Allen Show*, *I Married Joan*, *Life of Riley*, *The Jack Benny Program* and *Hey Jeannie!* (BBC); and *My Hero*, *Topper*, *My Little Margie*, *Father Knows Best* and *The Bob Cummings Show* (ITV).

11. *Hancock's Half-Hour* – first series: 6 July–14 September 1956; second series: 1 April– 10 June 1957; third series: 30 September–23 December 1957; fourth series: 26 December 1958–27 March 1959; fifth series: 25 September–27 November 1959; sixth series: 4 March–6 May 1960; *Hancock* series: 26 May–30 June 1961. Dates and details from Roger Wilmut, *Tony Hancock – Artiste* (London: Methuen, 1978), which also contains synopses and cast lists for each episode.

12. Quoted in David Nathan, *The Laughtermakers* (London: Peter Owen, 1971), p. 133.

13. Galton and Simpson, quoted in Barry Took, *Laughter In The Air* (Second Edition, London: Robson/BBC, 1981), p. 128.

14. Freddie Hancock and David Nathan, *Hancock* (Third Edition, London: Ariel Books/ BBC, 1986), pp. 59, 65. Listener research surveys included a measure of 'intensity of appreciation'. The average for a variety show at this time was 62.

15. Ray Galton, quoted in Wilmut, *Tony Hancock – Artiste*, p. 83.

16. Hugh Lloyd, quoted in Roger Wilmut, *The Illustrated Hancock* (London: Queen Anne Press/Macdonald, 1986), p. 53.

17. Galton and Simpson, quoted in *The Times*, 2 March 1959, p. 12.

18. In 'Situations Vacant', *Contrast* vol. 1 no. 1, Autumn 1961, p. 57.

19. Jim Cook, 'Narrative, Comedy, Character and Performance', in Jim Cook (ed.), BFI Dossier 17: *Television Sitcom* (London: BFI, 1982), p. 16.

20. Mick Eaton, 'Laughter In The Dark', *Screen* vol. 22 no. 2, Summer 1981, pp. 22–25.

21. Quoted in Barry Curtis, 'Aspects of Sitcom', in Cook (ed.), *Television Sitcom*, p. 7.

22. Hancock and Nathan, *Hancock*, p. 86.

23. John Le Mesurier, *A Jobbing Actor* (London: Elm Tree Books/Hamish Hamilton, 1984), pp. 91–93.

24. Quoted in Wilmut, *Tony Hancock – Artiste*, p. 134.

25. Rick Mitz, *The Great TV Sitcom Book* (Expanded Edition, New York: Perigee Books/ Putnam, 1983), p. 36.

26. Patricia Mellancamp, 'Situation and Simulation: An Introduction to *I Love Lucy*', *Screen* vol. 26 no. 2, March/April 1985, p. 33.

27. Quoted in Stuart Laing, *Representations of Working Class Life 1957–1964* (Basingstoke and London: Macmillan, 1986), p. 147.

28. *Radio Times*, 14 September 1951, p. 47.

29. Duncan Wood, quoted in Wilmut, *Tony Hancock – Artiste*, p. 100.

30. Ibid.

31. Galton and Simpson, quoted in *The Times*, 2 March 1959, p. 12.

32. Ibid.

33. Quoted in Philip Oakes, *Tony Hancock* (London: Woburn-Futura, 1975), p. 25.

34. Film was more attractive to producers in the USA because the extra cost could be better absorbed in the much larger American market and film offered the extra advantage of allowing a show to play at the same hour in all four time-zones.

35. BBC internal memo, 31 December 1957, quoted in Wilmut, *Tony Hancock – Artiste*, p. 96.

36. For a full description see Wilmut, *Tony Hancock – Artiste*, pp. 91–95.

37. BBC internal memo, 1 April 1959, quoted in Hancock and Nathan, *Hancock*, p. 196.

38. Wilmut, *Tony Hancock – Artiste*, pp. 102–3.
39. Oakes, *Tony Hancock*, p. 45.
40. One third of the BBC's output was recorded by 1961: Gordon Ross, *Television Jubilee* (London: W. H. Allen, 1961), p. 198. As late as 1963, certain ITV companies refused officially to recognise the possibility of cutting tape: see David Robinson, 'Shooting on Tape', *Contrast* vol. 3 no. 1, Autumn 1963, p. 30.
41. Wilmut, *Tony Hancock – Artiste*, pp. 103–4.
42. Hancock and Nathan, *Hancock*, p. 86.
43. 21 July 1962, p. 4.
44. See, for example, *Radio Times*, 16 May 1952, pp. 5–6 (Gale Pedrick); 16 January 1953, p. 9 (Eric Sykes); 28 August 1953, p. 6 (Pat Hillyard).
45. Interviewed in *Radio Times*, 28 March 1958, p. 4.
46. See Laing, *Representations of Working Class Life*, pp. 6–13.
47. Eric Midwinter, *Make 'Em Laugh: Famous Comedians and their Worlds* (London: George Allen and Unwin, 1979), pp. 122–6.
48. Hal Burton, *Acting In The Sixties* (London: BBC, 1970), p. 47.

Television and Pop
The Case of the 1950s

JOHN HILL

While the Postmaster General (PMG) may seem an unlikely candidate for a place in the history of rock'n'roll he did, nonetheless, make a small but important contribution to its advance in the 1950s. Under the terms of the Television Act of 1954, which had paved the way for commercial television, the PMG was responsible for the allocation of television hours. Up until 1957, the most striking consequence of this arrangement was the closed period on television between 6–7 pm. Known colloquially as the 'toddler's truce', it was designed to allow parents to put their children to bed free of the distractions of television. When ITV was launched in September 1955, the commercial companies had complied with this requirement but, in the face of financial losses the following summer, had petitioned the then PMG, Charles Hill, for the ban's removal. Hill, who felt 'it was the responsibility of parents, not the State, to put their children to bed at the right time', was sympathetic and persuaded the Government to agree to a change, with the result that the 'toddler's truce' on Mondays to Saturdays was formally ended on Saturday 16 February 1957.[1] At 6 pm that evening, the BBC broadcast a five-minute news bulletin, followed by a new programme aimed at young people and featuring live music. *Six-Five Special* was born and a small piece of both television and rock'n'roll history was made.

Although *Six-Five Special* is often regarded as a watershed in television's treatment of pop music it was not, of course, without precursors. The growth of the record industry during the 1950s and the compilation of the charts on the basis of record sales, rather than sales of sheet music, had already aroused television interest. The BBC itself had launched its own version of the US TV show, *Hit Parade* in 1952 and revived it in October 1955. This consisted of a selection of songs from those currently featuring in the Top Twenty as well as one 'standard'. The songs were not performed by the original artists, however, but by a team of residents, led by Petula Clark and Dennis Lotis, who not only sang, but also acted out the songs in an appropriate setting ('dramatic, humorous, tearful or sentimental').[2] *Hit Parade*'s producer, Francis Essex, was also responsible for the BBC's *Off the Record* launched in May 1955. This attempted to deal with various aspects of the record industry, providing news, 'behind the scenes' interviews and even small features (such as a 'Life of a Disc' profile recorded at EMI). The bulk of the show, however, was devoted to a varying roster of singers and bands performing in the studio, introduced by the veteran bandleader Jack Payne.

90

These included, in the first show, Max Bygraves, the Four Aces (then in the charts with their version of 'Stranger in Paradise'), Ronnie Hilton and Alma Cogan (performing her subsequent No. 1, 'Dreamboat'). As these performers and titles suggest, both shows, although linked to the charts, were showbiz in orientation and tied to the popular music traditions of Tin Pan Alley.[3]

This was also true of ITV's first venture into the field, ABC TV Music Shop, which appeared on their third day of transmission. This too consisted of current recording stars performing in the studio, although with more of an emphasis on US performers than in *Off the Record* (Teddy Johnson, Pearl Carr and Josh White, for example, all put in an early appearance). The bias of these shows, however, was hardly surprising. Although Bill Haley and the Comets had entered the British charts as early as January 1955 with 'Shake, Rattle and Roll', it was not until relatively late the following year that rock'n'roll was to make major inroads into the British Top Twenty. As a result, it was not until the end of 1956 (December 31, in fact) that the first show to register this musical shift appeared.

Made for Associated-Rediffusion, *Cool for Cats* was initially only to be seen in the London region, first on Mondays at 7.15 pm and then on Thursdays. The idea for the programme belonged to the Fleet Street journalist, Ker Robertson, who not only selected the records to be played, but also presented the opening shows. However, the fact that he was 'balding, bespectacled and middle-aged' was not, perhaps, the ideal qualification for the host of 'a teenage disc show' and by the end of the first month he had handed over to the marginally more youthful Kent Walton (aged thirty-eight).[4] The show itself was short – only fifteen minutes – and consisted of the presenter's comments on the discs plus visual interpretations of the music, devised and directed by Joan Kemp-Welch. These usually consisted of dance sequences, employing a regular troupe of dancers choreographed by Douglas Squires, but they could also be more abstract in nature. 'Sometimes I'll use just hands miming', Kemp-Welch told the TV *Times*, 'or close-ups of bowls of flowers for a sentimental number.'[5] The show proved sufficiently successful to be nationally networked twice a week in June 1957 and continued to run, in one form or another, until December 1959.

Cool for Cats' lead in the televising of pop was, however, short-lived. *Six-Five Special* followed it only six weeks later and quickly established itself with an audience of between six and seven million. Although the programme soon became a corner-stone of the BBC's Saturday evening schedule, its appearance was largely fortuitous. The Corporation had actively opposed the ending of the 'toddler's truce' and, when it became clear that the ban would end anyway, sought to delay its implementation. Failing to do so, their response was to look for stop-gap programmes which could be mounted both quickly and cheaply. Thus, *Six-Five Special* was intended to run for only six weeks (on a budget of £1,000 per show), and was still at a relatively early stage of planning at the end of January 1957. *Tonight*, the news magazine programme called upon to fill the gap on Mondays to Fridays, was still without a title a week before its launch.[6]

The benefit of this haste, however, was that it not only created openings for young programme-makers (Jack Good, the co-producer of *Six-Five Special* was only twenty-six while *Tonight*'s producer, Alasdair Milne, was twenty-seven), but also allowed them a relative freedom to experiment with new programme ideas. It was thus with some surprise that both programmes were greeted by the press. 'Yes, it was BBC, not ITV', observed one review of *Six-Five Special*, 'just the kind of thing, in fact, you might have expected from ITV.'[7] The irony, in this case, was that ITV had shown none of the same enterprise and had opted instead for an episode of *The Adventures of Sir Lancelot* followed by a repeat of a short play, *The Stolen Pearl*. That the BBC had apparently stolen a march on their commercial rival, however, was less the result of competitive vigour, at a time of falling audience figures, than the unexpected by-product of an initial reluctance to change.

But, while the association of pop on television with six o'clock on Saturday was largely coincidental, it did have a significant influence on the way televised pop developed in the 1950s. The ending of the 'toddler's truce' had forced broadcasters to anticipate the kind of viewer who might watch at this hour. Thus, the magazine format of *Tonight* was orientated towards those returning home from work and who might be expected to 'switch on at any time'. This would not be the case on a Saturday and here a programme aimed at young people seemed the natural choice to fill the gap between children's television in the late afternoon and proper 'grown-ups' TV in the evening.

However, it was also unlikely that only teenagers would be watching at this hour and any programme occupying this slot could not afford to be too exclusive in its appeal, especially given the importance of the hour for 'catching' the audience for the evening (one of the possible titles for *Six-Five Special* was, in fact, 'Start the Night Right').[8] In the cinema, 'teenpics' could be successfully targeted at the increasingly important youth audience, but television, with only two channels, had to make more of an allowance for the domestic and familial context in which it was received and hence the more heterogeneous nature of its audience.[9] This was especially true, perhaps, of what the press had dubbed 'tea-time TV', with its implied image of the family gathered around the television set while eating. With the launch of *Six-Five Special*, it was also Saturday tea-time when pop music was most likely to be seen on TV in the years which immediately followed. As a result, the programmes called upon to fill this slot were engaged in a balancing act, attempting to satisfy a specifically teenage audience on the one hand, and a more generally adult one on the other. It was thus with some pride that the BBC were able to report in their annual handbook that while 'primarily designed for a teen-aged audience', *Six-Five Special* had become, nevertheless, 'a national institution equally enjoyed by the parents'.[10]

This desire to cater to both young and old was already implicit in the show's early billing as the 'bright "new look" programme' aimed not simply at young people but 'the young in spirit of all ages'.[11] It was also evident in the show's format, which was much more of a mix than is commonly remembered. This took the form of a cross between a variety show and a magazine programme, in which musical acts, of various kinds, were interspersed with comic turns and special items. This mixture was designed not only to broaden the show's appeal, but also to temper, in the appropriate Reithian manner, the programme's offerings of entertainment with small doses of information and education. The programme's design, in this respect, is often regarded as something of a compromise between the show's main inspiration and co-producer, Jack Good, and the BBC. Whereas Good wished to bring the excitement and energy of rock'n'roll to television, the BBC management were clearly reluctant simply to indulge what it still regarded as no more than a passing fad. Only a month after the programme's start, for example, the Assistant Head of Light Entertainment, Tom Sloan, was anticipating rock'n'roll's demise and warning the show's producers that, 'as Rock and Roll diminishes it is important to introduce ... more items of general interest'.[12]

The nature of this compromise was well illustrated by the very first show. This was presented by Pete Murray and the show's co-producer, Josephine Douglas. Like so many pop programmes before and after, both hosts, and especially Douglas, were too 'old' and too obviously 'professional' to be entirely convincing to a teenage audience. 'Several viewers ... suggested that neither was really suitable, either in age or personality, for this particular job', the BBC's Audience Research Department subsequently reported. 'In their opinion a programme for teenagers should be introduced by teenagers.'[13] However, Douglas, middle class and smartly dressed, did provide the show with a sensible presence, reassuring older viewers that they were not excluded from the programme and that it was unlikely to get out of hand. Her role, in this respect, was well brought out by her opening exchange with Murray, in which the programme's twin forms of address were clearly presented:

Pete: Hi there, welcome aboard the Six-Five Special. We've got almost a hundred cats jumping here, some real cool characters to give us the gas, so just get with it and have a ball.

Jo: Well I'm just a square it seems, but for all the other squares with us, roughly translated what Peter Murray just said was, we've got some lively musicians and personalities mingling with us here, so just relax and catch the mood from us. . . . [14]

This judicious balancing of young and old, the entertaining and educational, was also apparent in the show which followed. The musical numbers, for example, were deliberately varied and designed to provide a balance of pace and style. Kenny Baker and his jazz band played the show in and out, while the singer Michael Holliday contributed a couple of ballads. The rock'n'roll meanwhile was provided by Bobbie and Rudy and the King Brothers. The most unexpected musical item, however, was undoubtedly the appearance of the classical pianist, Pouishnoff, performing a selection from Beethoven and Chopin. Although a member of the audience was enlisted to voice her approval ('It doesn't matter what sort it is ... if the music's good I like it'), it was evident that, whatever the desire of the programme to provide musical uplift, classical music did not really fit the bill. The programme persevered with a classical item for a few more weeks, but then it was quietly dropped.

Other regular features were also begun. There was a film extract (Little Richard in *Don't Knock the Rock*) and a 'Star Spotlight' featuring a light-hearted interview with the film actress Lisa Gastoni. More unusually, the boxer Freddie Mills was recruited to present a sports item featuring lesser-known activities. This began somewhat comically with a demonstration by two Hungarian muscle-men, the Herculean Balancers. 'If you're going to rock'n'roll properly you need to have your muscles in pretty good shape', Freddie Mills explained, after he had been carried in by the two Hungarian heavyweights.

Finally, the programme included a filmed feature profiling the Brady Boys' Youth Club choir, who performed a selection of folk songs. Along with the sports spot (which subsequently featured judo, swimming and boxing), it was the filmed feature (usually narrated by Josephine Douglas) which was most charac-teristically dedicated to educating the audience or encouraging them to more active and sensible pursuits. These could, however, give the impression of being rather artificially grafted on to the show. In one edition (31 August 1957), for example, the bandleader Ray Anthony was encouraged to demonstrate the new 'American dance sensation', the Bunny Hop. This he proceeded to do before leading his fellow dancers in a conga-like bunny hop around the studio. No sooner had this rather bizarre activity been concluded, however, than the pro-gramme was off to Wales to join a climbing expedition.

It was, however, the music which was the show's most important feature. Although this was varied, four main types of music tended to predominate: rock'n'roll, skiffle, traditional jazz and ballads. The show, in fact, developed a particularly strong association with skiffle – its eventual theme tune was per-formed by the Bud Cort skiffle group, Lonnie Donegan, Chas McDevitt and Willie McCormick all made regular appearances and the show even launched its own skiffle competition – but it was its links with rock'n'roll for which the programme became most famous. It was only a few months before the start of the programme that rock'n'roll had really arrived in Britain. Elvis Presley had enjoyed his first British hit with 'Heartbreak Hotel' in May 1956, *Rock Around the Clock* had reached the cinemas in September, while Britain's first native rock'n'roller (and an early guest on *Six-Five Special*), Tommy Steele, had entered the charts for the first time with 'Rock Around the Cavemen' in October. And, it was precisely because rock'n'roll was so new in Britain that *Six-Five Special* was able to play such an important role in its growth.

This was evident both in the programme's ability to influence record sales (The Diamonds' 'Little Darlin', for example, was an early beneficiary) and to provide an important stepping-stone to success for individual artists. Partly because of the show's budget and partly because so few American rock'n'rollers were visiting Britain (Presley refused to come at all), the show was heavily dependent on British talent. As, at this stage, few enough British rock'n'roll acts existed, or were established, the show became an important launching-pad for new discoveries. The programme's power, in this regard, was quickly demon-strated by the case of the hapless Terry Dene, Britain's first rock'n'roll star after Steele but also its earliest casualty.[15] Appearing on *Six-Five Special* in April, he entered the charts shortly afterwards with his cover of Marty Robbins' 'A White Sports Coat'. More hits and even a film, very loosely based on his career, *The Golden Disc*, were to follow. Other singers were also to benefit. Jim Dale, who subsequently became the show's presenter, and Marty Wilde were two of the best known, but there was also a string of *Six-Five* regulars, such as the King Brothers, the Mudlarks and Don Lang, who were to achieve chart success as a result of appearing on the show.

However, for at least one reviewer it was not these performers but the teenage audience who were 'the real stars of the show'.[16] For central to the show's conception, and an important part of its appeal, was not just the live music but the dancing in the studio. This idea was not entirely new. In Philadelphia, *Bandstand* (subsequently *American Bandstand*) had already used teenage dancing to good effect.[17] However, in the context of British television the innovation was striking and, if Palmer is to be believed, the source of some consternation at the BBC who initially opposed Good's plans for scenes of 'wild abandon'.[18] If this was the case, the objections quickly dissolved and by the time of the programme's anniversary the Controller of Programmes, Kenneth Adam, was even lamenting the loss of time devoted to watching the audience, the very feature, he observed, which had 'put the programme on the map in the first place'.[19]

The appeal of the studio audience, in this respect, was not just their contribution to the informal party atmosphere enjoyed by many viewers, but also their role as unofficial guides to the latest fashions in clothes, haircuts and, above all, dancing. The programme encouraged this last interest, in particular, by running dance competitions (offering LP vouchers to the couple who could 'cut the coolest capers' in the first show) and recruiting 'experts' to demonstrate the latest dance crazes (or, as in one show, the difference between 'rock'n'roll' and 'jive dancing'). Dancing was also integral to the show's presentation of the music. The bands generally performed on slightly raised rostra while the audience danced in front. During musical numbers the cameras would cut between the performers and the dancers, who were usually shot either from above or by cameras roving the studio floor. Singers would also join the dancers and occasionally perform surrounded by members of the audience while having, as one viewer put it, to 'fight their way towards the cameras'.[20]

In order to maintain the energy levels of such scenes, rehearsals for the show were kept to a minimum. There would be a band-call on Friday morning but, apart from that, all the rehearsal took place on the Saturday. The various acts would be rehearsed during the day, followed by a preliminary session – 'more of a try-out than a run through' – at 3 pm.[21] A final run through then took place at 4.30 pm, leaving half an hour to spare before the actual show. This schedule became even more exhausting once the show began touring. The programme's normal home was Lime Grove, subsequently the Riverside studios, in London, but the programme also took to the road at an early stage, broadcasting a special, for example, from Glasgow in May 1957.

The most famous of the programme's outside broadcasts, however, was undoubtedly its trip to the 'birthplace' of British rock'n'roll, The Two I's Coffee Bar in Old Compton Street on 16 November. With cameras placed both upstairs and in the basement, performers, audience and crew cheerfully jostled for position. Owner Paul Lincoln dutifully defended rock'n'roll against its detractors, Terry Dene was seen in a clip from *The Golden Disc* and teenagers hand-jived happily. Meanwhile, an assortment of *Six-Five* regulars and Two I's residents belted out a succession of numbers, culminating in a version of 'Rockin' at the Two I's' by the unlikely combination of Two I's favourite, Wee Willie Harris, the King Brothers and Mike and Bernie Winters. Even the Deputy Director, Cecil McGivern, was aroused. 'This edition', he wrote the following Monday, 'was not only extraordinary but extraordinarily good. It was first class television as well as first class entertainment.'[22]

Ironically, this show was also destined to be one of Jack Good's last. Good and the BBC had never seemed entirely at ease with each other and it was possible that the arrival of a new co-producer, Dennis Main Wilson, in November (following the decision of Josephine Douglas to go freelance) had been the source of some friction. The immediate cause of Good's departure, however, appears to have been his decision to proceed with a *Six-Five Special* stage show against the wishes of the BBC, and, on 9 January 1958, the Corporation announced that it was not renewing Good's contract. Duncan Wood was brought in to replace him and share production duties with Main Wilson. Billy Cotton Jr joined them later.

The BBC's attitude towards Good's departure was surprisingly complacent. Only days after Good's dismissal, the Controller of Programmes, Kenneth Adam, announced that he had been concerned about the way in which the programme had been developing anyway, mentioning, in particular, its excessive reliance on rock'n'roll, and called for a review of the programme's policy.[23] Once this was completed, he felt happy that the change in producers had been made 'only just in time'.[24] Subsequent events, however, were to prove him badly wrong. Once Good had left, the show never regained its full momentum, despite (or perhaps, because of) a succession of changes in personnel and format. More importantly, Good himself was subsequently to join the opposition and it was his new show, *Oh Boy!* which was finally to deal a death-blow to the programme he had once created.

Oh Boy! was made for ABC and began with a trial run in the Midlands in June 1958 (not long after The Crickets had enjoyed a three month run in the charts with the song 'Oh Boy'). It was nationally networked from 12 September and scheduled in direct competition with *Six-Five Special* at 6–6.30 pm. The programme represented, in some regards, what Good had wanted all along. Apart from the occasional piece of comic knockabout courtesy of the show's two hosts, Tony Hall and Jimmy Henney, *Oh Boy!* discarded all of *Six-Five Special*'s variety acts and magazine features in favour of non-stop music. The programme was broadcast live each week from the Hackney Empire and, whereas *Six-Five Special* had tried to recreate a party atmosphere, *Oh Boy!* sought to generate the excitement of a live stage show. Its central tactic, in this regard, was speed. Billed in the *TV Times* as 'an explosion of beat music', the programme aimed to pack as many musical numbers into each show as possible (managing seventeen in twenty-six minutes in the very last one) and nothing was allowed to interrupt the flow.

This was particularly noticeable in the case of the presenters, who were allowed none of the limelight enjoyed by Pete Murray and Josephine Douglas in *Six-Five Special*. They generally appeared at the beginning and end of the show but were otherwise kept out of sight. Their introductions to the acts, if they existed at all, were simply heard. Instead, the cameras cut, without pause, from one act to the next, or a singer would just appear and take over the microphone before the previous song was barely completed. This rapid succession of numbers also left no time to dwell on the audience, who rarely appeared in front of the cameras as they had in *Six-Five Special*. A shot of a group in the balcony was used to accompany the opening titles, but after that, bar the very occasional view from the stage, the audience remained unseen. They were, however, heard. A constant barrage of applause and screaming carried on throughout the programme and did much to add to the overall sense of frenzy.

The music itself was provided by a mix of guests and resident performers. The residents were led by the show's musical director, Harry Robinson, and his band. Lord Rockingham's XI (whose constant appearances on the show helped them to a No.1 hit with the novelty number, 'Hoots Mon'); The Vernons Girls, a song and dance troupe originally recruited from employees of the pools company; and The Dallas Boys (in fact, a five-piece from Leicester) also provided regular support. Although the show, like *Six-Five Special*, was obliged to make the odd concession to musical variety (the occasional ballad, comic number or song and dance routine), the emphasis was firmly on rock'n'roll. *Six-Five* veteran Marty Wilde was also a resident and many of the new acts with which the show became

Six-Five Special, 1957: Don Lang and the Frantic Five take a break in rehearsal.

associated – Billy Fury, Dickey Pride, Vince Eager, Cuddly Dudley – were drawn, like Wilde, from the Larry Parnes stable of rock'n'rollers.

The show's greatest discovery, however, was undoubtedly Cliff Richard. He appeared on the very first show and within two weeks had entered the charts with 'Move It'. He joined the show as a regular and quickly moved to top billing in the *TV Times*, originally having come last. Good himself took a keen interest in the youngster and reputedly helped to groom him for stardom.[25] But, important as the show was in breaking individual acts, it was in its ensemble playing that it really excelled. The resident musicians not only performed their own numbers, but also played together and with most of the guests (the groups were the usual exception). Guests, moreover, were not merely provided with backing, but were also incorporated into productions involving other members of the cast. This was particularly true of the show's opening number, or medley, which would characteristically begin as a solo but end as a rousing ensemble.

The drama of such numbers was increased by an appropriately striking visual style. Although broadcast live, the programme aimed to do more than simulate the appearance of a live concert and staged its numbers and conceived of its effects specifically in terms of the television cameras. The casual camerawork and general air of informality which had been a feature of *Six-Five Special* was thus dispensed with and replaced by a carefully choreographed and visually arresting use of cutting, light and composition in depth. The design of the stage itself was kept simple, with the band to the right, steps and rostra at the back and a central microphone at the front. It was usually only at the end of the big ensemble numbers, however, that the camera would pull back to reveal the whole set and most of the performers were shot in either close-ups or mid-shots.

A typical number would, therefore, begin with shots of a singer at the microphone before the rest of the performers were revealed on both sides of the rostra behind. This would be done either by cutting directly between different parts of the set or, more strikingly, by cutting to a new shot of the original singer (usually a slightly angled mid-shot) to enable the artists who were behind to be seen. The same effect could also be achieved by a movement of the camera or, more commonly, a change of lighting. Without any resort to cutting, singers could be dramatically brought into view through the introduction of light. They could then, just as readily, be plunged back into darkness or transformed into silhouettes. And while most of the numbers relied on a combination of quick cutting and lighting changes, the show could also dispense with both and present a whole song (usually a slow number) in one simple and unbroken close-up. It was a striking and visually accomplished achievement which the press was quick to acknowledge. 'The three-dimensional sets, clever lighting and fast, exciting atmosphere of *Oh Boy!*', observed the *Daily Herald*, have 'confirmed Jack Good as ITV's most imaginative producer of "pop" shows.' The BBC, on the other hand, would 'have a nerve to show *Six-Five* again'.[26]

The BBC had, in fact, been aware of preparations for *Oh Boy!* as early as July and had attempted to meet its challenge. Despite his confidence in the changes made to the show in January, Kenneth Adam now led the call for 'a new look, a new noise (and) new faces'.[27] Russell Turner was brought in to take over production and have a revamped show ready for *Oh Boy!*'s launch in September. His recipe for the show, however, consisted less of a 'new look' than a reversion to the old showbiz tradition of *Off the Record*. Described in the press as for 'adults only', the programme was primarily aimed at an older audience and practically dispensed with rock'n'roll altogether. In its place, Turner inaugurated a 'big band policy', involving two resident big bands (Tony Osborne and Tito Burns), as well as a regular big band guest (such as Ted Heath or Eric Delaney).

But, despite this dramatic expansion of the cast list, it was clear that the new show was no match for its ITV rival. The press quickly declared 'the battle of the TV programmes' in ITV's favour and although the BBC bravely declared that it was maintaining its audience, doubts were soon to emerge. 'I have been making enquiries among the younger generation about the interest in *Oh Boy!* and *Six-Five Special*', Adam informed the Head of Light Entertainment in early November, 'and there is no doubt the former is preferred. At this I am not surprised. Its formula is better, more punchy, its camera work simpler and faster than ours.'[28] His view was reinforced not long after by Cecil McGivern: 'This programme (*Six-Five Special*, Saturday, 22nd November) was another reminder of the sad present of this once excellent programme', he observed. 'The content was poor, the presentation and camera work very poor and the whole thing had no reason for its existence on our screen.'[29]

By some peculiar historical twist, this edition is one of only two that the BBC now hold. Looking at it again, it is not difficult to see how the show had lost its way and become entirely disconnected from teenage tastes and attitudes. The music, the audience and the atmosphere, which had originally been the basis of the show's success, had all changed in character. In line with the programme's new policy of abandoning the teenage audience, the programme was broadcast from an American air-base. Most of the dancers were well past their teens and in uniform and a group of officers and their wives sat awkwardly to the side watching the proceedings with an air of parental indulgence. Nearly all of the performers were kitted out in evening dress (including the two hostesses whom Turner had added to the show in the interests of 'glamour') and delivered a style of music to match: big band numbers, ballads, novelty numbers and, when things got really lively, the cha cha. Unlike the early days, the show now consisted almost entirely of music but, in comparison to *Oh Boy!*, the proceedings were slow, visually dull (Lita Roza on a forklift truck notwithstanding) and entirely lacking in energy and drive.

It was inevitable, therefore, that the programme would fold soon after. The Head of Light Entertainment, Eric Maschwitz, agreed with McGivern that the show's formula was now 'exhausted' and unveiled plans for a new show to be produced by light entertainment veteran, Francis Essex. Although Essex's original idea was for a cross between *Six-Five Special*, *Off the Record* and *These Wonderful Shows*, it was evident that the new programme was going to try and emulate the example of *Oh Boy!*, especially its speed and ensemble playing. 'The idea is to get as much life, movement and noise out of a simple presentation', Maschwitz informed Adam, 'without cluttering up the studio with juvenile delinquents.'[30]

Entitled *Dig This!*, the new show retained its predecessor's 6.05 pm start time but, as a means of injecting pace, was trimmed to half *Six-Five Special*'s length. Launched on 3 January 1959, the *Radio Times* underlined the show's determination to be fast. It will be 'a swift moving, up-to-the-minute show', it promised, 'with all the latest pop music presented in a new streamlined manner'.[31] Like *Oh Boy!*, the show also employed a regular troupe of musicians. These were led by Bob Miller and his seventeen-piece band, the Millermen, who, in addition to accompanying most of the numbers, were required to jump off high platforms and generally maintain an urgent sense of activity. Ex-serviceman and Sandhurst graduate, Gary Marshall, was recruited to act as the show's presenter and did his best to give conviction to the show's immortal lines of welcome: 'Hi, Kids! Dig This!' It was clear, however, that despite the show's efforts, it was unable to stem the tide of falling audience figures. Cast changes were made in February before the show was finally dropped at the end of March.

At this point, the BBC conceded defeat in the battle for the six o'clock audience and scheduled the programme's replacement, *Drumbeat*, at 6.30 pm. The popular American Western series, *Wells Fargo*, was brought forward to fill the gap. Although a new, and more youthful, producer, Stewart Morris, was put in charge of the show and the programme itself was described as 'the first of the new "beat" programmes', all the evidence suggests that *Drumbeat*, like *Dig This!* before it, was still in awe of *Oh Boy!*'s accomplishment and could do no better than imitate it.[32]

The show retained the services of Bob Miller and his band but added a new line-up of regulars, including a second resident band, the John Barry Seven, the seventeen-year-old Sylvia Sands, former *Oh Boy!* star Vince Eager and the show's main discovery, Adam Faith. Faith was, in fact, a former protégé of Jack Good's, who had opened the famous *Six-Five Special* Two I's show with his skiffle group, The Worried Men. Despite Good's efforts to groom him as a 'singing James Dean', success had eluded him until his appearances on *Drumbeat*. By the end of the year these had helped him to a No.1 hit with 'What Do You Want'. Like *Oh Boy!*, the show aimed to be fast-moving and pack in as many artists as possible. According to Adam Faith, the music demanded a good twenty arrangements and, in a clear example of the programme's indebtedness to its rival, a further seventy changes of lighting.[33] Morris was soon claiming to have more viewers than *Oh Boy!* and, while this was unlikely, the programme did well enough to justify an extension of its initial run. Although this was only a matter of months it was, in fact, just long enough to outlive its great rival.

The reasons for the ending of *Oh Boy!* are not entirely clear. The last edition was broadcast on 30 May 1959 and, although it displayed an end of term exuberance, the show's hosts still expected to be back the following September. The fact that the BBC had now stolen the show's formula, however, appears to have prompted the idea for a replacement, while ABC's wish to vacate the Hackney Empire and use studios in Manchester probably made the decision inevitable. The result was a new show, *Boy Meets Girls*, on 12 September 1959, at the new time of 6.30–7 pm. Many of the *Oh Boy!* regulars were still involved. Marty Wilde was the 'Boy' in question while the Vernons provided the 'Girls'. The organist Cherry Wainer and saxophonist Red Price also retained their roles as residents. The actual conception of the show, however, appears to have altered.

In a self-conscious retreat from the freneticism of *Oh Boy!*, the idea was to feature more ballads and quieter numbers as well as introduce a greater variety (the Vernons Girls, for example, were to figure much more prominently). This 'soft-pedal technique', as it was described in the TV *Times*, suggested that Good may have come under some pressure to tone his show down. Certainly, his comments at the time were unpromising: '*Oh Boy!* taught me that there is no substitute for personality in entertainment ... We shall use an occasional, wild number but the accent is on friendliness and the programme is aimed at a wider audience. We are out to capture the elder brothers and sisters of the teenagers. And the mums and dads too.'[34] Ironically, this dilution of the original formula appears only to have lessened the show's appeal without appreciably expanding its following among adults. This seems to have been recognised and the show made efforts to liven up the proceedings by importing some major American acts. Eddie Cochran made his UK television debut on the show, as did Gene Vincent, whose appearance as a 'malformed Richard III' has been lovingly recalled by more than one commentator.[35] Cochran and Vincent even shared the same bill, along with Billy Fury, Adam Faith and Jess Conrad, no less, but by this time it was too late to save the show and it ended two weeks later.

The Jack Good team, however, were back the following month with a replacement. Billed as 'a fistful of songs', *Wham!* attempted to return to the quickfire style of *Oh Boy!* with a mixture of guests and regulars led by the Vernons Girls, Billy Fury, Jess Conrad and Joe Brown (whom Good had discovered amongst the backing musicians on *Oh Boy!*). Keith Fordyce, subsequently to front *Ready, Steady, Go!*, acted as compère. The time, however, no longer seemed right and the show came to a rapid end, lasting only eight editions. With it, Good's contribution to British television also came to a halt. He went on to produce an updated version of *Oh Boy!*, *Shindig!* for ABC in the United States in 1964, while *Oh Boy!* itself was revived for British television in 1979 with Good as executive producer. By this time, however, the programme had lost all sense of immediacy, and, in an era of punk, was relegated to the ranks of comfortable nostalgia.

The demise of both *Boy Meets Girls* and *Wham!* had also been precipitated by an unexpected resurgence of the BBC's fortunes in the battle for the tea-time audience. Their answer to *Oh Boy!*, *Drumbeat*, eventually came to an end on 29 August 1959 when it was immediately replaced, at a slightly later time, by *Juke Box Jury*. Based on an American idea and produced by Russell Turner (this time hitting gold), *Juke Box Jury* had originally begun in June on Mondays at 7.30 pm. Switched to an earlier time on Saturdays, it seemed to provide the perfect formula for combining teen appeal with entertainment for all the family. 'When it made its début in this country there were many criticisms', observed one writer, 'but a successful format was quickly found and soon caught the imagination of televiewers from 4 to 94!'[36] It was a format which was also exceptionally simple (not to mention cheap).

A resident dee-jay, the avuncular David Jacobs, sat next to a fake juke-box, introducing excerpts from the week's latest record releases. A guest panel of four and a studio audience of young people sat and listened, while the cameras recorded their reactions. The panel were then invited to give their opinions on each record and vote it a hit or a miss. Should the vote be a tie, a teenage panel, chosen from the studio audience, would be called upon to decide. One of the artists whose record was featured in the show would make a guest appearance, remaining out of view until the panel had voted (in many cases, declaring the guest's record a miss). A simple formula it may have been, but it was one which was to prove immensely popular. The show quickly acquired a regular following of nine million viewers, rising to twelve million by early 1962, and, even more obviously than *Six-Five Special*, became something of a 'national institution'.

More so, perhaps, than any of its predecessors, the show appeared to have fulfilled the schedulers' requirements for a successful match of teenage tastes and adult interest. The role of the panel, in this respect, was crucial. The programme had initially begun with a panel loosely connected to the world of popular music. The very first show, for example, had featured the two singers Alma Cogan and Gary Miller, former *Six-Five Special* presenter, Pete Murray, and the youthful Susan Stranks, whom the *Radio Times* assured its readers represented 'a typical teenager'.[37] It was not long, however, before the panel acquired an increasingly showbiz flavour involving guests, such as Eric Sykes or Diana Dors, with only the most tenuous of links with the music business or, indeed, teenagers.

The result, and presumably part of the appeal for that section of the audience who didn't care for the music in the first place, was an increasing emphasis on the personalities of the guests at the expense of the show's musical content (a whole record, for example, was never played). This was a tendency that also led to one of the most regularly voiced criticisms of the show: that a panel consisting of comics, film-stars and crooners were hardly well-qualified to pass judgement on pop music (or, indeed, predict its commercial potential). Lack of familiarity with the music was certainly a regular feature of the show. In one edition (29 October 1960), for example, the journalist Nancy Spain confused Lloyd Price with Frank Lloyd Wright, while singer Carmen McCrae, on hearing Roy Orbison's 'Blue Angel', announced that she detested 'this type of music', but thought that because it was so 'terrible', it would be a hit. However, it was precisely this type of ignorance which also served the show so well.

For the guests on the show not only enticed the parents to watch, but also came out with the comments on pop music that parents themselves might be expected to make in the living room ('terrible', 'what a noise' and so on).[38] While this could undoubtedly be irksome to younger viewers, it could also add to the show's appeal. For teenagers did not necessarily want the guests (any more than their parents) to like the music; indeed part of the pleasure of the show undoubtedly lay in its confirmation that pop music was not generally understood or appreciated by adults. The art of *Juke Box Jury*, in this respect, was to have it both ways, both confirming adult and youthful prejudices at the same time. Iain Chambers, for example, describes David Jacobs' 'smirk' as he pressed the hooter for a 'miss' as 'a rather irritating reminder of a sober-suited, short-haired, responsible, adult "No"!'[39] But, while this adult put-down may have been enjoyed by the parents, it did, as the quote suggests, irritate other sections of the audience, who not only came to expect it but also, given how long the show survived, to enjoy it themselves. A large part of the pleasure was, indeed, the irritation and many of the show's most famous moments depended on this, such as when Johnny Mathis appeared and criticised *all* the records.

By the same token, when the tables were turned and the Rolling Stones replaced the usual assortment of showbiz worthies on the panel, the parents may have been outraged, but for many others the pleasure derived from the Stones' refusal to conform to the show's normally stuffy conventions. As Lawrence Grossberg observes: 'Different audiences may watch the same program but interpret it differently, not only because of their own history and relations to rock and roll, but also because of the use to which they put particular images in the larger context of their cultural lives and rock and roll fandom.'[40] *Juke Box Jury*'s success, in this regard, lay precisely in its ability to generate these different, and even opposing, responses and interpretations.

Juke Box Jury is, nonetheless, conventionally regarded as marking the end of an era. 'In less than four years rock'n'roll television had flourished and died,' writes Bob Woffinden. 'Like rock'n'roll *per se*, it had arrived boldly but was soon emasculated and re-cycled as family entertainment.' *Juke Box Jury*, in this respect, is singled out for rebuke because, 'unlike *Six-Five Special*', it 'was meant to appeal to the whole family'.[41] In fact, the history of rock'n'roll on television was more complicated than this argument suggests. In part, due to historical accident (the ending of the 'toddler's truce') and, in part, because television, with only two channels, could not afford to target its programmes too narrowly, rock'n'roll television had been involved from the beginning in winning over the family audience.

This was as true of *Six-Five Special* as it was of *Juke Box Jury*, although there were, of course, variations in the degree to which programmes were prepared to make concessions to the adult audience. If *Oh Boy!* made the least, then *Juke Box Jury* undoubtedly made the most and it was only with the arrival of *Ready, Steady, Go!* in 1963, on a Friday evening rather than at Saturday tea-time, that the pendulum swung back in favour of the youth audience. With its mix of music, dancing and competitions and successful creation of an informal party atmosphere, in which the audience were as much the stars as the musicians, *Ready, Steady, Go!* was also the first of many subsequent television pop programmes (including *Top of the Pops*, *The Tube* and even the dubious *Club X*) to demonstrate the lasting influence of the *Six-Five Special* format.[42]

This is not, of course, to imply that the pop programmes of the 50s did no more than make rock'n'roll safe for family consumption. Unlike so many subsequent musical trends, television, in this case, was not simply catching up with rock'n'roll, but actively involved in its promotion. British rock'n'roll was still at an embryonic stage of development when *Six-Five Special* first appeared and television not only provided the music with a national platform (providing access to the Two I's, for example, to those who would not otherwise have expected to go there), but also advanced the careers of numerous rock'n'roll singers. British rock'n'roll, in this respect, was far more dependent upon television for its success than American rock'n'roll (which in Britain, was more commonly heard on the radio – on Radio Luxembourg rather than the BBC – or seen in the cinemas) or, indeed, subsequent British pop movements (whose origins have tended to be rather more 'spontaneous').

This did mean, of course, that television, and television producers such as Jack Good, played an important part in the presentation and packaging of British rock'n'rollers. While this could lead to attempts to make them more acceptable to a family audience (the BBC, for example, attempted to stop Marty Wilde 'belly-swinging'), this was not necessarily so.[43] Indeed, in the case of performers such as Wee Willie Harris and Gene Vincent, Jack Good seems to have attempted to exaggerate, rather than play down, the apparent grotesquerie of their performances. Television undoubtedly paved the way for a more general acceptance of many of the early rock'n'rollers by incorporating them into traditional showbiz variety shows (*Sunday Night at the London Palladium*, *Saturday Spectacular*, *Billy Cotton Band Show*). However, on the rock'n'roll shows themselves the best of British rock'n'roll (the early Cliff, Billy Fury, Johnny Kidd and the Pirates) could be seen on television with only the minimum of cosmetic tinkering and often to better advantage than in the cinema, where the constraints should in some ways have been less.

Notes

I am indebted to a number of people and institutions for their assistance in the preparation of this article. My thanks to Debbie Whittaker of the BBC Written Archives Centre, Caversham, Reading for her help with written material and to Simon Radcliffe of the BBC for arranging screenings. Thanks also to the staff of the National Film Archive, London and the Weintraub-Pathé Film Library, Elstree for their help with screenings. My thanks too to Noleen Kennedy for her typing. My thanks, in particular, to Pamela Gibson for her help and advice on the writing of this article.

1. Lord Hill of Luton, *Both Sides of the Hill* (London: Heinemann, 1964), p. 170. The ban on Sunday broadcasting at this time was to continue until March 1958 when programmes of a religious nature were permitted to be broadcast. For a survey of the debates over television hours, see Bernard Sendall, *Independent Television in Britain Volume I: Origin and Foundation, 1946–62* (London: Macmillan, 1982).
2. Anon., 'At the Top of the List', *Radio Times*, 14 October 1955, p. 21.
3. *Off the Record*, which carried on until 1958, did begin to include some rock'n'rollers, although these were introduced with some disgruntlement by Payne. With respect to vocabulary, I am using the term 'popular music' to refer to the Tin Pan Alley tradition of 'light' music and the term 'pop music' to refer generally to the new styles and techniques of youth-orientated music which first began to emerge in the 1950s. In this respect, I am using 'rock'n'roll' in its specific sense (as a species of 'pop' music) rather than as a general category synonymous with 'rock'.
4. David Griffiths, 'Ker's no Kitten – But He's Real Cool', *TV Times*, 14 June 1957, p. 27.
5. Ibid.
6. For details, see Gordon Watkins (ed.), *Tonight* (London: British Film Institute, 1982).
7. *Birmingham Mail*, 18 February 1957.

8. Other titles considered included 'Hi There', 'Live It Up', 'Take It Easy' and 'Don't Look Now'. 'Six-Five Special' was preferred because of the popularity of allusions to trains in 'jazz-parlance'. Memo from Josephine Douglas to Assistant Head of Light Entertainment, Tom Sloan, 2 January 1957, BBC Written Archives Centre (WAC), File index number T12/360/3.

9. The importance of television's 'familial' viewer is discussed in more theoretical terms by John Ellis, *Visible Fictions* (London: Routledge and Kegan Paul, 1982) and Jane Feuer, 'The Concept of Live Television: Ontology as Ideology' in E.A. Kaplan (ed.), *Regarding Television* (Los Angeles: American Film Institute/University Publications of America, 1983). Simon Frith's discussion of the importance of 'hearth and home' to radio light entertainment also suggests a parallel; see 'The Pleasures of the Hearth: The making of BBC light entertainment', in *Formations of Pleasure* (London: Routledge and Kegan Paul, 1983).

10. *BBC Handbook* (London: British Broadcasting Corporation, 1959), p. 99.

11. *Radio Times*, 22 February 1957, p. 4.

12. Memo to Josephine Douglas and Jack Good, 18 March 1957, WAC T12/360/3.

13. Audience Research Report on *Six-Five Special*, 5 April 1957, WAC T12/360/6.

14. As no copy of this particular edition appears to have survived, this quote is taken from the script for the show held at the BBC Written Archives Centre. Despite the programme's reputation for apparent spontaneity, the show was rigid in its adherence to a script and it is unlikely that the broadcast show deviated significantly from the agreed script (and Pete Murray's speech is, in fact, quoted as it appears in the script in the *Sunday Times* review of 17 February 1957). All subsequent quotes, from this edition only, also derive from the script.

15. The rise and fall of Terry Dene is eloquently recalled in Nik Cohn, *Awopbopaloobopalopbamboom: Pop from the Beginning* (London: Paladin, 1970).

16. *Punch*, 3 April 1957.

17. Unlike *Six-Five Special*, however, most of the performances on *Bandstand* were mimed. For the details of the programme, see Michael Shore (with Dick Clark), *The History of American Bandstand* (New York: Ballantine Books, 1985). This famous American show is not, of course, to be confused with the half-hour jazz programme, *Bandstand*, launched by ITV in September 1959.

18. According to Tony Palmer, Good was obliged to resort to subterfuge for the first show and had 'a set constructed for the show that looked harmless and was approved by management'. The set, however, was on wheels and, during rehearsals, 'the entire set was quickly moved around so that the audience for the show was in front of the cameras as Good had planned'. See, *All You Need Is Love: The Story of Popular Music* (London: Futura, 1976), p. 215. Internal BBC memos, however, suggest that the BBC management were less distressed by the show than this story implies. The Head of Light Entertainment, Ronald Waldman, for example, wrote to Douglas and Good following the second programme and praised them for 'a good show'. His concern was less with the studio audience than the contrivance of the star spotlight interview, the over-exposure of Josephine Douglas and the rough and ready nature of some of the camera work. (Memo, 25 February 1957, WAC T12/360/3.) The Deputy Director of Television Broadcasting, Cecil McGivern, wrote, in turn, to Waldman about the seventh show, an 'exuberant programme' which he apparently enjoyed. Once again, he was unhappy about the camera-work but was mostly put out by Ian Carmichael's use of a 'chamber pot' in a comedy sketch. (Memo, 1 April 1957, WAC T12/360/7.) The issue of the audience did arise later in the year when the Television House Manager complained about their 'generally rude and aggressive behaviour'. (Memo to Light

Entertainment Organiser, Television, 25 September 1957, WAC T12/360/3). This complaint was referred to Good and Douglas, who were informed by the Assistant Head of Light Entertainment, Tom Sloan, that 'the actual nature of this programme' could not be regarded as an 'excuse for bad manners on the part of the audience'. (Memo, 25 September 1957, WAC T12/360/3).

19. Memo to Head of Light Entertainment, 7 February 1958, WAC T12/360/4.
20. Cited in BBC Audience Research Report on *Six-Five Special*, 1 January 1958, WAC T12/360/12.
21. Rowan Ayers, 'The Studio Was Jumpin''. *Radio Times*, 5 April 1957.
22. Memo to Head of Light Entertainment, 18 November 1957, WAC T12/360/9.
23. Memo to Assistant Head of Light Entertainment, 13 January 1958, WAC T12/360/4.
24. Memo to Head of Light Entertainment, 7 February 1958, WAC T12/360/4.
25. George Melly, indeed, blames Good for turning Cliff into 'acceptable family entertainment' by removing his guitar and sideburns and suggesting a new repertoire of arm, leg and hip movements: see *Revolt into Style, The Pop Arts* (New York: Anchor, 1971), p. 56 (Orig. London: Penguin, 1970). This is undoubtedly overstated. Good did make changes to Cliff's image but, as his appearance on the final *Oh Boy!* indicates, these were not designed to make him appear wholesome so much as to add an air of insolent, if somewhat studied, sexuality. Indeed, according to Chris Welch, Cliff was attacked for 'obscenity' after appearing on the show in December. See 'Rock '58', *The History of Rock*, No. 11, (Orbis, 1982), p. 205.
26. Mike Nevard, *Daily Herald*, 15 September 1958.
27. Memo to Head of Light Entertainment, 1 July 1958, WAC T12/360/4.
28. Memo, 4 November 1958, WAC T12/360/4.
29. Memo to Adam, 24 November 1958, WAC T12/360/4.
30. Memo, 25 November 1958, WAC T12/360/4.
31. *Radio Times*, 19 December 1958, p. 11. Despite this emphasis on speed, it was also clear that the BBC did not want to embrace entirely *Oh Boy!*'s freneticism. As Essex explained to the press, the show was to be 'good clean fun with no hysteria', *Swindon Evening Advertiser*, 3 January 1959.
32. *Radio Times*, 27 March 1959, p. 4.
33. Adam Faith, *Poor Me* (London: Four Square, 1961), p. 44. Jack Good's conception of Faith as a 'singing James Dean' is described on p. 26.
34. *TV Times*, 25 September 1959, p. 16.
35. The most detailed account is provided by Ian Whitcomb, *After the Ball: Pop Music from Rag to Rock* (London: Penguin, 1973). It is, perhaps, of some concern, however, that Good's insistence that Vincent exaggerate his limp has been recorded with nothing other than admiration by all those who have described it.
36. Ken and Sylvia Ferguson (eds.), *Television Show Book* (London: Parnell, 1964), p. 102.
37. *Radio Times*, 29 May 1959, p. 13.
38. This phenomenon was already noted by the BBC Audience Research Department in its report on the very first edition of *Six-Five Special*. A 'teenage Mill Tester' is reported as commenting on the programme: 'This is what many of us have wanted for a long time and I just cannot say how much I enjoy it. But my dad was grumbling all the time. He said it was "just a lot of noise."' (7 March 1957, WAC T12/360/5).
39. Iain Chambers, *Urban Rhythms: Pop Music and Popular Culture* (London: Macmillan, 1985), p. 53.
40. Lawrence Grossberg, 'MTV: Swinging on the (Postmodern) Star' in Ian Angus and Sut Jhally (eds.), *Cultural Politics in Contemporary America* (London: Routledge, 1989), p.

258. My argument is, of course, that the characteristics of *Juke Box Jury* facilitated different responses, not simply that different audiences could interpret the programme in whatever way they liked.

41. Bob Woffinden, 'Hit or Miss?', *The History of Rock*, No. 19, (Orbis, 1982), p. 380. Woffinden's somewhat doubtful use of the term 'emasculation' echoes similar remarks made by George Melly concerning 'the castration of the first British pop explosion' in *Revolt Into Style*, p. 56. Their resort to such terms, however, is not entirely unexpected insofar as it has been one of the more problematic features of pop music, from rock'n'roll to rap, that its rebelliousness has characteristically been encoded in the language and style of male aggression.

42. Ironically, the best and most exciting of the 50s shows, *Oh Boy!*, set an example that television was unable to repeat. This was due not simply to the absence of a successor to Jack Good, but the changing character of British pop. *Oh Boy!* was a supreme example of television d'auteur in which individual performers were subordinated to the programme's overall concept and design. As the emphasis of pop shifted from solo performers to groups, and pop stars acquired a growing sense of their own artistic self-importance (including the writing of their own material), the possibilities for the carefully drilled ensemble playing which characterised *Oh Boy!* diminished accordingly.

43. The Controller of Programmes, Kenneth Adam, wrote to the Assistant Head of Light Entertainment, Tom Sloan, in January 1958 complaining that he had found the number of 'Presley-type "bellyswingers"' on *Six-Five Special* 'offensive'. (Memo, 13 January 1958, WAC T12/360/4). The 'main offender' was identified as Marty Wilde and Tom Sloan threatened to drop him from the show (Memo to Controller of Programmes, 13 January 1958, WAC T12/360/4). A concern of a slightly different kind was aired later in the year by Cecil McGivern, the Deputy Director of Television: 'Apart from the general chaos, there was another fault in this programme which is unacceptable. That was the number of girls who wore very abbreviated skirts, and several who wore practically no skirts at all, and one, I think, who seemed to be wearing simply a pair of black pants. I know how kids feel and act and I sympathise with them but they must not be allowed complete licence. If this is a tendency in *Six-Five Special*, it must stop.' (Memo to Dennis Main Wilson, 8 April 1958, WAC T12/360/4).

Wise Scientists and Female Androids
Class and Gender in Science Fiction

JOY LEMAN

The post-war push by the authorities in Britain to relocate women back in the home, along with the desire to restore 'stable' family units and to increase the birthrate had, by the 1950s, given way to a recognition that more women workers were now needed, due to labour shortages in crucial industries – both white and blue collar. We could expect this to be reflected in the television fictions of the period. Similarly the more public, active role taken by women generally during the Second World War could be expected to affect the television depictions of the 1950s. Cinematic representations had shown, for crucial reasons to do with morale and the war effort, a different image of women during wartime. Radio programmes to some extent and certainly women's magazines had reflected the more active role of women. Since television had only just become properly established at the point when transmission ceased altogether in 1939, it is impossible to gauge how TV programmes might have dealt with those factors so crucial to the war effort – gender and class.

As a separate but related issue, there were very few women involved in the making of television programmes in the 1950s, either as writers, producers or in 'executive' roles. Grace Wyndham Goldie and Mary Adams in Talks and Current Affairs were the exceptions to the general rule. In the field of Drama in the 1960s, Irene Shubik became an innovator in television approaches to science fiction (SF) with her anthology series – initially, in 1962, *Out of this World* for ABC TV and later, in 1965, *Out of the Unknown* for BBC 2.

Towards a TV Convention of Science Fiction
Science fiction dramas had a remarkable impact on television audiences of the 1950s and 60s. Single plays such as Nigel Kneale's adaptation of Orwell's *1984* led to extensive controversy and questions in Parliament. Serialised science fiction offered adult viewers a weekly experience of serious, exciting, dramatic television over six or seven episodes. In television today the full dramatic potential of science fiction is rarely explored. Long running 'family favourites' like *Dr Who* tend to dominate the output. Science fiction programmes are mainly targeted towards viewers under the age of twelve and often in the form of animation blandly tailored to an international market.

Science fiction as a genre in literature, film and television offers the possibility of moving beyond the dominant narrative constraints of realism and natu-

108

ralism in exploring political ideas, visions of an alternative reality and domains of fantasy. These conceptual areas are an integral part of the genre and deserve more serious and imaginative treatment than television science fiction usually provides. In general, issues of class, race, gender and sexuality are incorporated into stereotyped characters, with narrative structures and production codes drained of more complex dimensions.

If television programme-making has been dominated by white middle-class males, then certainly SF as a genre has been gendered masculine if not necessarily white and middle class. Science fiction literature of all kinds has recently been transformed by women writers both feminist and non-feminist and some interesting shifts of emphasis in gender representation are taking place in science fiction films.[1] But the institutional controls, high investment, and industrialised production modes of television have made this a slower process in an industry not renowned for risk-taking. A masculine characterisation of SF still predominates in children's television in particular. In spite of the action-oriented female companions featured in television's longest-running SF series, *Dr Who*'s fan club seems to consist mainly of young men and boys fascinated by special effects.[2]

I intend to focus here on two corner-stones of the television output of science fiction directed towards the adult audience in this early period. Firstly, the *Quatermass* serials transmitted intermittently throughout the 1950s, when television was becoming established as a part of the cultural experience of the majority of people in Britain. Secondly, *A for Andromeda*, a serial broadcast in 1961, at the beginning of the Hugh Greene 'liberal' era. By considering these two it is possible to trace some important changes in television presentation of science fiction and, in particular, the inflections of gender and class which have formed an integral part of the genre in the visual media.[3]

When British television resumed service in 1949 the drama output was largely limited to reproductions of West End theatre presentations. According to Briggs, the setting up of the TV Script Unit in 1951 led to a fundamental reappraisal of what was possible in TV drama. The entry of science fiction into British television took place in 1953, when the first *Quatermass* series was broadcast. The adoption of a popular culture genre in the sphere of drama seemed, to its credit, to be an attempt by one part of the BBC to speak to a wider audience. The TV Script Unit was an important part of the BBC reappraisal of the potential of TV drama as more than a vehicle for stage play adaptations. The confidence shown in Nigel Kneale by giving him a large part of the modest budget accruing to the new Drama Section suggests that the BBC was willing to take risks in trying to establish a wider appeal for TV drama.[4] One of the results of this was the *Quatermass Experiment*, broadcast in 1953. The success of the first series led to *Quatermass II* in 1955 and *Quatermass and the Pit* in 1958. Kneale's motivation in wanting to write science fiction drama was to break new ground, to move away from a theatrical format and towards 'something different, something fast moving and adventurous'.[5] While much has been written about these series, including extensive interviews with the writer and producer Nigel Kneale, little reference has been made to issues of representation and, in particular, to the way in which images of class, gender and the family are constructed.

From the perspective of the 1980s and 90s, one of the interesting aspects of the *Quatermass* serials is the way in which established stereotypes of class, gender and the family are integrated into what was perceived at the time as a new and exciting television genre. The dominant characters are upper class and male. These men are often presented as negative, authoritarian figures, obsessed with bureaucratic concerns and power struggles – familiar characters indeed to a population emerging from the tightly government-controlled conditions of wartime. Professor Quatermass and his various male confidants offer more sympathetic identification points, being sensitive, perceptive and concerned, even when the confidants are junior army officers. The benevolent paternalism of Professor Quatermass provides the dominant perspective within the narrative. It is his point of view with which the audience are asked to identify. Trust in him is invoked, both in terms of his position as an educated, knowledgeable individual, and as a 'leader', carrying the responsibility with which only the upper class, educated man could be entrusted in the imagery and narratives of British broadcasting in the 1940s and 50s.

Of course, the demands of the system during wartime and after had changed some aspects of that hegemony, but what is surprising is that it had not changed more fundamentally in the 'new' dramas such as *Quatermass*. Instead, we have the same working-class stereotypes used as comic relief. The male characters, often soldiers, or occasionally workers, show a long suffering heroism; the women are more limited still: often no more than Elsie and Doris Waters' 'gossips'. Upper-class women featured more prominently, but still had to focus the 'love interest' and service the brilliance of the Professor, even though academically well equipped themselves.

'Bring something back . . .'

The Quatermass Experiment, at first entitled 'Bring something back . . .' was produced and directed by Rudolph Cartier and written by Nigel Kneale. The serial was broadcast in 1953, live from the studio in six episodes of approximately thirty minutes each. The plot centred on the story of a space flight which had gone wrong. Seven years before the first moon shot was launched, the dire consequences of a British/Australian space project were depicted in this 'Thriller for Television'. The space rocket crash-lands in a London street and an Ealing comedy scene of cheery chaos is soon subdued by the strange behaviour of the only surviving astronaut. It quickly becomes clear that he has been contaminated by an 'alien' organism which thrives to become a much wider threat to human life.

While suffering from the material limitations of the studio, *Quatermass* makes extensive use of familiar cinematic and radio references in establishing an (in)credible science fiction narrative. This was the first serialised TV SF in Britain to be aimed at adult viewers. Genre conventions were not yet set out in the new medium, though the serialised suspense thriller was a popular part of radio drama output. There were of course cinematic models, ranging from *Metropolis* and *War of the Worlds* to the output of Hollywood during the 1940s and early 1950s against which Kneale was reacting. The substantial print output of science fiction maga-

110

zines and novels seems to have had little bearing on either the narrative or visual qualities of TV science fiction in this period. On the contrary, the intention of Rudolph Cartier, the producer of *The Quatermass Experiment*, was to 'lift this production above the level of strip cartoons and magazine thrillers'.[6]

Cartier was concerned that viewers should be cued in to the serial structure and so introduced the cinematic 'trailer' by inserting telerecorded extracts of previous instalments at the start of each episode. This was probably the first use of this convention in British television and significantly was established in the pre-ITV era. Audience response was generally favourable according to the BBC Audience Research Department, and was clearly an important factor in the decision to make another *Quatermass* serial.[7]

'Normality' and Class in 'Quatermass II'

The start of ITV in September 1955 was the cue for *Quatermass II*, in which the writer/producer team of the first serial were clearly expected by the BBC to repeat their success in the face of commercial competition. *Quatermass II* was transmitted live in six episodes at 8 pm on successive Saturdays in October 1955. The plot centred on an attempted invasion of earth by aliens who illicitly establish control of human minds by toxic gases released from meteorites falling from space. Alien nourishment was manufactured on a moorland site in a secret reprocessing plant, which was finally attacked and destroyed by workers and local villagers together.

Nigel Kneale compared the second *Quatermass* with the first: 'Instead of a normal world with one sinister element moving in it, as before, we have one normal protagonist (Quatermass) moving in an increasingly abnormal world'.[8] One of the underlying themes of *Quatermass II* concerned the nature of 'normality', a theme powerfully inscribed in a Hollywood movie, *Invasion of the Body Snatchers*, released one year after *Quatermass II*. While a dominant motif of the film is the construction of a sinister and uniformly submissive workforce, the TV serial highlights the ruling élites as a 'push over' for brainwashing. It is not so much the 'crowd', workers, villagers, or idealised family units who appear easy prey to mind takeovers in *Quatermass II*, but rather the upper-class characters with vested interests embedded in rigid power structures – army officers, top civil servants and scientists. 'Normal' elements, represented by the village community, workers at the plant, and by family domesticity provide here the context for Quatermass to exercise his benevolent paternalism. Ultimately, the Professor saves the planet with assistance from these 'marginalised' groups.

Curiously, the BBC Controller of TV Programmes considered many scenes in *Quatermass II* 'improbable' and criticised the serial as a whole for complicated dialogue and insufficient action. These criticisms were vigorously repudiated by Kneale with evidence from press reviews and BBC Audience Research Reports.[9]

'Quatermass and the Pit' and the 'enemy within'

By the time the third *Quatermass* serial of the decade was broadcast at peak viewing time across six Mondays from December 1958, the Professor was shown doubting his own confidence. Not only is the wider environment disquietingly metamorphosed, but the stable element constituted by Quatermass, the father figure, is shown as flawed and vulnerable.

The publicity for *Quatermass and the Pit* suggested a confidence in the established cultural roots of the Quatermass stories and recommended that, as viewers would know what to expect, they should decide for themselves 'whether the serial is suitable for children or for people of a nervous disposition'.[10] The BBC Audience Research Report after episode one, while favourable overall, suggested that viewers wanted *more* 'spinechilling' and even more 'gruesome' events in what was seen as 'an absorbing piece of science fiction'.[11]

The presence of a black worker among the building workers featured in the opening sequence of *Quatermass and the Pit* sets the contemporary scene of Britain in the late 1950s.[12] This story of a mysterious and sinister sealed compartment, found buried deep in a construction site in central London, once again exposes the arrogance and opportunism of politicians and top civil servants. However, the psychic 'enemy within' is located as the major source of destructive social impulses and linked to supposed traces of 'race memory' preserved from a previous Martian presence.

There is a consistent topicality in some of the themes, such as the efforts by a construction company to eject archaeologists and palaeontologists from the site of an important discovery in order to commence building work. In the London building boom, and the struggle to preserve excavations of the 1980s and 90s, this issue still has cultural and political urgency. Similarly, the government plan to distort Professor Quatermass' scientific research intended for peaceful purposes, in order to establish military bases on the moon, foreshadows the madness of Reagan's Star Wars strategy. According to a War Office spokesman in *Quatermass and the Pit*, 'even if an aggressor nation should wipe out a neighbour in a nuclear attack they would themselves be obliterated by missiles from space'. Quatermass puts forward a clear reading of the situation when he says 'All this means we'll be going into space with one thought – war'. It is not the 'other' of the cold war who wreaks havoc and destruction but apparently primitive and ancient forces lying dormant from another aeon and now promoting mass hysteria and conflict in the population – including Professor Quatermass himself.

As the series concludes, an act of heroism and sacrifice by a fellow scientist finally saves the world. Quatermass, the 'wise man' who acknowledges self-doubt, puts the record straight for the future in a speech didactically addressed directly to the TV audience:

> If one of these should be found again we are armed with knowledge – including knowledge of ourselves and of the ancient destructive urges in us as our population increases and approaches in size and complexity those of ancient Mars. Every war crisis, witch hunt, race riot, purge, is a reminder and warning. We are the Martians – if we cannot control the inheritance within us this will be their second dead planet.

This dramatic speech, making reference to recent historical events – the Second

World War, the Nazi holocaust, the racist riots in Britain in 1956, offers a mystical, pessimistic perspective on social change.

A Gendered Discourse in 'Quatermass' Serials

While surface characteristics of gender and sexuality are presented conventionally in *Quatermass*, with heterosexuality as the 'norm', and generally male dominance of most scenes, there are interesting, implied criticisms of stereotypically 'masculine' behaviour. Professor Quatermass is portrayed as acting on 'masculine' promptings – rationality, material logic. This mode of response, particularly in *Quatermass II* and *Quatermass and the Pit*, seems to be posed in opposition to intuitive, emotional ways of responding, as represented by the female assistants and certain other characters, including a Welsh scientist and a skilled worker. However, the Professor fails to understand people and situations when he ignores in himself these stereotypically 'feminine' aspects of communication and understanding. He begins to acknowledge this in *Quatermass II*, as he becomes aware of moving in an 'abnormal' environment at the zombie dominated Ministry of Science, observing, 'I was afraid – perhaps I'm discovering new depths in myself – I was sharply aware of menace'.

Those depths are presented as double edged. Barbara Judd, the scientific assistant in *Quatermass and the Pit*, is shown to be clairvoyant and therefore able to 'tune in' to the destructive impulses of the Martian poltergeists. Quatermass says the diabolical vision she sees is 'a memory stored for thousands of years . . . and now picked up by a susceptible brain of a young woman'. The anti-intuitive, authoritarian character of Colonel Breen, denies totally these areas of perception, and is then suddenly and completely 'taken over' by the alien presence. In contrast, it is Judd's 'intuition' and initiative in following scientific and historical clues which leads to an explanation and solution to the paranormal happenings. As a scientific researcher, she is presented as the crucial link between the cold rationalism of science and the 'feminine' domain of emotional promptings, hunches and intuitive interpretations. The final *Quatermass* serial interestingly presents these 'repressed' levels of consciousness found, in particular, in a female character and in a male working-class character, as both to be feared and admired.

The women assistants in all three *Quatermass* series, while shown to be seriously involved in the scientific undertaking, are also bound into the standard narrative convention which uses heterosexual love interest to advance the plot. Generally, the leading female character is shown as highly educated and participating professionally in a scientific enterprise. Ultimately though, she opts for home and family. Predictably, she is mostly shown as upper class and, except for Judd, serves as a support to the Professor. However, other women characters suffer from depiction as working-class stereotypes, limited to an even narrower range of character dimensions than the working-class men in the serials. In this environment of science and bureaucracy, it is the 'career woman' who has prominence, with explicit references to family and children largely restricted to the community context of the working class. By the early 1960s, the female presence in scientific research was still seen as problematic, and good material around which to structure British TV science fiction as the national culture moved towards the mythic period of the 'swinging sixties'.

Female Androids and Angry Young Men

A for Andromeda is a particularly interesting example of science fiction drama made for BBC television adult audiences in the early part of the Hugh Greene era. It constitutes both a break with the predominant representation of women in television science fiction during the *Quatermass* era of the 1950s, as well as a link with older cinematic texts such as Fritz Lang's *Metropolis*. The serial was implicitly critical of government defence policy, with an angry young philosopher/ scientist as hero, and women in three of the leading roles – a cause for comment even today in the age of equal opportunities policies. The fact that one of these women was an android gives the serial a special relevance to popular culture assumptions and interests in the 1980s and 90s, given the current popularity of female android movies.

The changing position of women in British society was foregrounded both in casting decisions and frequent disputes on gender labelling depicted in the scripts. Issues of social class hovered beneath the surface at a time when industries (including armaments) depending on developments in scientific and technological research were drawing more working-class graduates from 'red brick' universities. The image of the 'angry young man' was prominent in the broader cultural context as representing a rejection of traditional authority and upper-class domination. Anger was also seen in political protest on the streets of Britain, as civil disobedience and CND brought the first cohorts of post-war students, together with a range of middle and working-class citizens, into direct conflict with the forces of law and order.

Production Details

A for Andromeda was a seven-part serial transmitted weekly on Tuesdays at 8.30 pm on BBC television during October and November 1961. The script was written by Fred Hoyle and John Elliot and the serial was produced by Michael Hayes and Norman Jones. The leading roles were played by Esmond Knight, Mary Morris, Peter Halliday and Patricia Kneale. Julie Christie, relatively unknown at the time, played a role which was unobtrusive at the start, but became central to the story by the last few episodes. The casting policy seemed typical of the time, employing actors well known in theatre as well as television – and likely to put in 'quality' performances – not 'stars' with glamorous images.

The setting is Britain in the future – 1970 – ten years ahead of the time when the serial was made. The story line concerns the response of scientists, governments and others to a set of messages apparently emanating from an extraterrestrial source and picked up at a scientific research base on a massive radio telescope. The scientists working on the project gradually see a pattern emerging from the messages. An international cartel bribes one of the scientists to give them information about the project. The scientist eventually dies in a cliff accident while escaping from a female government spy employed as press officer at the research station. Meanwhile, after debates between warring government

114

departments, a more sophisticated computer is installed to advance the work. Christine, the research assistant who primarily operates the computers linked to the radio telescope, is killed when the equipment appears to short-circuit. Scientists working on instructions picked up by the radio telescope discover and carry through a laboratory formula in which an embryo is developed. This rapidly becomes a fully formed female with superhuman powers. The conclusion of the story involves government attempts to use the 'girl creature's' powers, and the resistance to this by a talented young scientist concerned to oppose the abuse of scientific ethics.

The dialogue and action centre on an interlinked concern with bureaucratic control, military spending, the cold war, problems of new technology, the role of computers, and of course, attitudes to unmapped areas of knowledge and understanding. Contemporary debates and ideas concerning the complex interrelationship between science, politics and philosophy are cleverly woven into dialogue and plot, together with a discourse on gender and sexuality. These themes are also inscribed at a visual level, with intense close-up shots of the technology, computer print-outs and white-coated scientists, contrasted with bleak external landscapes featuring giant radar dishes and antennae.

Style and Meaning
The careless attitude of the BBC (and most other broadcasting organisations) towards popular culture genres means that most of the visual material for *A for Andromeda* has been lost.[13] The fact that all the programme files have disappeared as well seems more than a coincidence, particularly in view of the political issues and military defence questions raised in the serial. A commonsense approach would suggest that the files were junked in probably the same economy drive which led to the disposal of the visual material. Fortunately some of the film material has recently been rediscovered. This consists of fragments from seven scenes in episode two. The discussion undertaken here offers a textual analysis of this newly available film material in conjunction with a close reading of the scripts as broadcast.[14]

The scripts indicate a conventional narrative structure. Unities of time and place are observed and 'cliff hanging' moments at the end of each episode tie the viewer into the regular weekly serial structure 'stripped' across seven weeks. The barbed repartee of the script indicates the terms of debate with respect to gender, class and the overarching political issues of the day. Scientific processes are explained in simple terms through verbal exchanges. More significantly however, a discourse of ideas is offered in the dialogue which centres on science, politics and philosophy and deals with questions which normally occupied the 'intellectual' discussion slots of both TV channels. The writer Fred Hoyle, as a scientist, had primary knowledge of the issues, and a political commitment to many of the debates.

The recently discovered telecine fragments of *A for Andromeda*, when set against the scripts as broadcast, suggest an interesting use of aesthetic strategies which highlight issues of class and gender. The opening sequence of the film fragment (and of each episode) consists of the inscrutable look of Andromeda as in classical Greek sculpture, suspended in the galaxy and swinging around to face the camera. This is accompanied by ominous music, which becomes a cacophony of sound dominated by a heart beat.

The extract cuts to a close-up of a computer print-out, with figures emerging, printed out by large metal type pieces clacking forwards in front of the camera – which moves up gradually with the moving paper to show the woman working it (Christine, the research assistant). She has a functional, rather cold, non-expressive look, with short, dark, wavy hair and wears a simple, short-sleeved jumper with skirt. This image, together with the monochrome pictures, offers a stark, less glamorous, more serious look than we now associate with the 'star' Julie Christie. The camera cuts to a view from behind her as she pulls out the computer paper, and then reveals the background as a large, busy office.

Carefully constructed framing and slow camera movement convey an intense work process in computer room and laboratory. Visual emphasis in these word-less scenes suggests both an enigmatic relationship between the protagonists and a 'making strange' of mundane procedures in the use of computer technology – feeding in figures and retrieving information from computer print-outs. One such sequence involves a fade in to a close-up on hands operating the computer, which then becomes a montage of fingers pressing buttons, faces, computer dials, wires, diagrams, and circuit plans. Instructions in the script for a telecine insert match exactly with what has survived in this fragment – 'montage of sheets of figures, plans and wiring charts intercut with glimpses of Fleming's, Bridger's and Christine's faces at work'. This is an interesting use of visual codes in television drama and is not the standard naturalist approach. The effect of this aesthetic strategy is to suggest close team-work between the three scientists and an intense concentration on the human, intellectual effort required for scientific and mathematical problem solving. There are also moments when the woman assistant is somehow isolated from the two men; the camera privileges a view of her sitting at the computer keyboard looking up secretively – it is somehow *her* perspective, not one hostile to her, but disquieting nevertheless.

Gender in 'A for Andromeda': 'I call him "he" because he gives me the sense of a mind . . .'

While *A for Andromeda* is in the SF genre, dealing as it does with extra-terrestrial forces, a strong sub-text, particularly apparent in the dialogue, raises questions about the 'place of women' in the society of the 1960s – using everyday cultural reference points largely familiar to the audience. It is as if the writers and producers are laying clues for us and are testing out our assumptions about gender and appropriate behaviour, perhaps with a view to shaking these up a bit as the narrative progresses and confounds some of the obvious possibilities.

In assessing the presentation of women here it is important to take account of the fact that the producer (Michael Hayes) had quite positive and undoubtedly optimistic assumptions about the position of women in the period in which the drama is set. He writes in a letter to Mary Morris, who plays Professor Dawnay, that this part was originally written for a man, but that he changed it to a woman: 'because I wanted to set the scene more firmly in 1970, when I imagine there will

116

indeed be far more women in positions of responsibility'.[15] Hayes acknowledges here the changing position of women in the early 1960s in Britain. More women were in paid employment and more were entering further and higher education. Positions of power and eminence however, were, and still are, predominantly occupied by white, middle and upper-class men.

When Dawnay arrives at the scientific research station, it is believed that the Professor must be a man. She is introduced with a 'set piece' of gender misidentification in episode three, in which the military head of the research station, when asked for a pass for the visiting professor, assumes that it must be for a man. The initial response is 'A woman – ? . . . What's she here for?' However, he quickly accepts her as part of the old boys' network on discovering that they were at university together!

Comments from the male characters about women indicate the familiar, contemporary, sexist context in which the women work and live. In spite of their positioning as 'professional' career women, comfortable and powerful in comparison with the one working-class female character (Grace), Professor Dawnay, Judy the Press Officer and Christine/Andromeda are shown as the recipients of sexist treatment by the men. Fleming, the rebellious hero, sees Dawnay as a threat. Her professionalism as a scientist brings with it for him a denial of 'feminine' characteristics of warmth, emotion, humanity. He comments: 'Oh yes she's one of his biologist pals. All the charm of a test tube full of formaldehyde. What's he want to bring her for?'

The central conundrum of gender/sexual identity in the serial concerns the computer and the organism nurtured from the information offered by it. Fleming masculinises the computer, saying that, 'His normal thought processes are in binary arithmetic', to which Dawnay responds, 'How like a man'. Traditional gender attributes are underlined but not necessarily given credibility in Fleming's comment: 'I'm afraid I'm not a feminist. I call him "he" because he gives me the sense of a mind – a person almost'.

Clearly, for Fleming the feminine is not associated with minds, but rather emotions or bodies. The irony in the situation is that Fleming, partly working on (feminine) instinct, wants to stop the interaction with the computer, which he sees as having a devious and probably sinister purpose:

> With what was in the original programme, and what we tell him, he can learn anything he wants about us. And he can learn to act upon it. If that's not an intelligence I don't know what is.

Professor Dawnay dismisses Fleming as 'emotionally disturbed' and insists on prioritising the 'scientific' approach over the 'mystical'. She therefore continues, in the interests of science, to use the information mysteriously offered by the computer to build an organism. When asked if Professor Dawnay is attempting to create life, Fleming replies with a sexist jibe, 'That's a woman's function isn't it?'

The dialogue sustains the science versus mystery references throughout, with Dawnay, for example, referring to the state of the laboratory during the experiment as 'a witch's soup kitchen'. Similarly, when the organism multiplies itself, she can offer no scientific or rational explanation, but sees it as 'the miracle of life'. The climactic irony to all this is that Christine, the research assistant (played by Julie Christie), who quietly and unobtrusively carries out all the 'hands on' contact with the computer and later the experimental procedures with the organism under Dawnay's instructions, is revealed as the mediator for the extra-terrestrial intelligence emanating from Andromeda.

This is double-edged in its implications. On the one hand, all the references to the computer and the disembodied intelligence as 'he' are confounded when 'it' is shown to be feminine. However, feminine associations with mystery and enigma are reinforced both by the absence of rational scientific explanation for the whole phenomenon, and by the 'correct' reading of the situation by Fleming. As a male scientist he is shown nevertheless to be acting on his 'feminine' promptings, intuitively warning against the experiment almost from the outset. His passionate outbursts on the philosophical dimensions of science and his dire warnings against continuing to work on the messages coming from Andromeda, represent, traditionally, a 'feminine' mode of behaviour.

Christine, however, who becomes the mediator for Andromeda, is muted and somehow disembodied. The earliest description of her in the script is as 'a young post-graduate student, serious and pretty in a rather striking Baltic way'. This image is reinforced by Fleming when he offers Christine a description of the military computer recently made available to the research team as: 'Remote and beautiful like you. Also high powered, soulless, clueless – not like you, dear. Like the stuffed uniforms that run it'. Christine is treated by Fleming and Dawnay as an operative or a passive spectator to events, even though the privileged camera perspective puts her visually in significant juxtaposition to 'the machine', as described above.

This position of powerlessness appears to be reversed when Christine is metamorphosed into Andromeda as a result of the DNA experiment carried out on instructions from the computer. What emerges is a stereotypical beauty, 'a purified version of Christine', with blonde hair and cool demeanour. This 'girl creature' is given intensive tuition in human behaviour and thought processes. She grows rapidly, and, robot-like, accumulates information and knowledge without interruption from emotional responses or unpredictable impulses. While Dawnay is overawed by her success in 'making life', the government intend to use the 'synthetic wonder girl' to develop a sophisticated system of missile interception.

Fleming perceives Andromeda as the vehicle for an extra-terrestrial takeover of the earth, programmed by the computer for that purpose, and insists: 'It hasn't made a human being – it's made an alien creature that looks like one'. However, Fleming's strategy to undermine the threat is posed both at an emotional and a sexual level. His definition of what it is to be human is gender specific and invokes significations of sexuality intended to breach Andromeda's apparent invulnerability:

You want to make something of yourself if you're going to influence men . . .
You could push your hair back, then we could see your pretty face . . . or you

could wear scent ... You're made to register pain – and pleasure. We [human beings] live by our senses. That's what gives us our instincts for good or bad – our aesthetic and moral judgments. Without them we'd probably have annihilated ourselves by now.

The effectiveness of the appeal to 'feminine' responses is shown when Andromeda later enters 'looking stunning in a marvellous new dress' (description in script), and is subsequently kissed by Fleming 'sensuously but dispassionately like an experiment'.

Brummy Boys and Class Politics

The politics of class and power are also locked in a sub-text of *A for Andromeda*. This emerges in the biographical details and behaviour of characters. For example, the implied lower middle-class background of the two young male scientists and their involvement in CND or the Communist Party.

The character of Fleming carries through the 'angry young man' tradition of the 1950s. He is part of the post-war explosion in university education. In spite of an undercurrent of cynicism, he still makes positive demands of a system he assumes to be based on a tradition of humanitarianism. This is coupled with enormous confidence in his own capabilities and a personal code of loyalty and integrity shown in his comments on his friend and colleague:

We were Brummy boys together – the original red brick university. But I'm the best physicist in the country and he's the best developmental engineer. I have the ideas and he makes them work.

In constructing the character of Fleming as a physicist, the author Fred Hoyle may be drawing on his own experience as a leading astronomer, renowned for his advocacy of the steady state theory of the creation of the universe. Post-war discoveries in radio astronomy by British scientists led to the building of the world's first large-scale radio telescope at Jodrell Bank and clearly shaped the setting and narrative of *A for Andromeda*.

Fleming's friend Bridger, the other Birmingham University graduate at the research station, is a highly talented scientist/engineer. He provides the counterpoint to Fleming's heroic idealism in his 'yuppy' aspirations, which at this period cannot be fulfilled without corruption and exploitation. An ex-Communist Party member, he works in secret for one of the 'nastiest' international cartels, boasting: 'I could get five times my salary in industry'. He contemptuously dismisses Fleming with the observation that, ' ... before he's found what he's looking for he'll be old, respected and very poor'.

Nevertheless, Fleming occupies the moral high ground in the narrative and resists both material and emotional compromises. The speeches on the quality of life which he provokes in the dialogue can be seen as part of the 'two cultures', sciences versus humanities debate popularised by C.P. Snow in the late 1950s. Fleming expresses frustration at the obtuseness of the authorities and disdain for the judgment of politicians. As a brilliant but unappreciated scientist, he embo-

A for Andromeda: Christine (Julie Christie) at the computer terminal.

dies the anger and frustration of the newly educated scientist and engineer in early 1960s Britain. A low rate of economic growth and the slow development of science and technology in the final years of the Macmillan government followed the boom of the post-war period and led to Harold Wilson's emphasis on the 'scientific revolution'. Under the Labour government of the mid-1960s, this continued in the focus on the 'white heat of technology' and a technocratic recognition for those, like Fleming, previously stifled.[16]

Military Co-operation 'because we needed the money'

Bridger's lack of integrity is mirrored by the government's willingness to sell the scientific enterprise to the highest bidder. This is demonstrated when the representative of the Ministry of Science discloses that they had agreed to co-operate with the Ministry of Defence, because they 'needed the money' to continue with scientific research. Earlier in the serial, it was made clear that NATO and American military interests were also a part of the deal which even included the vicious Intel organisation. These corrupt alliances were justified with the excuse that African and Asian countries and cartels wished to keep their own raw materials. An authorial voice seems to speak in the warning to the scientists delivered by a military administrator:

> You're not in the university precinct. If this goes forward you're in the jungle. It may look like stuffy old public business, with lots of smooth talk and platitudinous statements from politicians and government officials . . . But it's a jungle all the same . . . secrets are bought and sold, ideas are stolen and sometimes people get hurt. That's how the world's business gets done.

Hegemonic power structures, and British government ministers in particular, are shown ultimately to be as unscrupulous as the international cartel in their misuse of scientific discoveries. The Prime Minister, for example, sees the 'girl creature' as enabling Britain to become the leading industrialised country in the world, saying: 'We want to be rich as well as strong'. He promises knighthoods to those who will effect this, even at the price of making trade agreements with the cartel. This ruthless, monetarist face of British government has been a central motif in the 1980s, both in the 'real world' and in TV dramas, which have keyed into the perceptions and experience of the population generally. But even in *Edge of Darkness*, a political thriller serialised on BBC 2 (and BBC 1) in 1985, the female Prime Minister is kept discreetly in the background. In *A for Andromeda*, the Prime Minister is male and presented with all the élitist paraphernalia of the traditional ruling class. Policy meetings take place at shooting parties with a 'grandiose picnic luncheon' and the 'PM in elegant shooting dress'.

The moral and political compromises made by the authorities almost lead to disaster, making Andromeda's threat seem well deserved as she tells Fleming: 'Our intelligence is going to take over and yours is going to die . . . you'll go down with the dinosaurs'. Finally, however, it is a *humanised* Andromeda who, with Fleming's assistance, saves the earth from annihilation.

Conclusions

In discussing the politics of class and gender in the *Quatermass* serials and *A for Andromeda*, it is clear that a crucial shift took place over the eight-year period during which they were broadcast. Political, economic and technological changes in the broader context also permeated the broadcasting organisations. The second of the *Quatermass* serials was one of the results of the new strategy by which the BBC sought to capture and address a wider audience following the start of ITV.

The *Quatermass* serials positioned women as supporters to the main action – always assistants and facilitators for the male characters, even when the key discoveries arose from perceptions associated with female approaches. The 'hard' science settings, laboratories, rocket sites and research stations, and the use of public arenas, inevitably sustained the general focus away from a domestic discourse. Children and the 'norms' of family life took place on the borders and generally in the working class. The female presence in these settings was restricted. The traditional authority of the male scientist was also under question, even though the demands of narrative closure put him back in place as the wise man improved by the addition of humility and self-doubt.

The scientists, the heroic young army officers, astronauts, detectives, and even journalists in *Quatermass* represented a middle- and upper-class voice. They protested against faceless bureaucracy and official brutality, but, as part of the officer class, did not seek fundamental social and political change. The working-class voice was structured primarily in comedy and also in striking moments of heroism. The resonances of wartime experience were refined and scattered across the three *Quatermass* serials. This might be seen as partly explaining their class and gender representations. Wartime disruptions of social organisation, the shattered urban landscape, and pressures on personal relationships provided those reference points around which the specificity of script and narrative structure was organised.

A for Andromeda offered an even bleaker environment than the *Quatermass* serials, with the addition of the stark natural landscape of Northern Scotland. The grimness was continued in the attitudes of the dominant power group – the political, military and administrative authorities. As a class, they were far more frightening than 'the alien'. The angry voice of the individual scientist substituted for working-class protest. The dominance of the 'wise (male) scientist' continued, but had a female counterpart in Professor Dawnay. While the female characters were in the forefront of the action, no longer the groupies of Quatermass, they were – had to be – flawed. The Professor by lacking femininity, Judy by being a spy, and Christine/Andromeda by being an android. Fleming the (almost) working-class hero had finally to sort it all out. The new man exemplified in Fleming was deeply suspicious of the new woman – with good cause.

The *new woman* of Andromeda was manufactured, synthetic, but an idealised perfect woman of the 1960s – invincible in terms of intellect and by contemporary ethnocentric aesthetic standards, perfect in form. *But*, she was controlled by an extra-terrestrial force and had no emotional responses. Andromeda can be read as the portrayal of the threat of the 1960s new professional woman – a woman who put intellect first and had to be taught, by *a man*, to express femininity and to respond to emotions. Fleming, as the new man, did not suppress his emotions or manifest contradictory positions in relation to his intellectual status and achievements. Only the women are shown as problematic in this respect. He protested against the system in order to make it work better for him.

An explanation for these formulations in the narratives of *Quatermass* and *A for Andromeda* has to be sought mainly in the economic, political and cultural contexts of the 1950s and 60s. This is not to minimise the central creative contribution of writer and director, but rather to acknowledge that the creative process is also shaped by material and ideological factors. In this study I have focused mainly on those factors and how they relate to the texts concerned, and not on the authorial creative process itself. That process worked within the constraints imposed by the organisation, routines, cultural assumptions, finance and technology of broadcasting at that time and in particular of the BBC. Above all, the representation of class and gender in television drama was – and is – determined by class and gender positioning in the broader social and economic structures of capitalism. The mediations of class and gender by established dramatists draw on images and myths set out by ideological structures which are, of course, far from neutral in their reference points.

Whilst science fiction would seem to take us outside these structuring elements of class and gender by a discourse of fantasy or futurism, the metaphorical transformations always speak about the historical time in which the production took place. The science fiction serials of the 1950s and 60s offered innovative possibilities both in form and content, but were finally limited to the dominant constructions of class and gender of their time – constructions similar, fundamentally, to those of the 1980s and 90s.

I wish to thank Tony Mechele, Brian Stableford, and Steve Edgell for helpful discussions in the early stages of preparing this article, and Mike Healy for encouragement in the final stage.

Notes

1. A useful survey of this trend in SF literature can be found in Sarah Lefanu, *In the Chinks of the World Machine* (London: The Women's Press, 1988). The archives of the Science Fiction Foundation at Polytechnic of East London contain a tightly packed and invaluable collection of literature in the genre. A discussion of some of the issues of representation of gender and sexuality in SF films can be found in the journal *Camera Obscura* no. 15 on Science Fiction and Sexual Difference.
2. The male domination of SF fan clubs is not an inherent characteristic of the genre. For example *Star Trek* in the late 1960s drew large numbers of female fans. A substantial study of the history and production processes of *Dr Who* can be found in John Tullock and Manuel Alvarado, *Dr Who, the Unfolding Text* (London: Macmillan, 1983). Very little is published in book form, but writing on the general area of television SF is

spread across a range of useful and informative television magazines for 'fans' and researchers. These include *Starburst* and *Primetime*.

3. I have drawn on the invaluable resources of the BBC Written Archives and on film and video material available for viewing at the National Film Archive (NFA). The staff at both establishments have been, as usual, extremely helpful in the project of piecing together the partially lost and fragmented map of popular broadcasting culture.

4. Asa Briggs, *The History of Broadcasting in the UK, Volume 4: Sound and Vision* (Oxford: Oxford University Press, 1979), p. 689.

5. Julian Petley, in *Monthly Film Bulletin*, vol. 56 no. 662, p. 91.

6. Letter from Rudolph Cartier to C. Moodie, Information Division Air Ministry, 12 June 1953, BBC Written Archives.

7. BBC Audience Research Department Report, 2 September 1953, BBC Written Archives.

8. Memo from Nigel Kneale to Cecil McGivern, Controller of TV Programmes, 5 November 1955, BBC Written Archives.

9. Memo from Controller of TV Programmes to Head of TV, 31 October 1955, see also memo note 8 above; BBC Audience Research Department Report, 9 November 1955, all BBC Written Archives.

10. Memo from Assistant Head of TV Drama to Controller of TV Programmes, 22 December 1955, BBC Written Archives.

11. BBC Audience Research Department Report, 7 January 1959, BBC Written Archives.

12. Lionel Ngkane, who played this 'one line' part, acted in many television productions and also directed *Jemima and Johnny*, an anti-racist film made in 1966.

13. According to Steve Bryant in his excellent BFI monograph, *The Television Heritage*, 'The destruction of television programmes by the organisations which produced them was due to a combination of technological, cultural and operational influences'. Important in this was the attitude that TV was 'ephemeral and therefore not worth preserving'. Fortunately most *Quatermass* programmes were preserved, and all quotations here are from the NFA prints.

14. Much of the following analysis has depended on access to the carefully preserved collection of scripts at the BBC Written Archives Centre. All *A for Andromeda* script quotations are attributable to this source.

15. Letter to Mary Morris from Michael Hayes, 7 June 1961, BBC Written Archives.

16. Useful historical analyses of the period include: V. Bogdanor and R. Skidelsky (eds.), *The Age of Affluence 1951–64* (London: Macmillan, 1970) and Arthur Marwick, *British Society since 1945* (Harmondsworth: Penguin, 1982).

Banging in Some Reality
The Original 'Z Cars'

STUART LAING

On the morning of 3 January 1962 Stuart Hood, the Controller of BBC Television Programmes, received an unexpected visitor:

> I was told that the Chief Constable of Lancashire was there and wished to talk to me. So he came into my office and said, 'You've got to take it off'. And I said, 'Why?' He said, 'Well, you show a policeman quarrelling with his wife and a policeman smoking on duty'. I said, 'Okay, I'll take it off and put up a notice saying I'm suspending the series because policemen never quarrel with their wives and never smoke on duty'. End of story. And he just walked out and banged the door.[1]

'It' was a new police 'drama-documentary' series, *Z Cars*, the first episode of which had been broadcast the previous evening. *Z Cars* – the original *Z Cars* – ran from January 1962 to December 1965. Within that period, the BBC broadcast 170 weekly episodes shown mid-evening on Tuesdays or Wednesdays. Additionally, from September 1962 there were regular repeats on Sunday afternoons; in all 118 episodes were re-shown. From January 1966, some of the production personnel and cast were transferred to *Softly, Softly*, a new police drama series, while the title of *Z Cars* itself was subsequently revived from March 1967 in an early evening twice-weekly format. This essay, however, is concerned with the original *Z Cars*' four-year run and considers the programme's origins, its distinctive formal and narrative properties, its modes of representation of the police and the community and its handling of the *series* as a particular kind of dramatic opportunity.

Within the four-year run there were three distinct periods, which will be discussed in turn. The initial 'season'[2] ran from January to July 1962, when a planned run of thirteen episodes was extended to thirty-one following the programme's immediate popular and critical success. The period of 'classic' *Z Cars* lasted from September 1962 to December 1964, during which time the series was dominated by the scripts and influence of John Hopkins. Finally, during 1965 the series began to lose both its coherence and its high audience ratings.

Origins of 'Z Cars'

As with any cultural product, *Z Cars* was the product of multiple determinations. By the beginning of the 60s the BBC had recognised the need to reconsider its programme policies in order to retrieve its audience share from ITV. Between 1957 and 1960, the numbers of viewers with sets which could receive both channels had tripled to nearly 75 per cent of the whole population, and throughout this period ITV was able to maintain a two-to-one lead over BBC in its share of their viewing time.[3] In April 1961 Stuart Hood was appointed Controller of BBC TV programmes as part of Hugh Carleton-Greene's new policy – a policy which implied that ITV must be beaten at their own game by the production of popular programmes which should be of sufficient quality not only to attract a mass audience, but also to ward off any potential criticisms concerning the lowering of standards. Within the BBC a recognition developed that in the area of drama this would not be achieved solely (or even predominantly) through single-play production, but rather by forms of continuing drama (series and serials) which could build up a regular and committed following.

Within the Drama Department this relative change of emphasis was among the factors leading to the resignation of Michael Barry as Head of Drama in September 1961. Barry had been in post since 1950 and, while allowing a good deal of experimental work, had retained an essentially theatrical model of the nature and role of TV drama. No immediate successor was appointed, but the existing Assistant Head, Norman Rutherford, became Acting Head, with Elwyn Jones (previously in charge of Documentary Drama) as his deputy. Jones was already planning the *Z Cars* series, of which he remained executive producer throughout. Overall, 1962 was to prove something of an *annus mirabilis* for the launch of new BBC continuous drama. The same evening (2 January) as the first *Z Cars* was broadcast saw the first episode of *Compact*, a twice-weekly continuous serial. Later that week, the pilot *Steptoe and Son* episode, 'The Offer' was broadcast. From June this became a series, while *Dr. Finlay's Casebook* was first shown in August.

Jones' key role in *Z Cars* reflected the extent to which its roots lay in the television story documentary tradition. The story documentary was a form quite distinct from the 'actuality' documentary, which was a filmed and edited report on some particular social or natural historical topic. The roots of the latter lay in cinema. The story documentary, by contrast, borrowed from the style and format of radio features and reflected the need throughout the 50s to produce most television broadcasting live in the studio.[4] The story documentary then used actors to reproduce a 'real-life' situation, typically reflecting a 'social problem' or depicting a particular occupational role, within the studio.

This form was a staple of BBC scheduling in the 50s and led to such police programmes as Robert Barr's *Scotland Yard* (1960), Colin Morris' *Who Me?* (dealing with police interrogation methods) and *Jacks and Knaves* (late 1961), dealing with the lighter side of police detective work within the Lancashire County Police Force. A further drama-documentary series shown in 1960, *Man at the Door*, had been scripted by the Lancashire born-and-bred Allan Prior. Jones, Barr and Prior were to become three core members of the *Z Cars* production team, remaining involved throughout the four years. Jones, in addition to his general overseeing role, wrote twelve scripts himself, while Barr was initially responsible for ensuring the programme's documentary credentials; he later served as script editor and contributed eleven scripts (including both the fourth and the fourth from last to be broadcast). Prior's twenty-nine scripts made him the second most prolific scriptwriter and the only one to provide scripts for all five seasons between 1962 and 1965.

The other two significant originators of *Z Cars* were Troy Kennedy Martin (the first scriptwriter) and John McGrath (the first director). Both had entered television in the late 50s and, according to McGrath's later recollection, they both saw *Z Cars* as a chance to break new ground by going beyond existing television forms:

> ... to use a Highway Patrol format, but to use the cops as a key or way of getting into a whole society ... two kinds of communities ... The first was called New Town, which was roughly based on Kirkby. The other was Seaport, which was based on the sort of Crosby-Waterloo waterfront. ... a kind of documentary about people's lives in these areas, and the cops were incidental – they were the means of finding out about people's lives.[5]

Highway Patrol was a highly formulaic American police series regularly broadcast in ITV regions from the late 50s; it was regarded as typical of the kind of popular low quality entertainment which the new BBC policy had to overcome. In January 1959 *Highway Patrol* was among the first night's scheduling on the new Tyne Tees regional station; by mid-1962 one Tyne Tees viewer was complaining to the *Guardian*, in ironic tones, of the 'privilege' of being able to see repeats of the programme, in preference to talks from Sir Kenneth Clark (showing in other regions).[6] At the time of its launch, however, *Z Cars*' main ITV competitor was *No Hiding Place*, which dealt (also through a tight and regular narrative formula) with the solving of crime in London. In the early months of 1962 these two programmes were directly scheduled against each other. Critical comparisons were generally favourable to *Z Cars*, the emphasis being on its greater authenticity; this corresponded with the production intention (as McGrath saw it) to 'use a popular form and try to bang into it some reality'.[7]

Reality is of course a relative concept, especially when it becomes implicated in notions of social realism in fiction. To speak of reality and realism in English culture and society at the beginnings of the 60s was most often to refer to a particular way of life; reality resided more than anywhere else in a Northern working-class industrial town. *Z Cars* was born from a cultural moment which also comprised British 'New Wave' cinema (the last major moment of black-and-white cinema). *Saturday Night and Sunday Morning* had been released in October 1960 and was showing successfully throughout Britain during 1961. *A Taste of Honey* was released in September 1961 and while Prior and Kennedy Martin were researching the first *Z Cars* scripts in Lancashire in late Autumn 1961, John Schlesinger was shooting *A Kind of Loving* in the same county.[8]

Even closer to home, however, was the example of *Coronation Street*, which had been launched by Granada in December 1960 and had developed from a regionally based run of thirteen weeks to become the most popular national television programme by late 1961. The success of *Coronation Street* undoubtedly influenced BBC scheduling on 2 January 1962 in two respects. While *Compact* (set in 'the hothouse atmosphere of women's journalism')[9] attempted to profit from the proved audience propensity for the twice-weekly continuous serial (or 'soap opera'), *Z Cars* sought to present an even more 'realistic' picture of Northern urban life from a quite different perspective.

The First Season, January–July 1962

Preparations for the thirteen-week series had begun in mid-1961. Contacts with the Lancashire County Police set up through *Who Me?* and *Jacks and Knaves* were further developed under the general guidance of Elwyn Jones. In late 1961, while Kennedy Martin and Prior researched and wrote the early scripts, David Rose (to become the regular producer throughout the four-year run) and McGrath undertook the casting:

'Before we began rehearsals,' says McGrath, 'I spent a clear week with them discussing the complete social background of every character – age, parentage, why they were in the police force, what they wanted out of it. We filled it all in, in great detail. Not one of these blokes would say a line without knowing why he was saying it.[10]

McGrath's influence was also decisive in establishing a distinctive *Z Cars* style of direction. The series was to be broadcast live. This had traditionally meant an emphasis on a leisurely paced sequence of long studio scenes. McGrath and Kennedy Martin however sought a style with much greater pace, involving up to six cameras and fifteen sets per episode, some film inserts shot on location, some pre-recorded film or tape studio inserts and the use of back-projection, with the Z-Car on rollers to allow scenes of the cars in motion on the open road to be broadcast live from the studio. This style led to a *Z Cars* camera shot lasting, on average, only twelve seconds.[11]

For McGrath and Kennedy Martin this style related to particular notions of how to tell a story, and what kind of story to tell. While Kennedy Martin 'wanted to break down the dominance of the story line and put in its place character and dialogue',[12] McGrath has emphasised the particular rhythm he aimed for:

Stylistically, I went for one rigid rule: no camera move, no cut, until the next piece of story was to be revealed. But the stories unfolded very quickly, so there were a lot of cuts, and a lot of locations. . . . a style that would make these stories move, hold the attention. We placed a conscious emphasis on narrative – society, real and recognisable, but *in motion*. No slick tie-ups. No reassuring endings, where decency and family life triumphed.[13]

According to Shaun Sutton (who directed nineteen episodes of *Z Cars*, more than any other director), the effect of *Z Cars* was that, 'Sort of overnight, link shots disappeared in drama'.[14]

The first episode, 'Four of a Kind' (scripted by Kennedy Martin and directed by McGrath) was broadcast from 8.30–9.15 pm on Tuesday 2 January 1962; the first four episodes were scheduled for forty-five minutes only (although the first episode is reported to have finished five minutes early), after which the standard time for the rest of the series became fifty minutes. The story line (typically for a new series) showed the setting-up of the Z Cars unit (following the murder of a foot-patrol constable) and the main aim was to establish the characters of the six key personnel – Inspector Barlow, Sergeant Watt and the four crime-car constables, Lynch, Steele, Weir and 'Fancy' Smith.

To introduce the series, the *Radio Times* drew on the McGrath/Kennedy Martin emphasis on a breadth of social context:

> Life is fraught with danger for policemen in the North of England overspill estate called Newtown. Here a mixed community, displaced from larger towns by slum clearance has been brought together and housed on an estate without amenities and without community feeling.[15]

The idea of a new estate community with little genuine 'community' exemplified *Z Cars*' difference from *Coronation Street* (and implied a greater contemporary realism). Realism was further 'guaranteed' by the reference to the help of the Lancashire police who, according to Rose, 'were as keen as we were to see that the atmosphere and feeling of the north were seen in the stories we used'. Rose went on to suggest the balance of concerns which he saw in the series – 'mainly about crime cars – but it is also about people and their problems, especially in a place like Newtown'.[16]

In 'Four of a Kind', viewers, and police, saw not only officers smoking, but also Lynch gambling, Smith womanising and Steele quarrelling with his wife (the episode showed the effects of their row – Janie Steele's black-eye and the stain on the wall where she had thrown his hotpot dinner at him). While the most senior police officers complained, reaction among junior ranks and general viewers was positive. Within eight weeks the audience had climbed from nine to fourteen million.[17] Episodes such as Kennedy Martin's 'Limping Rabbit' (9 January 1962), in which a girl disappears and Lynch and Steele face 'a conspiracy of silence in her broken family'[18]; Prior's 'The Big Catch' (30 January), dealing with whaling fishermen seeking a good night out in Seaport; and Kennedy Martin's 'Friday Night' (6 February), which interwove eight or nine small stories together, including a particularly powerful scene of the death of a young motor-cyclist surrounded by a helpless policeman and an unhelpful crown of onlookers – all continued the focus on the lack of community and the consequent problematic role of the police. In Prior's 'Threats and Menaces' (6 March) this extended to difficulties with neighbours for the police themselves (specifically for the Steeles).

By mid-February it became clear that the BBC had achieved a major success. The eighth episode, Kennedy Martin's 'Family Feud' (20 February 1962) was the first to contain the listing of a series Script Editor. This reflected the necessary expansion of the initial small team to cope with the decision to extend the run from thirteen to thirty-one episodes – running through to the conventional summer scheduling break at the end of July. The script editor was John Hopkins, an experienced television writer and script editor who had spent time with Granada as well as with the BBC.

Also during February, the BBC had begun to promote an idea which had already occurred to a number of television critics – that in *Z Cars* they had a valuable addition, rival and, if necessary, successor to their own *Dixon of Dock Green*. *Dixon* had been first televised in July 1955 (as part, therefore, of the BBC's first wave of response to the challenge of ITV); the character of PC Dixon (played by Jack Warner), however, originated in the Ealing film *The Blue Lamp* (1949), in which he was shot to death by a young tearaway. In the resurrected *Dixon*, life was generally more sedate. The initial theme tune, 'Maybe It's Because I'm a Londoner' and its later substitution by 'An Ordinary Copper' ('patrolling his beat') reinforced the core idea of a predominantly stable, 'traditional' East End working-class community being served by policemen who were part of it.[19] With its 6.30 pm Saturday scheduling, *Dixon* attracted an early-evening 'family' audience, and by early 1961 its audience of 13.85 million was only exceeded (in BBC programming) by *The Black and White Minstrel Show*.[20]

After only two episodes of *Z Cars*, Frederick Laws in *The Listener* had compared the 'professional ambition . . . enjoyment of a rough house and . . . frivolous opinions' of the *Z Cars* policemen with the 'sugary nonsense' of *Dixon*.[21] In mid-February, the *Radio Times* offered a more neutral comparison (although one clearly designed to provoke viewer response):

> Until the beginning of this year the most efficient station sergeant in television was Flint . . . of *Dock Green*. We feel now, however, that Flint had perhaps better look to his laurels, for in *Z Cars* he has a younger up-and-coming rival – Sgt Twentyman of the Newtown 'nick'. This North of England counterpart, though a somewhat rougher character, is no less human.[22]

A week later *The Times* critic repeated the comparison, but endorsed the valuation of *The Listener*. Dixon's habit of presenting an explicit moral conclusion (directly to the viewer) at the end of each episode tended to 'place PC Dixon and his doings just one degree further from reality than they can conveniently bear . . . *Z Cars* on the other hand is realistic to a fault.'[23]

By March, the *Radio Times* began to receive sufficient letters to stage its own viewers' debate. Lady Savile (London SW7) wrote to defend *Dixon*:

> The actors in *Z Cars* are good, but they never for one moment give me the impression that they are anything but actors, whereas the cast in *Dock Green*, especially Flint and Dixon seem to be utterly and entirely genuine policemen.
>
> And the same applies to the script; every film about police seems to rely on rushing about in cars, but the *Dock Green* script and personnel go steadily on their way, and I am sure none of them need to look to their laurels.[24]

Two subsequent replies suggested generational, regional and class differences in the respective audience response to the two series. B.E. Fargher (aged seventeen from Birmingham) considered *Z Cars* to be 'pulsating, lively and above all genuine. The rough tongue, the occasional display of bad temper, and the crafty "drag" at a cigarette all tend to reassure me that policemen can be portrayed as human beings with the same frailties as the rest of us'. Jane Halton (aged fourteen from Stockport) wrote that 'If Dock Green (which reminds me of a social club) is authentic I am not surprised at the high rate of crime in this country. ... there is nothing phoney about *Z Cars*. All the characters are solid and down to earth and typical of people in the North'.[25]

The debate continued. In May, Derek Hill in *The Listener* repeated the terms of a by now familiar comparison. *Z Cars* had 'broken with the bland tradition of Ted Willis, the policeman's PRO, and shows both sides of the law as equally human ...'; he contrasted the 'saintly Dixon, too good to be true' with 'the harassed *Z Cars* driver making the best of an unenviable job'.[26] These criticisms, as part of the general debate, provoked Ted Willis himself (the creator of Dixon, and who still played the dominant role, as scriptwriter, in the production of the series) to a reply, the terms of which, however, did nothing to damage *Z Cars*' claim to realism. *Dixon* showed more of the 'social work' side of police work: 'Go into any London police station and most others throughout the country, and you will find a Dixon'. Both programmes showed accurately different aspects of police work, but while all *Dixon*'s stories were based on fact ('the police files or from a newspaper clipping'), the scheduling was a limiting factor:

> *Dixon of Dock Green* is transmitted at 6.30 on Saturday evenings, when there is a large audience of children and young people viewing. ... We are bound by the BBC code on early evening programmes. At least 70 per cent of the material used in *Z Cars* could not be used in our programme.[27]

Willis's analysis was generally supported by a retired police officer in the *Radio Times* in the same month: 'the situations in *Z Cars* are so real that I find myself living all through my city experiences again ...', while *Dixon* was also accurate in showing 'an out-station where life does go on in that rather quiet friendly atmosphere ...'.[28] Throughout the first season a critical and audience consensus built up which reinforced strongly the BBC's own emphasis on *Z Cars* as a drama-documentary: authentic, genuine and 'real', drawing on the advice of policemen and ex-policemen (such as ex-Liverpool CID officer, Bill Prendergast, who had also advised on *Jacks and Knaves*). Notably, however, especially through the comparison with *Dixon*, *Z Cars* was praised particularly for its depiction of policemen, rather than of any more general social vision.

Meanwhile, the *Z Cars* first season had continued. The initial thirteen episodes concluded with Kennedy Martin's 'Sudden Death' (27 March 1962). Kennedy Martin had written six and McGrath directed four of these episodes (more than any other individual writers or directors). Of the remaining eighteen episodes in the first season, only three were written by Kennedy Martin and a further four directed by McGrath. Prior followed his initial five scripts with

Z Cars, 1963: The crews of Z Victor One and Two relax in the canteen. L. to r.: Brian Blessed, James Ellis, Joseph Brady and Colin Welland.

another five, but the most prolific contributor during this second section of the first season was John Hopkins, with seven scripts.

During this period, Peter Lewis researched and wrote an article on *Z Cars* for *Contrast* (a short-lived magazine of television criticism published during the early and mid-60s); Lewis found Kennedy Martin already concerned about the damaging effects of this extended run:

> It's like a meat factory ... The organisation isn't there to allow character development. You would need a far more closely knit team of writers and directors bound together with a common attitude and enthusiasm. It calls for living together, living for the series, which is the sort of thing that has never happened in television. A series is a living thing, always twisting and turning. But if they insist on this sameness week after week then the characters tend to become caricatures of themselves. After a time you just get hollowness and nothing.[29]

McGrath's retrospective views on this period were similar, but more specific:

> After the cops kept appearing week after week people began to fall in love

with them, and they became stars. So the pressure was on to make them the subjects, rather than the device. And when the BBC finally decided that's what they were going to do, then Troy and I decided we'd had enough.[30]

Both Kennedy Martin and McGrath left the *Z Cars* production team at the end of the first season, their last joint episode being 'Teamwork' (3 July 1962). A few weeks earlier, McGrath had (uniquely, as it turned out, during the four-year run) both written and directed the same episode, 'People's Property' (15 May). This episode, while not necessarily typical of the first season as a whole, does reflect many of the particular emphases which McGrath, together with Kennedy Martin, attempted to realise within the early *Z Cars*.

'People's Property'

'People's Property' is the story of two twelve-year-olds (Tommy and Jimmy) who engage in a crime-wave of petty theft. The episode opens with their capture at night on a warehouse roof and concludes (about fifty offences later) with their fourth appearance in a magistrates' court and their committal to an approved school.[31]

Even for the early *Z Cars*, this episode has an exceptional diversity of location. The boys' chosen environment is, significantly, outside home and school – in the playground, the streets, the docks, the park and, eventually, the country. The episode concludes with a chase as the boys take a bus to North Wales, pursued by Jock and Fancy. The chase ends on a hillside where Fancy looks up and back across a panoramic rural valley landscape. 'Look at that', he exclaims as the camera slowly pans through 180 degrees in a shot fully outside the normal grammar of contemporary television drama. Rather it recalls aspects of the British 'New Wave' films of the period – in the idea of escape outside the city, leading only to an inevitable return to urban conditions and limitations.

Within the narrative, the boys are positioned between the competing claims of four institutions – family, school, judicial law and the police. The family is significant mainly through its absence, in particular that of the father. Tommy's father is weak, 'soft as soft soap' (according to his wife) and suffering from a disability which makes walking difficult. The mother reproves him for his weakness and threatens (implausibly) to 'knock the living daylights' out of Tommy – 'If you can't, I must'. Jimmy has only a (heavily pregnant) mother; in one scene she persuades Fancy to take Jimmy to school to stop him playing truant. Here the police, and Fancy in particular, take on the role of the absent father – mixing authority and care. This view of the police as a paternalist institution recurs when, after John Watt has attempted to explain the boys' actions in terms of the 'rotten world' they live in, Barlow comments that Watt 'should have had three sons', since he 'would make a good father'. The irony of this lies in the fact that one of Watt's defining character elements is that his own marriage has broken down because of the excessive demands of the police service. The idea of the police as the agency for restoring (or substituting for) broken family and community structures remained a recurring topic throughout the whole series.

A more explicit response to family breakdown occurs through the magistrates' court. McGrath's style of directing typically involved speedy cutting between geographically dispersed settings, and here the scenes within the magistrates' court provide a rhythmic punctuation (through repetition) which marks the progress of the narrative. Each of the four scenes has an ordered sequence of shots (alternating the point of view of the magistrates' bench and of the boys facing them), and is accompanied by a parallel commentary from Jock and Fancy outside the court-room. Initially, the chairman of the bench criticises the police for keeping the boys overnight at the police station, rather than returning them to their families. On their second appearance they are remanded for reports, but no remand home has space to accept them, so on a third appearance they are put on bail. Their crimes intensify and they entice other boys to join them in truanting and spending the stolen money; their final court appearance takes them beyond the social world which *Z Cars* depicts.

During the boys' third court appearance, Watt is instructed to talk to their headmaster and enlist his support in controlling them. With the failure of the family, the school becomes the major hope for socialising the boys into legitimate behaviour. The dominant representation of the school is through the headmaster's study. Here the head talks to Watt and to the boys' friends, although not to the two boys themselves. For them, school is an institution which, whatever its civilising intentions or its attempted discipline, has little relevance. Between the boys and the police, however, there is a greater complexity of relations. First, the boys are a nuisance, causing a rise in the annual crime statistics. Secondly, they are an embarrassment; the episode opens with three vehicles, eight policemen and a dog descending on the warehouse only to discover two boys on the roof. This sense of inappropriateness (the police having to deal with a problem that demands a less heavy-handed solution) runs throughout the episode. Finally, there is some element of complicity between the boys and the crime car policemen; as Jock tells Fancy, 'a few years ago that could have been you . . .'. Certain qualities displayed by the boys – independence, ingenuity, daring, bravado (the attributes of masculinity) – are recognised and half-admired.

The episode illustrates McGrath's view that there should be 'No slick tie-ups. No reassuring endings . . .'. Rather, just below the surface of the narrative, is a level of latent critical social analysis. The headmaster, in talking to Watt, points out that Higgins is not vicious or violent, he only harms 'people's property'; it is very hard, he remarks, to educate children in the concept of property. In the immediately previous scene Watt himself offers the bitter comment that it is not surprising that children steal when they can see 'other people knocking off property legitimately and making easy money on the right side of the law'. Later on, he remarks that 'these two kids have suddenly become affluent . . .' – a word, in 1962, which carried many connotations concerning the development of a new consumer society with a problematic morality at its heart. Overall, while the dominant police view remains (as Jock remarks) that, 'it's not our job to decide what should or shouldn't be done . . .', there is sufficient evidence to substantiate Peter Lewis's contemporary view that the early *Z Cars* constituted a 'dry-eyed lament for life as it is messily lived in Britain in affluent 1962'.[32]

134

Classic 'Z Cars', 1962–64

The period of classic *Z Cars* lasted from the opening of the second season in September 1962 to 2 December 1964, when John Hopkins' last *Z Cars* was first shown. During that period, ninety-five original episodes and eighty-eight repeats were broadcast; of these forty-six and forty respectively were written by Hopkins, who also acted as script editor for the second season (forty-two episodes concluded in July 1963). Allan Prior wrote twelve scripts for the second season, although during the third (a further forty-two episodes from September 1963 to June 1964) he only contributed four. However, seven scripts from Robert Barr and two from Elwyn Jones maintained the core team's dominant role. This level of continuity had particular significance for *Z Cars*, certainly according to David Rose who later recalled that:

> If there was a quality for that series of *Z Cars* it was to do with our respect for the writer. We didn't bugger about in rehearsal and lines weren't changed without the script-writer being advised and told.[33]

As both main writer and script editor, Hopkins' influence was the most significant during this period in maintaining and developing the programme's established style and standards.

This was also the moment of *Z Cars'* peak audiences. BBC figures for the early months of 1963 indicated 16.65 million average weekly viewers, higher than for any other BBC drama series – more than 3 million higher than *Dixon*, although a million less than *The Black and White Minstrel Show* and some way behind the massively successful *Steptoe and Son*'s 22 million.[34] In recognition of this central role within BBC programming, *Radio Times* ran a twelve-part *Z Cars* serial ('Murder in Milltown') by Allan Prior from December 1962 to March 1963.

Organisational changes within the BBC also helped to secure and give recognition to the programme's success. In late 1962, the BBC continued its successful offensive against ITV by appointing Sidney Newman as Head of Drama (he took up the post in early 1963). Newman's record in heading ABC's Armchair Theatre, where he combined popular success with serious single-play drama, made him particularly suitable for the new model BBC. His subsequent reorganisation of BBC Drama into separate Plays, Serials, and Series sections recognised the role of such series as *Z Cars* as integral to the BBC's strategy for drama. By mid-1963, it was clearly one of the Corporation's flagship programmes and the *Radio Times* could announce the arrival of its third season by boasting that: 'Just as the start of a new series is a national event, so the main characters in this police epic have become national figures'.[35]

Crucial to its occupation of this flagship role was the fact that *Z Cars* could be presented as not only popular, but also of cultural and educational value. The early 60s was a period of particularly intense concern among educationalists and politicians about the effects of television (particularly of the newer 'commercial television'). The most striking result of this concern was the strong moral tone of the Pilkington Report (June 1962), in which the BBC was clearly preferred to ITV as the more responsible broadcasting service. While *Z Cars* itself did not entirely escape some implied criticism for its violence (implied, that is, by some press interpretations of the Report), in general it was taken up in the mid-60s as an example of how television could produce popular entertainment with a serious content.

An early instance of this was Albert Casey's essay 'Blood Without Thunder' in *The Schoolmaster* in mid-1962 (reprinted in *Screen Education* later in that year). Casey saw *Z Cars* as 'of quite remarkable quality, very far in advance of anything in this field' (he compared it favourably to the predictability and 'deadness' of *No Hiding Place* and the 'fantasies' of *Dixon*).[36] Specific points praised were the technical achievement, casting and sensitive treatment of violence ('nothing glamourised').

Similar points were made at a conference in Liverpool in mid-1963, attended by delegates from the WEA and the Townswomen's Guilds, by Elwyn Jones and David Rose and by the Lancashire Deputy Chief Constable. Here an officer from the Society for Education in Film and Television (SEFT) praised both the 'naturalism or comparative realism' and the 'social comment' – with particular emphasis on the programme's ability to provoke dialogue and discussion.[37] In Hall and Whannel's *The Popular Arts* (1964), many of Casey's points were reiterated in a more comparative context (as against, for example, *Coronation Street*).[38] Finally, in 1967 Michael Marland re-presented similar judgments within a more particular educational context in his article 'Z Cars and the Teacher' in *The Use of English*, followed in 1968 by an edition of *Z Cars* scripts (three from the third season and one from the fourth) specially 'selected for reading in a Secondary School'.[39]

There were obviously major continuities between the early *Z Cars* of the first season and the programme in its classic period. If McGrath and Kennedy Martin had left, then Prior, Jones, Barr and Rose remained and Hopkins himself had become involved at a very early stage in February 1962. However, in McGrath's view a significant shift of emphasis did take place – away from his and Kennedy Martin's original aims: 'the series was very lucky, in that it got John Hopkins, who actually managed to write about policemen in a way that was interesting – but we didn't want to write about policemen'.[40] Hopkins' view in mid-1963 was that the heart of the programme was 'the conflict between the police and the public'.[41] Increasingly however, the emphasis fell on the characters and moral dilemmas of the police themselves. In introducing the first episode in January 1962, the *Radio Times* had recognised the role of the 'mixed community' of Newtown and 'people and their problems' within the programme's concerns; by contrast, when the hundredth episode was broadcast in March 1964 it saw matters rather more simply:

It is a programme about police. It is not about crime; it is not about criminals; it *is* about those men and women, who are paid by us to do on our behalf work we are too weak, or too frightened, or too fastidious to do ourselves.[42]

As if to exemplify this, the hundredth episode (written by Hopkins and directed by Rose himself) was titled 'A Man ... Like Yourself' (4 March 1964) and centred on the death of PC Sweet, the boyish, mainly desk-based assistant to the station sergeant and a character who had tended to provide some light relief within the series.

In mid-1962 Albert Casey had suggested that an increasing problem for the series could be that 'the critical distance, already too narrow, between the creators and their police heroes will diminish'.[43] In retrospect, Stuart Hood views this process as one which subtly turned the potential critical edge of the programme into a way of implicitly endorsing what might previously have been seen as questionable police practice. The police came to like the programme because it produced a public perception that 'You don't have to pretend to be Dixon of Dock Green anymore. You can play it down and say "Oh I've seen that on TV ... on Z Cars". So eventually, in my view Z Cars became an instrument which could confirm police practices and was no longer critical ...'.[44] For the viewers too, the programme became comfortable, as Francis Hope's comments in July 1963 in the New Statesman implied: 'Z Cars has a problem just because it has created such a superb picture of men at work ... one could switch on week after week merely for the pleasure of joining the gang ...'.[45] It was this high level of identification and empathy with the problems, perspectives and experience of professional policemen that formed the core of the classic Z Cars formula.

Classic 'Z Cars' Narrative – 'Happy Families'

A consideration of one episode from the third season will show how this formula worked through into particular narratives. John Hopkins' 'Happy Families' (18 March 1964) concerns the investigation of the circulation of pornographic photos among boys at a primary school. The whole episode takes place in a single evening as the Z Cars team trace the source to the Shields (parents of one of the boys), who are themselves taking the photographs and selling them to a London distributor. Connected sub-plots are the disappearance from home of one of the other boys involved (Reg Sargent) and the impact of the police investigation on the marriage of the nude 'model'. A parallel sub-plot (activated from the 'memory' of the series, running back to the first episode) is a meeting between John Watt and his estranged wife (a meeting which leads to an apparently final separation).

Formally, there is a sharp contrast between 'People's Property' and 'Happy Families'. In the latter, there is no outside film; the characteristic pace is maintained by the alternation of scenes within the police station, a number of domestic interiors and a stationary Z Victor One outside various homes. The emphasis is on dialogue and on the police entry into the domestic space of (especially) the Shields and the Sargents in order to restore normality. In this restoration, a number of core Z Cars themes are brought together in a particularly condensed manner. In an echo of 'People's Property', within the two main families concerned the proper exercise of masculinity is hard to locate. It is Mrs Sargent's response to the discovery of the pictures (brought home by the eight-year-old

Reg) which opens the episode. Mr Sargent (although mentioned) is absent throughout and (in his absence) Mrs Sargent calls the police in order to find a way of dealing with Reg. She greets Fancy Smith's arrival by telling Reg: 'They'll know what to do with the likes of you. Lock you up, that's what . . .'. When Fancy vigorously protests that she is scaring the boy, she replies, 'Well that's what you're there for isn't it . . .'. At the end of the episode, it is Jock and Fancy who find Reg hiding in the gang hut, where Fancy both comforts him and gives him a stern talking-to about having anything to do with the photographs.

Masculinity is even more clearly at risk in the simpering, lisping, bespectacled, soft-spoken and clearly affluent Mr Shields (a cameo performance from Joss Ackland), whose son Tommy has stolen some of the photographs to sell at school and to get in with 'the gang'. Shields finally protests to Barlow that he didn't know that his son had been able to get hold of the photos, to which Barlow replies: 'He lives in the house doesn't he, you don't expect to keep something like that locked in one room'.

The 'something like that' is explicitly the photos, but more generally suggests an issue running across the whole episode – the problem of the social management of sexuality. When Fancy shows the photos to Jock, Jock chuckles and says, 'Look at that . . .', before his attitude is altered by the knowledge that they have been looked at by children. The level of Fancy's anger and personal disturbance is one of the main threads of the episode – anger at the way young boys have become involved. 'They should have let me take the Shields down to the station', he growls, with an implied threat of physical violence. His view is summed up in Barlow's much colder assessment of Shields (to his face) as 'stupid as well as vicious and depraved'.

Throughout the episode, there is an implication that it is the fact of female sexuality that is causing the disturbance. A contributory factor to Fancy's annoyance is the belief that John Watt has gone out with 'a bird', rather than staying on duty to see the case through. In fact, Watt is meeting his estranged wife. In a lengthy scene (five and a half minutes – very lengthy indeed for *Z Cars*, where an average scene lasts about forty seconds), powerful Hopkins dialogue provides the background to their separation and shows the impossibility of reconciliation (she is expecting another man's child). While the theme fits the episode (the characteristically ironic title suggesting the four *un*happy families depicted), and the conflicts caused by giving police duty priority over family ties remain a recurrent staple of police series, the length, style and intensity of the scene are much less typical and look forward to the concerns of Hopkins' *Talking to a Stranger* quartet of plays screened in 1966 after his departure from *Z Cars*.

In terms of the series as a whole, however, this is a scene which closes options rather than opens them; while there is no simple distribution of blame for the breakdown, Watt's long search for his wife, his wish to have her back and his commitment to his work ('the thing I do . . .' – 'because I want to, I have to . . . ') reinforce that sympathy for the difficulties of a policeman's lot (rather too simply summarised by the *Radio Times* in its comments on the hundredth episode), which came to embody the programme's central point of audience identification.

1965 and After

In December 1964 John Hopkins left the series to work on a number of projects for the new BBC 2 (which had opened in April), including a dramatisation of Ford Madox Ford's *Parade's End* trilogy (broadcast in 1965) and *Talking to a Stranger* (1966). During 1965, Alan Plater emerged as *Z Cars'* most prolific scriptwriter of its last year. Plater however never dominated *Z Cars* as Hopkins had done. During each of the second and third seasons, only eight writers had been used and for both Hopkins had written nearly half the scripts. During the fourth season (September 1964 to June 1965), seventeen writers contributed to the forty-three scripts, with Plater writing less than a quarter. The fifth and final season (October to December 1965) contained twelve programmes from seven different writers.

By early 1965, viewing figures suggested that *Z Cars'* popularity was on the decline; the audience had dropped to 11.8 million, barely ahead of *Dixon* and clearly below the 13.2 million of *Dr. Finlay's Casebook*.[46] Television critics were now increasingly taking the view that the series was neither able to maintain its quality nor to innovate successfully. In the *New Statesman* in December 1964, John Russell Taylor suggested that, 'the feeling continues that the series is noticeably running down',[47] while in the *Financial Times* (January 1965), T. C. Worsley asked for, 'Courage, too, please from the producers of *Z Cars*. Isn't it sad to see this once brilliant series teetering out in fumbling ineptitude?'[48]

Later that year Worsley got his response when in May the *Radio Times* told its readers that *Z Cars* would end in December, commenting that 'the same treatment of another aspect of police work would be refreshing for writers, directors and the public'.[49] Alan Plater's 'That's The Way It Is' (21 December 1965) was the last episode of the original *Z Cars* to be screened. Within a fortnight it had been replaced by *Softly, Softly*, based on the work of the regional crime squads, with Rose and Shaun Sutton among the production team, Plater among the scriptwriters and Barlow, Watt and Blackitt among the original characters. *Softly, Softly*, or *Softly, Softly Task Force* as it later became, continued for a ten-year run until December 1976 (barely outlasting *Dixon* which closed in 1975 when Jack Warner reached eighty). The title of *Z Cars* was revived from March 1967 and reverted to its single episode fifty-minute format in 1971. It continued until 1977, with a final episode ('Pressure') in which Kennedy Martin and McGrath were recalled as writer and director to produce a mixture of parody and black comedy, with a vision of an armed and fortified police station needed to combat the potentially riotous civilian population of the late 70s.

The Series Format

Within television history, the original *Z Cars* has multiple significance – as a final achievement of the story documentary and of live television drama, as a part of the BBC's striking stylistic transformation in the early 60s and as the opening of new possibilities in the televisual representation of the police. At a more general level, the programme also constitutes a particularly interesting case-study of the intrinsic possibilities and limitations of the dramatic *series* as narrative form for television.

The dramatic requirements of the series are necessarily different from those of the single play, the continuous serial or the serial pure. As with most situation comedy, the close of each episode must return the regular characters to the position they occupied at the beginning, ready for another self-contained episode the following week, in which constant frames of reference for the viewer are retained. The great difficulty then is to avoid, as Kennedy Martin put it in 1962, 'sameness week after week ... the characters tend to become caricatures of themselves'.[50] Among the reasons given by Kennedy Martin and McGrath for leaving *Z Cars* was that, given the extended run the BBC now planned, this result was inevitable. In 1964 T. C. Worsley put this point another way:

> There ought to be a law to protect addicts, a law against any series or serial continuing for more than a dozen episodes; after that it can't have the one necessary ingredient of a good programme – surprise.[51]

Ironically, however, one of the factors which prevented *Z Cars* from falling too quickly into this pattern was precisely the departure of McGrath and Kennedy Martin and the shifts of emphasis towards the style and concerns of Hopkins. In discussing his early scripts, Kennedy Martin referred to being 'frightened' by the 'alien' quality of the North of England – 'in the new town one felt the rawness of the Wild West':

> It's a man's country all right, with fights in the pub and husbands hitting wives. There's a hard brand of humour. The women have a self-contained independence ... It's *Room at the Top* and *Saturday Night and Sunday Morning* country, but television hadn't caught up with it.[52]

These perspectives are clearly reflected in a short novel[53] by Kennedy Martin, published in 1962 and based on the first and eleventh *Z Cars* episodes ('Four of a Kind' and 'Jail Break'). The verbal style is frequently pastiche Sillitoe (factories are 'Dark towering menageries of steel which ... gave the people of this New-town money to save, to buy, to eat, to court, to bear children, to get drunk, beat their wives, have holidays in Blackpool ...), while the characterisation of the police is unsentimental and frequently unattractive – Fancy Smith is first seen with 'his mouth open like the Mersey Tunnel ... emitting snores of great loudness'.[54]

Kennedy Martin felt that there was a '30 per cent loss of his intentions in the series as it has emerged on the screen'.[55] According to Peter Lewis, police scrutiny of the scripts (in order to get 'procedures' right) tended to soften some of the language and attitudes. He also detected:

> the whittling away of class attitudes. The crime patrol began with a firmly working class crew ... There was some pressure to make them £1,000-a-year men. One week Sergeant Watt got a shiny new raincoat. Another, Janey, the policeman's wife, got a snazzy new cooker to replace the old stove.[56]

140

The characters themselves also changed. An early feature of the series was Barlow's rudeness and intolerance. One ex-policeman told the *Radio Times* in April 1962 that, 'A snarling bully such as Barlow would not have remained a CI in any of the police forces with which I have had associations ... ';[57] he was answered by another viewer who perceived 'a high degree of understanding between senior officers and men' and suggested that in any case the PCs were not 'very sensitive little flowers'.[58] By April 1963 however, Barlow's character had been toned down; in the *Radio Times* Stratford Johns explained that his portrayal of Barlow 'was much tougher at the beginning, and necessarily so, because the four Z-Cars lads were pretty raw material ...'.[59] In the same year, Allan Prior offered a rather different explanation for why character changes had taken place:

At the very beginning, before the actors were cast, we wrote words on paper that one day somebody would speak. They had no reality. When the actors arrived all that changed ... once Joe Brady was cast, we forgot the rugby bit ... Joe has a likeable manner. He isn't a rugger tough ... Fancy Smith we first visualised as a bit of a dandy. After Brian Blessed was cast, we forgot that one, too – he's just the wrong shape![60]

Such an account of the casting was in sharp contrast to that offered by McGrath to Lewis a year earlier, when he emphasised the actors' immersion within the scripted characters. However, Fancy Smith's character certainly developed well away from Kennedy Martin's creation who (in the manner of Sillitoe's Arthur Seaton) liked 'a crafty kip after his lunchtime pint' and was famed for 'the Italian cut of his civilian gear, his combed hair and his way with women'.[61] According to the *Radio Times*, in a feature on Fancy's character at the opening of the third season, 'he seems to have been dogged by children. This has slowly forced him to think beyond his duties as a policeman to his responsibility as a person for anyone who is a victim of violence'.[62] In episodes such as 'Happy Families' (during which Barlow remarks that Fancy has 'got a nose for kids ... ') and 'A Place of Safety', Hopkins drew on this, by then established, characteristic in his construction of the narrative. Such character transformations may seem to lend credence to Hopkins' claim in September 1963 that, 'Z Cars is like a serial rather than a series. Each story is progressive; there's a growth in the characters'.[63] This claim might suggest that *Z Cars* was moving towards what Shaun Sutton has called the 'series-al': 'a long running series with a strongly built-in continuing element, which at the same time skilfully gave the impression of offering a complete story each week'.[64]

At times, certainly, *Z Cars* took on aspects of this construction, particularly when actors left. At the end of 1962, the actor playing the station sergeant (Twentyman) suddenly died and a replacement had to be drafted in; the departure of Jeremy Kemp (the actor who played Bob Steele) in February 1963 was able to be explained dramatically and the replacement, Dave Graham (played by Colin Welland), was gradually woven into the *Z Cars* pattern over a number of weeks. A more sustained attempt to maintain such a 'continuing element', and the character development that went with it was the promotion of Lynch to the CID in 1965.

Sutton, however, has identified the 70s as the period of origination of the 'series-al' – giving such examples as *The Onedin Line* and *When The Boat Comes In*. Compared with such programmes, the narrative form of any single episode of *Z Cars* was always substantially self-enclosed. There clearly was considerable character development (or at least transformation) within the series during 1962 and early 1963, but this was essentially a process of gradual adjustment away from the rough, raw and untidy social project of Kennedy Martin and McGrath towards Hopkins' concern with the humanity, strains and personal dilemmas of individual policemen, when faced with problems for which they held no solution. Once this latter position had been achieved and explored there was little further character development available. In T. C. Worsley's view, 'more than a year before [*Z Cars*] closed it had reached the end of its possibilities for the development of its resident characters'.[65]

The programme's loss of direction and demise was not, however, only a matter of its own internal development. By 1965 much had changed within British television, and British culture generally. Major changes in facilities for editing videotape meant that live television drama seemed increasingly anachronistic and clumsy; also, the regular use of film within television drama had now become accepted (traditionally in British television, a clear distinction had been drawn between drama and film – based on the difference between theatre and cinema). Thus a young director such as Ken Loach, who directed three episodes of *Z Cars* in early 1964, could move on in the summer of that year to direct a six-part serial called *Diary of a Young Man* written by McGrath and Kennedy Martin. This was a consciously experimental work, embodying Kennedy Martin's rejection of what he defined as 'naturalism' and relying heavily on editing to achieve effects of montage, manipulation of time and counterpoint between language and pictures.[66]

Loach himself then went on to direct Nell Dunn's *Up the Junction* for the Wednesday Play in November 1965. The Wednesday Play series began in October 1964 (the idea for a named series and a regular slot being a clear policy decision from Newman) and swiftly became the new focus for BBC mid-week drama scheduling. *Up the Junction* was an essentially naturalistic work in the sense of dealing in documentary-drama fashion with working-class life in South London, but, as against *Z Cars*, it was based on the techniques of documentary film-making, shot on location and edited together into a pre-recorded whole. This process was used again by Loach in the production of *Cathy Come Home* in November 1966. Such plays as these made the techniques and sets which had made the original *Z Cars* appear 'realistic', now seem artificial and stylised.

At its best, *Z Cars* had operated along a borderline of tension between McGrath's idea of using 'the cops as a key or a way of getting into a whole society' and the view (as expressed by a former Head of Lancashire CID in introducing the final episode) that 'the purpose was to depict the "ordinary policeman" going about his every day work . . .'.[67] By 1965 (and with the departure of Hopkins), this tension had relaxed and, with the development of new televisual forms and

142

the waning of the early 60s cultural fashion for Northern working-class subject-matter, the moment of the original *Z Cars* had passed.

Notes

1. Personal interview with Stuart Hood, October 1989.
2. In this essay the term 'season' is used to describe an unbroken run of weekly episodes, while the more usual term 'series' is used generically to refer to *Z Cars* as a whole.
3. R. Silvey, *Who's Listening* (London: Allen and Unwin, 1974), p. 187.
4. For discussions of the story documentary see P. Scannell, 'The social eye of television 1946–55', *Media, Culture and Society* vol. 1 no. 1, 1979, and S. Laing, *Representations of Working-Class Life 1957–64* (London: Macmillan, 1986), ch. 6.
5. J. McGrath, 'Better a bad night in Bootle', *Theatre Quarterly* vol. 5 No. 19, 1975, pp. 42–3.
6. B. Sendall, *Independent Television in Britain Volume II: Expansion and Change in Britain 1958–68* (London: Macmillan, 1983), p. 9.
7. McGrath, 'Better a bad night in Bootle', p. 43.
8. See Laing, *Representations of Working-Class Life 1957–64*, ch. 5.
9. *Radio Times*, 26 December 1965, p. 27.
10. P. Lewis, 'Z Cars', *Contrast* no. 1, 1961–2, p. 309.
11. This estimate is based on the analyses of Lewis, of A. Hancock, *The Silver Screen* (London: Heinemann Educational, 1965), ch. 3 and of the present author.
12. Lewis, 'Z Cars', p. 313.
13. J. McGrath, 'TV Drama: The Case Against Naturalism', *Sight and Sound* vol. 46 no. 2, Spring 1977, p. 103.
14. J. Bakewell and N. Garnham, *The New Priesthood* (London: Allen Lane, 1970), p. 100.
15. *Radio Times*, 28 December 1961, p. 26.
16. Ibid.
17. Lewis, 'Z Cars', p. 308.
18. *Radio Times*, 4 January 1962.
19. J. Warner, *Evening All* (London: Star Books, 1979), p. 191.
20. BBC *Handbook 1962*, p. 51.
21. *The Listener*, 18 January 1962, p. 145.
22. *Radio Times*, 15 February 1962, p. 26.
23. *The Times*, 24 February 1962, p. 4.
24. *Radio Times*, 8 March 1962, p. 29.
25. Ibid., 29 March 1962, p. 55 and 12 April 1962.
26. *The Listener*, 3 May 1962, p. 787.
27. Ibid., 17 May 1962, p. 787.
28. *Radio Times*, 31 May 1962, p. 28.
29. Lewis, 'Z Cars', p. 315.
30. McGrath, 'Better a bad night in Bootle', p. 43.
31. 'People's Property' is available for hire from the BFI.
32. Lewis, 'Z Cars', p. 310.
33. Cited in B. Millington and R. Nelson, *Boys from The Blackstuff* (London: Comedia, 1986), p. 25.
34. BBC *Handbook 1964*, p. 29.

35. *Radio Times*, 29 August 1963, p. 33.
36. A. Casey, 'Blood Without Thunder', *Screen Education* no. 16, September–October 1962, p. 27.
37. 'Z Cars and their impact: a conference report', *Screen Education* no. 21, September–October 1963.
38. S. Hall and P. Whannel, *The Popular Arts* (London: Hutchinson, 1964).
39. M. Marland (ed.), *Z Cars: Four Television Scripts* (London: Longman, 1968).
40. McGrath, 'Better a bad night in Bootle', p. 43.
41. 'Allan Prior and John Hopkins talking about the *Z Cars* series', *Screen Education* no. 21, September-October 1963, p. 12.
42. *Radio Times*, 27 February 1964, p. 33.
43. Casey, 'Blood Without Thunder', p. 27.
44. Personal interview with Stuart Hood.
45. *New Statesman*, 5 July 1963, p. 22.
46. *BBC Handbook 1966*.
47. *New Statesman*, 3 December 1964.
48. T. C. Worsley, *Television: The Ephemeral Art* (London: Alan Ross, 1970), p. 38. This book is a collection of reprinted reviews from the *Financial Times*.
49. *Radio Times*, 13 May 1965, p. 41.
50. Lewis, 'Z Cars', p. 315.
51. Worsley, *Television: The Ephemeral Art*, p. 15.
52. Lewis, 'Z Cars', p. 313.
53. T. Kennedy Martin, *Z Cars* (London: May Fair Books, 1962 and London: Severn House, 1975).
54. Ibid. (1975 edition), pp. 7 and 22.
55. Lewis, 'Z Cars', p. 315.
56. Ibid., p. 314.
57. *Radio Times*, 26 April 1962, p. 59.
58. Ibid., 10 May 1962, p. 55.
59. Ibid., 18 April 1963.
60. 'Allan Prior and John Hopkins talking about the Z Cars Series', p. 10.
61. Kennedy Martin, *Z Cars*, p. 22.
62. *Radio Times*, 29 August 1963, p. 33.
63. Ibid., 5 September 1963, p. 37.
64. S. Sutton, *The Largest Theatre in the World* (London: BBC, 1982), p. 34.
65. Worsley, *Television: The Ephemeral Art*, p. 44.
66. A description of the ideas behind *Diary of a Young Man* and a short extract from one of the scripts are contained in T. Kennedy Martin, 'Nats Go Home', *Encore* no. 48, March-April 1964.
67. *Radio Times*, 16 December 1965, p. 25.

Filth, Sedition and Blasphemy
The Rise and Fall of Satire

ANDREW CRISELL

For *That Was The Week That Was*, BBC Television's most successful satire show of the 1960s, the transmission of 19 October 1963 created something of a record. Within the previous ten days, the British Prime Minister, Harold Macmillan, had announced his resignation on the grounds of ill health. His deputy, R.A. Butler, was widely expected to succeed him. But, after a mysterious process of consultation among senior members of the Conservative Party, the right man to lead the nation through this egalitarian, technology-conscious decade was mysteriously judged to be a quaintly spoken landed aristocrat: the 14th Earl of Home. *TW3*, as the show was known for short, marked the occasion in its own inimitable way, addressing the Earl directly:

> My Lord: when I say that your acceptance of the Queen's commission to form an administration has proved, and will prove, an unmitigated catastrophe for the Conservative Party, for the Constitution, for the Nation, and for yourself, it must not be thought that I bear you any personal ill-will. . . . You are the dupe and unwitting tool of a conspiracy – the conspiracy of a tiny band of desperate men who have seen in you their last slippery chance of keeping the levers of power within their privileged circle. For the sake of that prize, which can at best be transitory, those men are prepared to dash all the hopes of the Party they profess to serve: or rather the two nations which by their actions they seek to perpetuate . . .[1]

It was recited by the show's presenter, David Frost, as a Butlerian or Disraelian reaction to the appointment. He concluded: 'And so, there is the choice for the electorate; on one hand Lord Home – and on the other hand Mr Harold Wilson. Dull Alec versus Smart Alec'.[2] The attack provoked six hundred phone-calls and three hundred letters of complaint – more than the BBC received in any other week of the programme's run.[3] The show ran from 24 November 1962 to 27 April 1963, and from 28 September to 28 December 1963, but a rather more telling statistic than the number of complaints is the number of viewers: over twelve million a week at its peak.[4] Satire on television was not only extraordinarily popular: it was wholly unprecedented. What were the cultural origins of *That Was The Week That Was*?

Contexts of 60s 'Satire'

The programme was in fact only one, and effectively the last, manifestation of a fashionable interest in satire which had already been well indulged in theatre and print and was dubbed by journalists 'the satire boom'. It arose at the end of the 50s and the beginning of the 60s, and might now be seen as a somewhat bizarre and distant consequence of the radical new social and economic measures which were taken at the end of the Second World War by the newly elected Labour government. These measures eventually led, via 'austerity' and a change of the party in power, to an overall increase in the national standard of living. One consequence of this was a modest increase, too, in the amount of leisure that people enjoyed. They had more time for 'consuming' the media they had purchased, hence the opportunity to learn in a direct or indirect way more about what was happening in the world, not simply the relatively clear-cut world of political events and current affairs, but also the vaguer, yet no less influential, spheres of social trends – of attitudes and values, life-styles, formations of taste in clothes, music, furniture, private transport and countless other concerns. Television, particularly after the national focus it attained during the 1953 Coronation,[5] was central to the shift, and statistics showing licences more than doubling during the mid-1950s support this.[6]

The increased public awareness of events and phenomena in politics and society at large seems to have had a further consequence, which was also, possibly, the effect of another measure taken at the end of the war – the passing of the 1944 Education Act; that consequence was the development of a more critical disposition among large numbers of people. This new mood or spirit took various forms which might be broadly expressed as: an increasing scepticism about politics and public affairs; a need to question or challenge traditional values or 'the received wisdom'; a growing distrust of, even an impatience with, certain notions of authority; and a sharper awareness of social differences and divisions.

1956 seems to have been the year in which the new mood became apparent, albeit in diverse ways and at different social levels. In July of that year, President Nasser of Egypt nationalised the Anglo-French controlled Suez Canal Company, as a consequence of which British, French and Israeli forces bombed and occupied the Canal Zone. In a previous era, the British public might well have united behind its government, regarding the occupation as no more than a legitimate measure to protect the interests of an imperial power, but instead there was fierce opposition from both within and outside Parliament, as well as from Britain's ally, the United States. It was felt by many that an imperial role was one which Britain neither should, nor could, continue to assume. The crisis broke the health of the Prime Minister, Sir Anthony Eden, and by the end of the year the British and French troops had given way to a United Nations peace-keeping force.

A few months before the development of the Suez Crisis, certain apparently fixed British values and customs had come under attack in the theatrical world. At the Royal Court Theatre the English Stage Company performed *Look Back in Anger*, a play by a new writer named John Osborne. Its hero was a ranting young misfit called Jimmy Porter and it consisted very largely of his tirades against the British Establishment as embodied by his middle-class wife. The play was a success with audiences and critics alike, and the following year Osborne collaborated with Lindsay Anderson, Kenneth Tynan, John Wain and Colin Wilson on an essay entitled *Declaration*, a wide-ranging attack on national institutions and on what the authors perceived as the endemic British diseases of snobbery and complacency.[7] As a result they became known as 'the Angry Young Men'.

Perhaps more important was the fact that the rebellious spirit of the time was also apparent among the newest beneficiaries of wealth and leisure, the young. In previous periods of relative prosperity, the benefits had largely accrued to the older generation, but in the 1950s young people became for the first time affluent enough in their own right to constitute a significant consumer group, and the decade saw a commensurate growth in the importance of youth culture. The appearance of new words is often a useful barometer of changes in social values and so it is not surprising that 'teenager' was well established by the late 1940s. The word is a monument to the process whereby adolescents became a coherent and demanding group in their own right, rather than incomplete adults.[8] Indeed teenagers soon developed their own words as a badge of exclusivity, regarding themselves as 'cool', 'hip' and 'with-it' and deriding their elders as 'squares'. Yet so well-publicised were they as a social group that, by an irony that greatly exasperated them, their private language passed rapidly into public parlance. The main manifestations of youth culture were in clothes – the Teddy Boy cult from around 1955 – and a new kind of music called rock'n'roll, whose first exponents were an American band, Bill Haley and the Comets. The band's records had been popular in Britain since 1954, but in the late summer of 1956 the release of their film 'Rock Around the Clock' caused enthusiastic disturbances in the nation's cinemas, the fans setting off fireworks, ripping out seats, and jiving rapturously in the aisles. On many occasions the police were called and a number of youths were charged with insulting behaviour and fined.

It is not surprising that this general mood of critical rebellion, iconoclasm even, should find eventual expression in the cultural life of Britain's oldest and best-known universities, Oxford and Cambridge, and notably in the latter's revue society known as the Footlights Club.[9] Footlights had long been something of a nursery for the West End stage and so its reputation extended beyond the University. However, it would not be too crude a generalisation to say that before the 1950s its revues consisted of rather anodyne musical comedies, the stock-in-trade of which was boaters, blazers, canes and toppers.[10] Perhaps the best-known Footlights products from this earlier era are Jack Hulbert and 'Professor' Jimmy Edwards. By the end of the decade, though, the wind of change was blowing even through Oxford and Cambridge (February 1958, when the Campaign for Nuclear Disarmament was founded, is another significant date). Like the other universities, they were now admitting the first products of the 1944 Education Act, ex-grammar school pupils whose humbler origins were likely to sharpen their social observation. There was also an influx of ex-servicemen, some of whom had fought in the war or in Korea, and of men who had completed national service, all of which made for a rather more worldly and cynical generation of students than had been admitted hitherto.[11]

The Last Laugh (1959), with a cast which included Eleanor Bron and Peter

Cook, was the first Footlights revue to attempt political satire;[12] but the pinnacle of achievement in university revue was *Beyond the Fringe*, which after initial runs in Edinburgh, Cambridge and Brighton opened in London in May 1961 and was an enormous success, moving to New York in October 1962. The cast showed an interesting symmetry of academic and social backgrounds: Alan Bennett and Dudley Moore were grammar school boys and Oxford graduates, while Peter Cook and Jonathan Miller came from public schools and Cambridge. Michael Frayn saw the show as a symptom of the general rise of prosperity, not only in the sense that wealth gave many people access to a clearer, less romantic view of the socio-political world and consequently a zest for satire, but because satire absolved them from any feelings of guilt about their less wealthy brethren:

> Conceivably the demand arose because after ten years of stable Conservative government, with no prospect in 1961 of its ever ending, the middle classes felt some vague guilt accumulating for the discrepancy between their prosperous security and the continuing misery of those who persisted in failing to conform by being black, or queer, or mad, or old. Conceivably they felt the need to disclaim with laughter any responsibility for this situation, and so relieve their consciences without actually voting for anything which might have reduced their privileges.[13]

Some six months after *Beyond the Fringe* opened in London there were two other important developments: a satirical magazine called *Private Eye*, which was produced by Richard Ingrams, Christopher Booker and William Rushton, began to circulate in fashionable restaurants in Kensington, Knightsbridge and Chelsea; and a satirical night-club, 'The Establishment', was opened in Soho by Peter Cook and Nicholas Luard.[14] The revue, the magazine and the nightclub would, together with *TW3*, which came on-air in November 1962, constitute the basis of 'the satire boom'.

Of course, the BBC could – and doubtless to a large extent did – ignore such movements in popular culture as Teddy Boys, Angry Young Men and satiremongers. Since the days of Lord Reith there had been a pervasive assumption that the Corporation's function was to shape values and attitudes, rather than merely to reflect them. The imperatives of its Charter – to inform, educate and entertain – imply its active, somewhat paternalistic role. But during the second half of the 1950s there were factors which made for a more populist approach within the Corporation – a concern not so much with what might be good for its audiences as with what presently preoccupied them and with what they actually wanted to watch and hear.[15]

The huge popularity of ITN news on the Independent network[16] forced the BBC to pay closer attention to the mood of the times, which was in favour not just of a more vivid presentation of news and current affairs, but also of a more critical attitude *towards* the news and those in the news – and, as we have seen, sceptical of the concepts of authority and expertise. At the end of 1956 it therefore launched the *Tonight* programme, which ran for five evenings a week and was to continue into the early 1960s. Its philosophy has been well summarised by Grace

Wyndham Goldie: whereas *Panorama*, for instance, drew its strength from being authoritative:

> The immense popularity of *Tonight* was due ... in part to a kind of national explosion of relief. It was not always necessary to be respectful; experts were not invariably right; the opinions of those in high places did not have to be accepted. In Britain, broadcasting, even television broadcasting, had seemed hitherto to be dominated by Reithian attitudes. These were suffused by intellectual condescension. Broadcasters knew the best when they saw it; it was their duty, with the help of the experts they selected, to pass on to the listening and viewing masses this privileged perception.
>
> *Tonight* was different. It stood, so to speak, the accepted communicative process on its head. It looked at those in power from the point of view of the powerless; it examined the effect of the judgments of experts upon specific cases; and of administrative policies upon the human beings who were at the receiving end of the administrative machine.[17]

It was a philosophy from which *TW3* was to grow, due largely to the fact that the programmes shared the same production team.[18]

Nevertheless, while the BBC might wish to reflect and even provoke the scepticism of its audiences through *Tonight*, it did not need to go so far as to cater to the growing demand for satire by broadcasting *TW3*, especially as satire ran somewhat counter to its statutory duty to provide balance. How, then, did satire come to be included in its programming?

The 'TW3' Idea

The answer to the question posed above seems largely to lie with its Director-General, Sir Hugh Greene, who was appointed in 1960 and was, in personal disposition, very much at one with the 'debunking' energies of the age. Three aspects of his personality and life-history seem to have been propitious. First, he was a news man by profession, with a sceptical and investigative temperament and with that need which the satirist shares to get behind facades and probe the discrepancies between appearance and reality. Allied to this, he seems to have had an imaginative sense of mischief, bordering at times upon the nihilistic.[19] And thirdly, he had a long-standing love of political cabaret, which he had seen in both Nazi and post-war Germany.[20] He also had a close relationship with a German cabaret actress, Tatjana Sais, whom he later married. It was not surprising, then, that his thoughts should turn to some form of political cabaret on the television:

> I had the idea that it was a good time in history to have a programme that would do something to prick the pomposity of public figures; I've always had a considerable degree of confidence in the power of laughter. I thought it would be healthy for the general standard of public affairs in the country to have a programme which did that. *How* it did that was, to my mind, not my

affair. All I did was to start talking about this idea, to start putting it in people's minds.[21]

If the idea was Greene's, the BBC was just the right organisation to carry it into effect, for, as we have seen, the satire boom was very largely the creation of Oxford and Cambridge graduates and the relations between these two institutions and the Corporation had always been extensive and intimate. They were over-whelmingly the largest source of recruitment for the BBC's managerial and pro-duction staff and for many of its broadcasters, journalists and entertainers. Ned Sherrin, who had produced the *Tonight* programme and was also to produce *TW3*, was himself an Oxford alumnus. From this perspective, then, it seems almost inevitable that the BBC should have devised a satire show in the early 1960s.

According to Sherrin, its title was coined by John Bird: 'We wanted to purge the memories of the week that had been, shrug and look forward to the next'.[22] The show itself has been wittily described by Sherrin as the offspring of a rape performed upon the *Tonight* programme by *Beyond the Fringe* and *Private Eye*;[23] but *Tonight* too was something of a hybrid – an interesting collocation of politics and entertainment. As Grace Wyndham Goldie puts it:

> I had always believed that the departmentalised structure of the BBC's pro-duction departments was in a sense a barrier to creativity in broadcasting. It was based on a bricks-and-mortar mentality which had become out of date, a lecture room with visual aids for 'talks', a music hall for light entertainment. But in both radio and television the whole air was free for imagination and for a new appreciation that to most people in the electronic age it was possible to move easily from entertainment to politics. They could like both, and both could be combined in a single programme. This was the idea of *Tonight*.[24]

As a consequence of this, *Tonight* became a kind of nursery for other pro-grammes that cut across the departmental structures of the BBC.[25] Both Donald Baverstock and Ned Sherrin went from *Tonight* to *TW3*, and from the former programme sprang the philosophy of the latter:

> *That Was The Week That Was* took the relationship between audience and programme a step further. From the beginning we were looking for a 'them' and 'us' polarisation. Our 'us' constituted both the programme-makers (per-sonified for the viewer by the actors) and the sympathetic part of the audience. 'Them' were represented by the public figures or establishment forces whom we investigated, challenged, mocked or pilloried. If *Tonight* was establishing a conversation with its audience, *TW3* was engaged with it in a conspiracy.[26]

In this respect, then, *TW3* was even more irreverently populist than *Tonight* had been, and one of the first things that strikes the modern viewer of the pro-

150

gramme, however trivial in itself, is the demotic nature of the performers' accents, whether Cockney, Brummie, or, in the case of the presenter David Frost, an indeterminate South-Eastern (this was at a time before his American commitments obliged him to affect a mid-Atlantic drawl). Received Pronunciation was mainly confined to Lance Percival and William Rushton, but was almost invariably parodic – comically 'posh' or blimpish.

The proven ability and well-defined aims of the *TW3* production team help to explain the overall quality and 'watchableness' of the programmes, despite the unevenness of their material, the haste with which they had to be put together, and the necessary absence of elaborate sets. Each show opened with the excellent title tune, which was punctuated by jokes and quick-fire sketches. David Frost was the presenter, and the cast consisted of Millicent Martin, who sang the opening tune, David Kernan, Roy Kinnear, William Rushton, Kenneth Cope and Lance Percival, whose calypsos, extemporised from current events which were shouted out by the studio audience, were a vehicle for instant and up-to-the-minute satire. In most of the shows, too, there were lightning cartoons and patter from Timothy Birdsall, and Bernard Levin in confrontation with his *bête noire* of the week. Sherrin shrewdly assembled his cast in almost equal measure from the university and public school network, where the satire craze had its roots, and from mainstream show business. The result was a fruitful blend of new ideas with traditional performance techniques, rather than the grotesque mismatch it might have been.

The show's closing sequence is another example of how the imaginativeness of the production communicated itself to the viewer despite the unavoidable bareness of the studio ambience. Among the final credits a funny 'fact' or anecdote was run across the screen rather like the print-out from a ticker tape machine: in the show of 8 December 1962, for instance, the viewers were informed that Gladstone's wife used to make him a cup of tea every morning – with water taken from his hot water bottle. The bareness of the studio resulted from the show being compiled so hastily. There was little time to build sets or for technical rehearsals, so that the television cameras themselves were often seen in shot; but Sherrin perceived a virtue in this, feeling that it gave the show a sense of freshness and topicality.

It seems, however, to have achieved more, because the permanent features of the show, such as the opening and closing sequences, together with the panache of such performers as Millicent Martin and Lance Percival, gave the more rudimentary aspects of the production a kind of cachet – made them seem a *part* of the show's imaginative, innovative nature. The lack of style became a kind of style in itself and started a vogue for 'brutal production' which was rather irritably attacked by Andrew Miller Jones, a former producer of *Panorama*, in an essay entitled 'The Impact of Vision':

The success of *TWTWTW*, which in the stress of topical production broke all previously accepted rules and conventions, is held in some quarters to indicate that they were of no importance. It does not seem to have occurred to these pundits that *TWTWTW* succeeded for quite other reasons and in spite of its disregard of established techniques. Its *enfant terrible* character, its lack of inhibition, topicality, good writing, cast, variety of image and pace were sufficient to compel attention. But the production was rough, the composition often bad, geography sometimes confusing. In the fantastic rush of production it could scarcely be otherwise. But this is no argument for ignoring these things.[27]

Good writing there certainly was, although since much of it had to be topical the material was inevitably variable. From time to time the show attracted contributions from such writers as John Antrobus, Christopher Booker, John Braine, Willis Hall, Richard Ingrams, Gerald Kaufman, Frank Marcus, John Mortimer, Peter Shaffer, Kenneth Tynan and Keith Waterhouse. Its themes fell into two main categories. The first might vaguely be described as 'the contemporary scene', politics in the broadest sense – the three main parties (but especially the Conservative Government) and individual politicians of all hues; Britain's lingering pretensions to be a world power, whether through nuclear weapons, colonial endeavours or the 'special relationship' with America; the church; the judiciary; the class system; and so on. The second common theme, and one which has become an increasing preoccupation of popular satire, was what might be termed 'media culture' – parodies of various aspects of newspapers, film, advertising, and notably television itself. By the early 60s, the themes and conventions of television were familiar to everyone and the subject of much conversation. The satirists' attentions were therefore overdue, although television's parodies of its own genres and conventions have often turned out to be as exasperating as they are cathartic: they hit their targets, certainly, but are almost inevitably no more than a kind of inverted compliment – just another manifestation of the medium's obsession with itself.

Post-mortems and Legacies

Given the soundness of the programme concept, the talents of its performers, the overall quality of the material, and the resourcefulness of its producer, what were the reasons for the demise of *That Was The Week That Was*? Richard Ingrams avers that it was doomed from the start because 'it blatantly defied the Corporation's obligation to be fair and provide balance'.[28] But did it die a natural death or was it killed? The answer seems to be, a bit of both – a kind of euthanasia was performed. What is universally agreed is that almost any reason for ending the show would have been more convincing than the official one offered at the time: that a General Election was imminent and that this would make the programme's political content difficult to sustain. The Election had in fact been known about for some time and there had been no threats to the programme from the main political parties. The immediate cause of its death was the Vice Chairman of the BBC Board of Governors, the upright and forceful Sir James Duff, who made it clear that he would resign if *TW3* were not dropped. Fearing a collapse of the Governors and a weakening of the Corporation's position if Duff went, Greene decided to take the programme off.[29]

Nevertheless, it would have been difficult for Duff to prevail had public support not dwindled by the third or fourth show of the second series. There is general agreement, even among the show's scriptwriters, that there was latterly a decline in quality – not so much flatness as a vapid striving after sensationalism.[30] This might, indeed, have been the consequence of that strange habit reality sometimes has of outdoing even the outrageous fantasies of satire: for during the show's summer break the nation had been treated to the sensational disclosures of the Profumo Affair, and when the show resumed it seemed to feel a need to rouse the jaded palates of its viewers by becoming ever more immoderate. In any case, Ned Sherrin feels that the show was inherently unsustainable over a long period:[31] yet other vehicles of topical satire have been able to survive for long periods, such as Radio Four's *Week Ending*, for instance, or *Private Eye* magazine.

A more reasoned and persuasive explanation for the show's demise has been offered by Grace Wyndham Goldie – essentially that it died from institutional causes. She points out that it was even more cross-departmental than *Tonight*: it was both politics and show-business.[32] Indeed, whereas the two elements had merely been juxtaposed in *Tonight*, they were positively superimposed in *TW3*: it was impossible to say where one ended and the other began. Although Goldie insists that the cross-departmentalism was highly creative in its way, she also argues that it caused serious institutional problems, because it was unclear as to who was responsible for the show's editorial content. Ultimately this meant the show was subjected to the partial and uncertain control of no less than four members of the BBC management.[33] Goldie therefore regards *TW3* as an unsuccessful and unconscious attempt to see if it was possible to work outside the conventional editorial control of the BBC yet still observe its statutory obligations.[34] As far as the production team were concerned:

> the suggested restrictions were at once incomprehensible and irrelevant. The problems of the BBC were not theirs. Theirs was a kind of private fun which they were sharing with a mass public. That was part of the charm of the programme. Watching it was like going to a private party rather than attending a public performance.[35]

In short, then, the programme's diverse elements were a consequence of its (and the *Tonight* programme's) cross-departmental locus: institutionally it was something of a freak, and when firm control was established it was bound to crush the creative vitality that cross-departmentalism had nurtured. In fact, Sir Hugh Greene felt that the programme was better taken off than too firmly controlled, for under firmer control 'the programme's own perceptible decline in vitality was likely to be accentuated'.[36]

This explanation is a compelling one, but I would also want to argue that the programme's fusion of politics and entertainment may not altogether have been a good thing, even in creative terms; that there are indications that the programme's near identification with politics and current affairs output encouraged inappropriate judgments of the show and needlessly damaged its standing.

The programme of 8 December 1962 contained two sharp attacks – one on Lord Cobbold, who was about to take up the post of Lord Chamberlain (which in those days also carried the responsibility of censoring theatrical performances), the other on the Prime Minister, Harold Macmillan. Part of the technique in both cases was to edit film of the victim, decontextualising his remarks in such a way as to make him look ridiculous. The Conservative Party protested and the senior management of the BBC forbade any further use of film in this way.[37] The episode prompts comparison with one recounted by Goldie,[38] who, as a current affairs producer, had objected many years previously to a similar transposition of news film. In a political documentary about post-war Vienna, she had used scenes from a local night-club to illustrate the squalor of life in an occupied city. She then discovered that the scenes were reused in a holiday series to convey the attractions of Paris, and objected on the ground that viewers who had seen both programmes would not have known whether the scenes had been shot in Vienna or Paris, but *would* know that one or both of the programmes was not to be entirely believed.

Goldie's objection is eminently reasonable, but it also illustrates how the close association with politics and current affairs may well have damaged *TW3*; for while political programmes (and holiday programmes, for that matter) stand or fall by their literal truth, satire, despite its frequent preoccupation with politics and current affairs, really deals in a different currency. As in the Macmillan item, it will readily *distort* a literal truth in order to allege a broader, moral truth against its victim, to make a general statement about his or her character or function. This is universally accepted as a legitimate technique, though we can perhaps discern it most clearly in visual art as the technique of *caricature*, the exaggeration (and thus, in effect, distortion) of a person's physical features in order to assert an essential truth about that person. The test of the assertion is quite simply whether the audience finds the caricature amusing, because their amusement is a sign of recognition. For politics and current affairs output the tendentious editing of the Macmillan film would have been absolutely unacceptable: for the BBC management to forbid it in *TW3* was rather like banning a caricature from an exhibition of satirical art on the ground that visitors to the exhibition would be naive enough to mistake it for an actual likeness. It would be surprising if this prohibition were still in force for satire shows, and the episode suggests that *TW3*'s inclusion within politics and current affairs production must in some respects have been a mixed blessing – that, had the show been placed under the less sensitive banner of Light Entertainment, it is likely to have been less misunderstood and, at the end, less rigorously policed.

The problem for the BBC in the 1960s was that, for some time after *TW3*, the connection between satire and current affairs programming was maintained, with predictable consequences. Its immediate successor, *Not So Much A Programme More A Way Of Life* (November 1964 to April 1965), was also in the hands of the erstwhile *Tonight* team of Baverstock and Sherrin and was inhibited by the criticisms that had been levelled at *TW3*.[39] The show was generally disappointing. Sherrin tried again with *BBC3*, which ran from October 1965 to April 1966, but again, the show lacked bite;[40] and with *The Late Show* (October 1966 to April

1967), which was not produced by Sherrin and lacked even that style that he had brought to its predecessors, BBC Television lost its way on satire entirely.

In fact, a rather fitting epitaph on the satire boom appeared in the guise of *The Frost Report* (March to May 1966 and April to June 1967). Its presenter was that arch-opportunist of the 1960s, David Frost, and the fact that the sketches which it included – performed by Ronny Barker, Ronny Corbett and John Cleese and some of them extremely funny – could scarcely by regarded as satirical was a sure sign that the boom was over.[41] Indeed the title sequence was an attempt to adjust Frost's image to new and more respectable prospects, for he no longer came across as the *enfant terrible* of *TW3*. The transition from David Frost the scourge to David Frost the darling of the Establishment is as ludicrous in effect as it is serious in intention, his chiselled features reflected in the radiator grille of a Rolls Royce and juxtaposed with images of Big Ben and the Union Jack.

What, then, is the significance of *That Was The Week That Was*? Its great achievement was simply to be the first satire show on television, for this enabled it to essay various *kinds* of satire and thus to discover which of them were viable on the medium and which were not. Consequently, while the modern viewer, inured to television satire, expects, and often finds, much of *TW3* to be rather more innocuous than contemporary viewers did, she or he occasionally gets a shock: some of it is stronger than anything that has been done since.

This is particularly true of its attempts at *invective*, for invective delivered vocally and by visible individuals, sometimes in confrontation with the victim,

Members of the *TW3* team just before going on the air. L. to r.: David Frost, Roy Kinnear, Kenneth Cope, Lance Percival and William Rushton.

seems much more trenchant than written invective or radio invective; and although *Spitting Image* seldom if ever resorts to this satirical technique, it is hard to imagine that invective would sound stronger in the mouths of puppets. I have already instanced the attack on Lord Home which occurred in the programme of 19 October 1963. The Director-General ordered cuts before it went on air,[42] but, even so, the attack provoked nearly 900 complaints and television has dared to do nothing similar since.

A more regular piece of invective in the show was provided by Bernard Levin in his face-to-face denunciations of individuals whom he held responsible for various deficiencies in British public life. His spot in the programme of 8 December 1962 is typical. On this occasion, the victim was Charles Forte, whom he treated as the embodiment of all that was wrong with Britain's hotel and catering trade. Levin's powers of denunciation are famous, and Forte was rapidly rendered a laughing-stock before the studio audience and several million viewers. Again, it is almost impossible to conceive of such a thing happening on television now. It happened then, not only because satire on television was new, but because the medium itself still had a relative novelty value. There were only two channels, BBC and ITV: performers, as well as viewers, were less blasé than they are now and Forte was evidently prepared to risk humiliation before a vast audience for the sake of gaining an appearance on television. It is difficult to believe that public figures in any subsequent, more televisually sophisticated era, would have allowed themselves to be placed in so vulnerable a position.

Thus, much of the satire of *TW3* was not only 'hard-hitting', it was unique – a one-off: however effective it was in terms of television it was culturally unrepeatable. On the other hand, some material which gave deep offence at the time does indeed seem innocuous now, good as it often is. As Bernard Levin pointed out some years afterwards, the excellent consumer guide to religions done in the style of the *Which?* reports ('This handy little faith [Anglicanism] ... optional extras ... if you want Transubstantiation you can have it, if you don't you don't have to ...') would hardly have affronted a subsequent audience to the extent that it affronted its contemporaries.[43] Indeed, a recent edition of *Spitting Image* (July 1989) showed a puppet caricature of Pope John Paul II, talking like an American pop star and doing a commercial for a brand of soap powder called 'Miracle', whose efficacy with respect to a stained garment (the Turin Shroud) was extolled over that of 'Brand X' (carbon-dating). In some ways much more extreme than the *TW3* sketch, it could be screened with perfect impunity.

The inference is clear. Since we now live in a climate in which satire is widely enjoyed, or at least tolerated, we can say that *TW3*'s second main achievement was to help turn satire – possibly for the first time in its history – into a genuinely popular art form. It is certainly true that the programme encountered great hostility in its own time and that its immediate successors on television were inferior; but in reaching a large and generally appreciative audience it had a far greater impact than literary or stage satire has ever had, and it seems likely that *Private Eye* magazine owed its unflagging popularity through the 60s and 70s to the appetite for satire created by *TW3*, even though it antedates it. Over the last two decades, broadcast satire has undergone something of a revival with programmes like *Week Ending* (BBC Radio 4) and *Spitting Image* (ITV). There is surely enough matter for ridicule in contemporary politics and culture to raise hopes that revival might soon turn into renaissance.

Notes

1. Quoted in Ned Sherrin, *A Small Thing – Like an Earthquake* (London: Weidenfeld and Nicolson, 1983), p. 78.
2. Ibid., pp. 78–9.
3. Christopher Booker, *The Neophiliacs: a Study of the Revolution in English Life in the Fifties and Sixties* (London: Fontana Books, 1970), p. 216, and Sherrin, *A Small Thing*, p. 78.
4. Bernard Levin, *The Pendulum Years: Britain and the Sixties* (London: Pan Books, 1972), p. 319.
5. Asa Briggs, *The History of Broadcasting in the United Kingdom, Volume 4: Sound and Vision* (Oxford: Oxford University Press, 1979), pp. 458, 466–7.
6. Peter Golding, *The Mass Media* (London: Longman, 1974), p. 35.
7. Booker, *The Neophiliacs*, pp. 121–2.
8. Brian Foster, *The Changing English Language* (Harmondsworth: Penguin Books, 1970), p. 56.
9. Robert Hewison, *Footlights! A Hundred Years of Cambridge Comedy* (London: Methuen, 1984), pp. 119–120.
10. See Hewison, *Footlights*, chs. 1–4.
11. Roger Wilmut, *From Fringe to Flying Circus* (London: Eyre-Methuen, 1980), p. 4.
12. Ibid., p. 8.
13. Quoted in Wilmut, *Fringe*, p. 22.
14. Richard Ingrams, *The Life and Times of Private Eye, 1961–1971* (Harmondsworth: Penguin Books, 1971), pp. 7–9.
15. See Michael Tracey, *A Variety of Lives: a Biography of Sir Hugh Greene* (London: The Bodley Head, 1983), pp. 160–173.
16. See the assessment in Grace Wyndham Goldie, *Facing the Nation: Television and Politics, 1936–76* (London: The Bodley Head, 1976), p. 197.
17. Ibid., p. 216.
18. Sherrin, *A Small Thing*, p. 56.
19. Tracey, *A Variety of Lives*, pp. 182, 205–6.
20. Sherrin, *A Small Thing*, p. 61; Tracey, *A Variety of Lives*, p. 115.
21. Quoted in Wilmut, *Fringe*, p. 58.
22. Sherrin, *A Small Thing*, p. 61.
23. Ibid., p. 58.
24. Goldie, *Facing the Nation*, pp. 210–11.
25. Ibid., p. 219.
26. Sherrin, *A Small Thing*, p. 57.
27. A. William Bluem and Roger Manvell (eds.), *The Progress of Television* (London and New York: Focal Press, 1967), p. 194.
28. Ingrams, *Life and Times*, p. 11.
29. Tracey, *A Variety of Lives*, p. 220; Wilmut, *Fringe*, pp. 70–1.
30. Booker, *The Neophiliacs*, p. 219.
31. Sherrin, *A Small Thing*, pp. 88, 90.

32. Goldie, *Facing the Nation*, p. 223.
33. Ibid., pp. 228, 231–3.
34. Ibid., pp. 234–5.
35. Ibid., p. 235.
36. Quoted in Goldie, *Facing the Nation*, p. 234.
37. Wilmut, *Fringe*, p. 64.
38. Goldie, *Facing the Nation*, p. 59.
39. Sherrin, *A Small Thing*, p. 96.
40. Wilmut, *Fringe*, p. 81.
41. Ibid., p. 139.
42. Booker, *The Neophiliacs*, p. 216.
43. Levin, *The Pendulum Years*, p. 319.

Television Memories and Cultures of Viewing, 1950–65

TIM O'SULLIVAN

Introduction

Today everybody talks about the everyday, even the empiricists.[1]

This is a short account of a project with which I have been involved for about two years. The work, which is decidedly 'in progress' and prompts more questions than it answers, is based on interviews with people about their recollections of early television in Britain in the period 1950–65.[2] It is intended to connect with several strands of recent television research and writing. The most general of these concerns the shift in emphasis and methodology from the study of television as a fundamentally textual phenomenon, to the study of the social contexts and relations of television viewing and the wider dynamics of cultural consumption.[3] I shall argue that, in terms of this shift, an adequate history of British television in the period under review must engage with the ways in which television – one of the most decisive cultural technologies of the post-war period – entered the culture of the British 'home', and with how television viewing cultures became established and 'domesticated' British TV. My major concern then, is less with the analysis of television *programmes* characteristic of this important and formative period, but more with people's early experiences of television and with their memories of the place of the medium in their lives during this time. O'Shea has recently commented on the importance of approaching 'television *as a whole*' and of researching the 'specificities of the *medium*'. Historically, as he notes,

> The institution of television must also include its technologies of distribution and consumption; how does their insertion into the domestic sphere affect *viewing cultures* and the (re)constitution of everyday life alongside other domestic priorities?[4]

Available historical accounts of the development of television in Britain have generally neglected the experience and contexts of television *viewing*. Studies of viewers and the domestic conditions under which television was acquired and watched have been largely absent from the picture. When they do appear, it is usually in the form of large scale quantitative data used to demonstrate the rapidity of the diffusion of this domestic medium or to exemplify the 'power' of the medium in its early period to amass large audiences, notably to participate in what Chaney has called 'civic rituals',[5] of which the Coronation in 1953 is the most popularly cited example.[6] With these exceptions, histories of British television tend to be more concerned with the inner workings of the broadcasting institutions themselves, the BBC and ITV, their production policies and practices, their early and developing presence in the public world of post-war politics, culture and social affairs. This kind of focus on the institutional production and organisation of television also predominates in many of the available biographical accounts from the formative years of television.[7] Other approaches are distinctive in that they concern either the development of the technologies of television broadcasting, or offer historical accounts and analysis of television programmes, personalities or selected genres from a range of critical or celebratory perspectives.

What is striking about these approaches, given the current direction of television theory and analysis,[8] is the relative absence of historical data and questions concerning the domestic, everyday presence and use of television. That is not to say that in their own terms they do not offer vitally important insights into the historical development and structure of aspects of the medium and its institutionalisation. However, the activities of television viewing and viewers are, by and large, assumed to have followed certain conventions and patterns, to have been determined from 'outside' the private, domestic sphere, primarily by television itself. Until recently, there has been no real need to take this up as an issue.

An important early exception here, in terms of historical data and research, resides in early work by the BBC Audience Research Department into the 'television service'. Daily surveys and regular responses from a viewing, in addition to a 'listening' panel, were established early in 1950. In the period prior to the inauguration of ITV in 1955, three important *ad hoc* research studies were carried out in 1948, 1950 and 1954 by the Projects and Developments section. In addition to gaining large scale representative data concerning the growth of the audience, this research was also designed to attempt an exploration of satisfactions and tastes characteristic of early television viewers, eliciting 'feedback' on the programme 'menu' provided. As Silvey, Head of Audience Research at the BBC in this period notes, the main aims were:

> to discover what kinds of people were becoming viewers, how much they were viewing, and how the way they spent their leisure hours was being affected – in particular how the possession of a television set was affecting radio listening habits.[9]

These studies (taken from Briggs[10]), and subsequent regular work stimulated especially by the introduction of the ITV service in 1955, provide in the first instance a measure of the growth of the TV public, and of increasing, daily amounts of private viewing.

At a general level, the data has been taken to suggest that television ownership and use in the 1950s rapidly spread 'downwards' through the social structure and that income and educational attainment influenced acquisition and typical

| | Proportion of the population* having: | | | |
	single channel receivers (a)	two channel receivers (b)	Total with TV (c)	no TV receivers (d)
	%	%	%	%
1955	35	5	40	60
1956	30	18	48	52
1957	31	25	56	44
1958	20	45	65	35
1959	14	61	75	25
1960	10	72	82	18
1961	5	80	85	15
1962	4	84	88	12
1963	2	87	89	11

* 1955–56 excluding children under 16; 1956 *et seq.* excluding children under 5.

SIZE OF THE TELEVISION PUBLIC, OCT–DEC. 1964–69

| | Proportion of the population (excluding children under 5) able to receive: | | | |
	BBC-1 and ITV only (a)	BBC-1, BBC-2 and ITV (b)	Total with TV (c)	No TV receiver (d)
	%	%	%	%
1964	88	3	91	9
1965	84	8	92	8
1966	81	12	93	7
1967	70	23	93	7
1968	61	32	93	7
1969	51	42	93	7

programme preference. Television viewing appeared to challenge the previous dominance of radio listening in the evenings, and to have had implications for some other leisure habits, notably family cinema-going. In terms of viewer tastes, some of the main findings are summarised as follows:

> We found that with each step up the income scale there was a sharply diminishing taste for all types of Light Entertainment and for Feature films and increasing taste for Ballet and for Documentary films. The tastes of men

Year	No. of new TV licence holders
1946–7	14,560
1947–8	57,000
1948–9	112,000
1949–50	344,000
1950–1	420,000
1951–2	685,319
1952–3	693,192
1953–4	1,110,439
1954–5	1,254,879
1955–6	1,235,827
1956–7	1,226,663
1957–8	1,123,747
1958–9	1,165,419

Source: BBC Handbooks (1946–59).

and women proved very much alike except that women showed more interest than men in Musical Comedy, Ballet and Magazine programmes while more than twice as high a proportion of men expressed enthusiasm for Outside Broadcasts of Sport.[11]

This type of research work, which sought to map the development and constitution of the single channel, BBC television audience, was given added focus and impetus by the availability of ITV services from 1955 onwards. The challenge to the BBC by ITV programmes became a particular pragmatic focus,[12] as did, at a later stage, the emergence of BBC 2 in April 1964. It is also clear from Silvey's account however, that audience research in the late 1950s and early 1960s had to respond to public claims and fears about the socially destructive or 'harmful' influences of the new medium. As a result, externally funded projects became preoccupied with assessing, and attempting to quantify, the 'impact' and 'effects' of television on children, held to be particularly at risk, and on the family.[13]

Despite limitations and shortcomings, the increasing amount and sophistication of research work carried out by broadcast institutions and other professional or market agencies in the 1950s and 60s provides an important resource for developing historical research on television viewing cultures in the period.[14] In contrast to the methods and objectives of that research, this study offers a different starting-point for exploring some of the assumptions concerning the entry and establishment of television viewing cultures in the home, and of issues involved in the transition from radio-centred to television-centred domestic leisure cultures. It is intended to complement recent work on the entry of radio into the household[15] and other current approaches to television and emergent leisure technologies in the domestic sphere.[16]

Memories of Television

It has been suggested that the development and mass availability of television 'suffused the private domain with a new order of experience.'[17] As a result, it is not surprising to discover that most people have memories of their early encounters with television. Often sentimentalised and fragmented, what is remembered tends to function as a point of symbolic, biographical reference, representing some aspects of the difference perceived between identity or circumstances 'then' and 'now'.

The majority of people who talked to me about their recollections of watching television in the 1950s and early 60s started by discussing programmes of the period. For all intents and purposes, the apparatus itself had become invisible, and to talk of television was to talk of programmes and, implicitly, the shared experiences of watching. Many of these recollections are embedded in the experience of the 'live' televised event itself – of the Coronation, the assassination of Kennedy, election of Harold Wilson, the Beatles, sporting or space spectacles and so on. They bear witness to the power of the medium in presenting itself as transparent, 'instant history',[18] or at least in constructing what appears at times to have been a very direct sense of contact with world affairs and public, 'historic' events. On this basis, television has clearly been a significant force in the formation of popular memory from the late 50s onwards.

These 'entry points' for discussion, did not, however, exclusively concern 'live' actuality coverage. Television presenters and personalities, drama, music and fictional programmes, especially situation comedies and serials were also foregrounded. Other memories frequently fuse television programmes and experiences to the rites of passage of domestic biography, serving as markers for remembered people and situations, of changing relations of kinship, lifestyle and shared experience.[19] For many, memories of early TV have in part been refashioned by broadcasting and popular culture's nostalgia for the relatively recent past. A central divide in these popular memories clearly relates to the age and the generation of the person remembering. British generations from the late 1950s onwards were born into domestic circumstances where television had less and less novelty as an apparatus or spectacle, as it rapidly became part of the accepted, everyday, familiar landscape of 'home'.

My own most memorable recollections of early television place me firmly in the post-war world, and are predictably dominated in the first instance by narrative images and senses. These combine the security of *Rag, Tag & Bobtail* (*Watch with Mother*, BBC), with the strange thrills of *The Lone Ranger* (BBC) or *Robin Hood* (ATV). They also encompass what feel like more idiosyncratic and contradictory recollections of stage coach wheels revolving the wrong way (especially *Wells Fargo*, BBC), of the bizarre litany of the football league results late on Saturday afternoons, of learning to be quiet while adults watched 'their programmes', and the place of television in the struggles over 'bedtime'.

The memories of preceding generations, however, those of people born before the war, differ in a variety of ways. Most significantly for the purposes of this study, their memories are in part constituted by 'pre-television' experience, and as a consequence have perspectives and resources absent from those of their

163

daughters and sons. As became apparent in many of the interviews, these memories do invoke a sense of the initial unfamiliarities with the cultural dynamics and practices of television viewing in either their own or others' homes. Early television viewing experiences can be placed and judged alongside those from pre-television culture.

Arguably, once domesticated, and in spite of subsequent innovations such as the development of colour transmission and reception,[20] cyclical refinements in design, or developments in scheduled content, television has never recaptured or replicated the early novelty of its initial appearance and presence. Indeed, it may be said that it has had to work harder and harder to produce novelty in terms of the internal dynamics of the cultural form and experience it has offered since that period.[21]

In the range of interviews that this article is based on, I wanted to gain insight into the following major themes and areas. These were used informally to structure and sequence the discussions and I have then used them to organise the accounts and memories which emerged.

Acquiring the set

All of the people who I talked with about television had acquired their first TV sets in the 1953–58 period. All of them had initially encountered TV viewing outside of their own domestic living space. In the main this had been in neighbours' or relatives' houses, and in some cases, large department stores, local electrical retailers or other types of promotional exhibition. The interviewees confirmed a sense of the public excitement that accompanied the initial spectacle of TV and many recalled the ways in which early television viewing was often an occasion for large numbers of people to gather at friends' or relatives' houses. For instance, one woman noted that her first view of television:

> Was like going to a cinema in Aunty Betty's house, it was in a room about as big as this – just packed full of people. The picture had a snowy effect – it wasn't very good.

I was interested to try to gain a sense of the economic and cultural 'pre-conditions' and 'pre-dispositions' which led to set acquisition and ownership and hence to the possibility for the development of domestic viewing cultures. In short, why and how did people acquire their first TV sets, and what factors were at stake in such a decision, were central issues here. The responses and discussion of this area in the interviews pin-pointed several interesting themes. In the first instance, purchasing the hardware for the majority of families was a considerable investment, and one that was not achieved without fairly explicit discussion of the likely benefits to be gained. Ambivalence towards the early growth of domestic consumerism, especially in the form of early rental or hire purchase methods of payment, were strongly marked in many of the interviews.[22] In general terms, most of the men I interviewed had been ultimately responsible for the decision to buy the set. They also tended to refer to the technicalities of fitting the aerial and the subsequent tuning in of the set which accompanied installation

Here it is:

The most sensational set of the year!

The outstanding new

Pam
Super-Slim
TV

It's TV's greatest idea yet. Only Pam could have done it—only Pam dealers can sell it! Stock up with this wonderful selling line. There's going to be big advertising in your local press to tie in with the Autumn selling period. Be ready to meet the demand! Pam Super-slim TV has 110° tube, exceptionally large frontal speaker, natural walnut veneered cabinet with Polyester non-scratch finish. The speaker fabric is in oatmeal Vynair and a brass trim surrounds the screen.

Super-slim TV 21″ model 821	75 gns
Plus-power version model 822F	82 gns
Super-slim 17″ TV model 804	64 gns
Plus-power version model 805F	71 gns

It's ready to bring you* BIG
new business and profits NOW!

PAM (Radio & TV) LTD · 295 REGENT ST · LONDON W.I

B

Super-Slim Fashion: Promising Profits to Dealers in a 1960 copy of *Wireless and Electrical Trader*.

and use. In some instances, this technical ownership extended into a form of possession over its use and deployment in the home. As one woman remarked:

> It was really his television, he turned it on, fiddled with it and turned it off. . . . but remember, in those days you couldn't argue about the choice of programme . . .

In many cases, decisions about getting a television were clearly bound up with factors beyond the level of the domestic budget. These concern the ways in which 'the value' of television, and hence the rationales for investment, appear to have been constructed in a number of quite distinctive ways. The dominant themes encountered in the interviews and discussions to date suggest a variety of ways in which TV ownership in the 1950s symbolised status and modernity, as well as a commitment to the values of viewing particular types of programme. The act of getting a television generally seems to be remembered above all as a sign of progress, a visible sign of joining, or at least of not being left out of, 'the new'. Moreover, some interviews demonstrate the ways in which early television ownership was a recognised mark of status in the family or local community, although that sense of status or distinction is inflected in often quite different ways. For example in the following two comments:

> We had one of the first sets in the village and at that time it was quite a status symbol really, everybody knew about it and used to ask what it was like, it was sometimes awkward because you didn't want them all trooping in and out of the living room.[W]

> You could tell from the aerials who had and who hadn't got sets. I remember that we were one of the first three in the road to get one. If you had a car and a TV set, you'd really arrived.[M]

In a significant number of cases, the acquisition of the set was planned in conjunction with other celebrations, most commonly Christmas.[23]

The domestic acquisition of television in the 1950s was also clearly motivated by other allied 'pre-definitions' of its cultural value and importance. Most of the interviewees remembered the fascination of having the broadcast picture 'in your own home', or as one put it, 'having a private cinema or newsreel'. Indeed, possessing the private, visual presence of the medium, in actuality and dramatic terms, appears as a common motivating theme. Also of note here is the large number of responses which suggest that the television had been bought 'for the children'. In these cases the acquisition of television appears to have been valued as intrinsically worthwhile and improving, most commonly in terms of the educational and 'horizon-expanding' images and commentaries provided. As one interviewee noted:

> We did buy it for ourselves, but I remember thinking that it would help the children to get on at school, that they would know more about the world and

what was going on, they'd be more 'in touch' and be able to see and understand things better – I'm not sure if it did, mind, but we certainly felt that at the time.[M]

This is an issue I shall return to under a later heading.

Television and Domestic Space

This second theme encompasses both the ways in which television was accorded a physical place in the home and any related ways in which its presence had implications for the structure and use of living spaces. For all of the interviewees, the arrival of their first TV set appears to have resulted in various rearrangements of domestic lay-out and organisation.

In the first instance, several interviewees remember arguing about which was the most appropriate room in the house for the television. This was particularly evident where there existed a strong division between a 'living' room, which was used for eating, relaxation and other everyday domestic activities, and a 'parlour' or 'sitting room', used for more exclusive and formal occasions. In the majority of these cases, the TV appears to have been installed in the latter space, and several of the interviewees noted that this contributed to a certain 'awkwardness' and formality which accompanied their early viewing and use of the set:

I remember, you had to go into the front room to watch it, and in those days, the front room was really only used for 'best' – for special occasions. The television changed that.[W]

This kind of response might be taken to indicate that in these early years, the practices of television viewing were not directly or simply assimilated into the everyday centre of the home. However, most accounts recognise that in a short time TV had 'colonised', not only domestic space, but also leisure time at home:

In the evenings, it (the living room) became the television room . . . it was 'what's on tonight?', and everything started to give way to television. It used to annoy me, you couldn't talk to people.[M]

In some cases, recollections suggest that there was a marked antipathy towards television viewing accompanying, or intruding into other domestic routines, notably household meal-times, or visits from family or friends. Early viewing in these instances appears to be remembered as a more deliberate, self-conscious activity, often requiring a move into a separate room for those who were allowed to watch. In general, the activity of watching the television was clearly negotiated and governed in a variety of ways by pre-existing sets of domestic codes. For example, the interviews also provide some insights into a range of issues concerning the reorganisation of rooms, particularly in terms of seating and lighting arrangements. The placing of the TV set demanded a form of spatial and domestic centrality, as one woman remarked:

167

I wanted to have it by the side of the fireplace because you know, I've always thought of it as the centre.

Most interviewees made reference to the rather cumbersome qualities of their early sets. Indeed, the size and design of the sets, especially those in the 1950s which combined wooden, 'furniture' solidity and cabinet aesthetics, appears as an important memory point.[24] In this context, several of the interviewees commented on the convention of TV cabinets fitted with hinged or sliding doors, designed to make the screen less obtrusive when not in use. Others refer to the size of the tube, the 'humming' and warming up time of early bakelite sets and one couple remember when, having moved to a new, modern house in 1959, the 'clash' of decor caused by their old cabinet style set.

In these and other ways, questions about the physical positioning of the television within the home, were, I found, difficult to separate from discussion of related issues, notably television and domestic time, emergent styles and patterns of viewing, and the priorities accorded to television viewing in the contexts of other competing domestic activities and obligations.

Television and Domestic Time

While the introduction of sets into homes was in many senses the essential prerequisite for the development of the television audience in this period, domestic availability of the apparatus had to be accompanied by its actual use. Not only did television occupy domestic space, it also sought to capture domestic time and focus. Average daily amounts of viewing in the evening have been calculated as increasing from about one and a half hours in 1955, to approximately two hours by 1963, as the following table shows:[25]

QUANTITY AVERAGE VIEWING, OCT.–DEC. 1955–63

| | *Daily average in the evening* per head of population with TV By the two-channel public* | | | | |
| | *Of BBC by single-channel public* | *BBC* | *ITV* | *Total* | *Two-Channel channel ratio* |
	hrs mins	*h: m*	*h: m*	*h: m*	*BBC: ITV*
1955	1: 34	0: 50	0: 43	1: 33	54: 46
1956	1: 37	0: 35	1: 06	1: 41	38: 62
1957	1: 41	0: 34	1: 07	1: 41	34: 66
1958	1: 41	0: 36	1: 11	1: 47	34: 66
1959	1: 41	0: 40	1: 03	1: 43	39: 61
1960	1: 54	0: 43	1: 13	1: 45	37: 63
1961	1: 56	0: 51	1: 04	1: 55	44: 56
1962	1: 53	0: 57	0: 57	1: 54	50: 50
1963	1: 50	0: 51	1: 01	1: 52	45: 55

* 1955–6, 7.00–11.00 pm; 1957 *et seq.* 6.00–11.00 pm
† 1955–59, excluding children under 16; 1960 *et seq.* excluding children under 5

In this section, I was interested to try to develop in the interviews a sense of how television viewing had entered the time economy of domestic life. In this context, most of the interviewees made the point that time spent watching television was clearly dependent upon a number of factors. Most obviously, what programmes were on offer, how watching them was valued, and how available they were to watch at a given time. In retrospect, some interviewees recalled the contradictions at work here, for instance:

In some ways, because there was less choice then and because it was new I think we watched things that we wouldn't dream of watching today. But because we weren't really used to it, it never seemed that important – we certainly didn't let it take over our time at home quite so much as it did later [laughing] – or does today.[M]

We seemed to have lots more things to do – you know important things – we were much less home centred and wanted to get out and about more, seeing our friends.[W]

It used to annoy me sometimes, it would go on and you'd know it would stay on, and that would be the evening.[W]

For many of the interviewees, unplanned and extensive amounts of time spent watching television in the evenings is something that was guarded against.[26] For many, television is remembered as having had a much lower priority on an agenda that encompassed more outgoing social and leisure pursuits and more demands associated with household maintenance and family work. The spectres of the indiscriminate use of TV, and of the guilt associated with 'unproductive', casual watching, are regularly referred to:

They used to say 'there's old square-eyes at the goggle box again', and that I'd wear it out if I watched it too much!

Memories of the period tend also to present a fairly uniform picture of a highly restricted schedule of programmes in terms of menu and daily duration. In addition, many interviewees did suggest that, following the initial excitement of television, they had been disappointed with the nature of early programme services.

In an important and suggestive analysis of broadcasting and social time, Scannell develops work by Giddens in proposing three principal and related levels for analysis. These are, in summary form:

First the temporality of immediate experience, the continuous flow of day to day life . . . *clock time* bounded by the twenty four hour day. Second, there is the temporality of the life cycle of living organisms . . . *life time*. Third, there is the *longue durée*, the slow, glacial movement of institutional time . . . *calendrical time*.[27][W]

169

Scannell goes on to note that these levels are fused and intertwined. Many of the recollections of TV in the period appear to function as 'markers' for remembered domestic situations or celebrations involving particular relatives or friendships. In this way, memories of shared viewing experiences appear to act as quite significant life time markers and generational indicators. In many of the interviews for example, TV programmes are remembered as 'favourites' (or in some instances pet 'hates') of husbands, wives, children, grandparents, friends and so on, at particular stages of family circumstance and history:

He never used to miss the big-band shows because he was very keen on that type of music then.

My favourites then were the dramas, they were more theatrical then, the plays, *Under Milk Wood* I remember, it inspired me.[W]

I always used to watch Broderick Crawford in *Highway Patrol* with the children, and we used to watch their favourite cowboys too.[M]

The very fact of being asked to talk about television in the period, as many of the interviewees noted, was an invitation to 'turn their clock back' and to self-consciously reminisce about their life times and biographies. In this process, comparison between senses of the past and the present state of television and of the past and present situations and qualities of life of the interviewee, were inevitable and important. At an explicit level, most accounts provide some insight into what, in retrospect, are recalled as the relative 'abnormalities' or 'datedness' of TV in the period, for example:

Well, we had to make do with black and white then obviously and the definition wasn't as good as it is now. What I remember most is the sort of 'stageyness' of the whole thing – a bit amateur dramatical – perhaps it was because it was more live then, but there always seemed to be something going wrong or on the verge of going wrong.[M]

Less explicitly perhaps, interview responses like this also suggest a series of changes concerning people's expectations of television. Most commonly, these reference aspects of change in technical quality of picture and picture management, choice of channel, programme types and styles, and of shifts in institutional formality and texture (the mode of address, 'personality' or 'feel' of different TV channels). In this latter context for example, many interviewees made reference to the stricter controls governing the use of language and representations of sexuality on television in the period. This involvement of television in the personal and generational construction of senses of leisure and family life time appears, however, to be powerfully interlinked with its activities at the other two levels.

All of the people I interviewed acknowledged that in various ways they had learned to pass and to 'fill in' time with television during this period. Most readily accepted that watching television had rapidly become an integral and valued part of their domestic routines, an accompaniment to their personal lives at home. For some, watching TV is remembered as a poor substitute for other more active or interactive pursuits, pastimes and hobbies, and in these cases there is the suggestion that the set was turned on for particular programmes only. For others, television viewing appears more rapidly to have become the dominant component of leisure time, becoming part of a process which several interviewees described as 'switching off' from work or other domestic priorities. As one noted:

> Well it made a difference in that you could stay in and to begin with it was like not staying in because there was television to watch. It could be relaxing and it could send you to sleep. It was another option I suppose, and we worked out what was worth watching pretty quickly.[M]

In a general sense, the interviews provide an insight into the daily routinisation of viewing, the 'meshing' of early schedules with family time patterns:

> We used to watch it after tea, and it became a regular thing . . . some nights were good nights on television, and we used to look forward to them.[W]

In this and related ways, television entered the cycles of clock time characteristic of domestic space. In addition to the beginning and ending of transmission, TV news was most often singled out as a major marking point in the typical evening's progression. The news on TV, like radio, formally told the time and appears to have rapidly become a significant, if not in some cases an obsessive, part of household ritual. More generally, interviewees' accounts offer some insights into the ways in which television programmes could contribute to the 'texture' or, as Raymond Williams has put it, to 'the flow', of an evening at home:[28]

> On some nights there would be a string of good programmes – you'd start with a comedy, *Here's Harry* or *The Army Game* or something like that, and that would get you off to a good start, and then a thriller or a play, some sport – [laughing] I seem to remember that Wednesdays were good nights at one time.[M]

The theme of 'good' and 'bad' nights on TV seems in many instances to connect across weekly or seasonal cycles, and offers some insight into how people negotiated a fit between television watching, early television schedules and other domestic obligations and demands. Particular regular programmes, in some instances, appear to have been regarded as the property of certain family members, 'their programmes', and in some cases this is remembered as a cause of routine domestic arguments between husbands and wives or parents and children. Other accounts point to the ways in which television watching was also capable of bringing the family together at particular points in the week. For example, some interviewees recalled watching films on a Sunday afternoon in the winter as a valued sign of cosy, domestic security and communality. Television viewing is also recalled as an important form of companionship, most significantly by women, when their husbands were absent from the home.

The sense that television was valued as a means of connecting the private, personal world with the public 'world out there' of historical events and process, comes through very strongly in many of the interview accounts of TV in the period. As I have noted earlier, many television memories concern the actuality of TV, the coverage of 'live' events.[29] I encountered numerous references to the elation and involvement which surrounded sporting and other types of historic spectacle and ceremony. Interviewees were able to recall in some detail specific ways in which television images of incidents of disaster, death and tragedy had at times demanded different kinds of emotional involvement and attention. In some instances, there was an incongruity between the order of the domestic world and that revealed 'live' on the screen:

> Well, I remember that someone was doing my hair at the time President Kennedy was shot.[W]

In most cases, it was clear that coverage of this kind of 'historic event' had sparked considerable discussion, as well as memorable feelings of emotional shock or outrage. Outside the home, it became a routine expectation that people would have seen television news coverage or other programmes from the night before. In this way, it seems that television punctuated household history by its ability to connect inner space and situation with the dynamics of the world 'out there'. The fuller implications of this have been taken up recently in the following terms:

> Not only has the development of communications technology been affected by the pre-existing organisation of domestic space but broadcasting for example, can be seen to have played a significant part in rewriting the relations between the domestic and public spheres – for instance, by increasing the attractiveness of the home as a site of leisure.[30]

Habitus, Cultural Capital and Cultures of Viewing
I want to conclude by introducing and framing a level of analysis which is the most challenging, and at this stage, the least complete. So far, I have tended to focus on some of the major common themes raised in the interviews concerning recollections of acquiring and positioning the set in the home, and of time spent watching television during the years being researched. In this final section, I want to turn to some of the major points of difference and discontinuity which appeared in different interviews. It became apparent in the discussions that the introduction and use of television in different households, and the contrasting ways in which it was managed and evaluated, were mediated in relation to what Bourdieu has referred to as distinctive codes of cultural capital. Furthermore, the interviews provide some qualitative insights into the operation of the family and domestic culture as a site for establishing and reproducing the primary *habitus*, defined by Bourdieu as that: 'system of schemes of thought, perception, appre-

172

ciation and action'[31] which provides the fundamental generative and classifying principles embodied in particular patterns of taste, life-style and class culture. As Featherstone has noted:

> By *habitus* Bourdieu is referring to the unconscious dispositions, the classificatory schemes, taken-for-granted preferences which are evident in the individual's sense of the appropriateness and validity of his/her taste for cultural goods and practices – art, food, holidays, hobbies, etc. . . . Each group, class and class fraction has a different habitus, hence the set of differences, the source of distinctions and vulgarity of taste, can be mapped onto a social field.[32]

Clearly, this project does not draw on the extensive range of empirical data which Bourdieu and his associates have amassed, analysed and sought to explain since the mid-1960s. It is also limited in the sense that it foregrounds those dispositions concerning television and TV viewing, to the exclusion of those relating to other leisure pursuits and forms of domestic consumption and arrangement. However, the accounts of TV presented in the interviews do suggest the operation of distinctive sub-systems of cultural classification, disposition and difference. Viewed from the 'inside', these provided the basic means whereby what television offered was subject to different types of appropriation, regulation, involvement and judgment. Some of these issues have been framed in aspects of the preceding discussion. For now, I want briefly to address questions concerning memories of BBC and ITV output; children and television; gender and viewing; and relations between TV and other leisure pursuits.

The majority of interviewees remembered early BBC programmes as having a great deal of formality, characterised above all by a mannered and serious mode of address. In retrospect, this was recalled as rather anachronistic and in some cases it was described as 'off putting' or 'unsettling'. As one interviewee remarked:

> It was really rather élitist and snobby, but that was the BBC in those days – there wasn't much of the familiarity and jokiness of later years, it was what they used to call 'high brow' and very 'plummy'. It was as if you had to be on your best behaviour to watch, we used to laugh at it sometimes – the airs and graces.[W]

The arrival of ITV services from 1955 onwards provided television viewers with an alternative to the established BBC style. Choice, in terms of television watching, became possible.[33] All of the interviewees recalled early ITV programmes, and the 'feel' of the network, as being very different from the BBC. As Bartlett has noted in a valuable analysis:

> To attract audiences so that advertisers would be encouraged to make use of the television medium, ITV transmitted programmes that conveyed the glamour of attainment in their production values (for example in light entertain-

173

ment shows), their goal orientations (in, for example, give-away quiz shows), and in the personalities who were featured. The values that were expressed had already been stimulated in audiences by American popular culture and by advertising seen elsewhere than on TV. Courtesy of the TV medium, personalities in both fictional and non-fictional programmes literally entered viewers' homes, week in and week out. The regularity of these appearances broke down any sense of remoteness and distance, fostering a relationship of intimacy between personalities and audiences . . . the informal approach enabled viewers to feel that they were being addressed on their own level rather than from above.[34]

For the majority of people I spoke to, ITV is remembered as providing a distinctive alternative to the BBC. Generally this was welcomed, though not without qualification. In some cases, it became clear that ITV services were regarded with a good deal of suspicion in the early period. The more consciously 'popular' programme formats, the use of Americanised personalities and informalities of address, the commercial nature of the channel as epitomised by adverts, represented for some of the interviewees a kind of 'popular vulgarity' which they distanced themselves from. In one, perhaps rather extreme case, ITV programmes were banned from the home, although the set was capable of two channel reception:

> Well, you could say it wasn't approved of in our house . . . I just thought it was a dreadful waste of time and I didn't like it . . . there was too much cheap entertainment and not really enough education. I didn't want the boys to get used to watching it so I used to ban it. It seems funny now, but I just didn't think it was a worthwhile way for them to spend time, but I know that they used to watch it when my back was turned, or at friends' houses.[W]

The differences between ITV and BBC programming were not always recalled in these terms. Many of the interviewees, for example, noted that the most important issue concerned the extension of choice:

> Well it meant that you had a choice, you could actually switch over and see what was on the other side, it was exciting, and seemed to be more in touch with the times. I think it took us some time to get used to it, the adverts were a novelty, it was lighter and I remember the quizzes.[W]

Some other comment welcomed the regionalism of ITV companies by comparison with the metropolitan, London basis of the BBC. In these and other ways, the arrival and subsequent development of ITV programming was subject to a range of viewer evaluations.[35] In part, these seem to demonstrate some of the ambivalences concerning notions of 'the popular', applied and negotiated for the first time in the context of television. They also indicate different kinds of domestic alignments and loyalties towards the BBC during the period.

All of the people I interviewed had young children growing up in the home during the 1950s. As I have noted, a significant number of them referred to children as a major reason for investing in a television set in the first place. In this sense, many of the interviewees valued television as a positive extension of schooling, as an important domestic resource for their children's educational and (in)formative experience and development. Most commonly in this context, reference was made, not initially to 'children's programmes', but to nature and wild-life documentaries and foreign or travel features.[36] These kinds of programmes appear to have been defined by parents as intrinsically valuable for children, and as memorable, recurrent vehicles for parent-child interaction.

More predictably, mothers, and to a lesser extent fathers, recalled in considerable detail the timing, contents and characters of 'children's television', mainly referring to BBC programmes. *The Woodentops*, *Bill & Ben*, *Andy Pandy* and others were frequently mentioned, and most interviewees made reference to the ways in which TV schedules had restructured their children's day. Television viewing in the afternoons, after school, had rapidly become part of established domestic routine. Children's television during the period is remembered fondly as a private point of contact with children now grown older, part of the parent-child relationship. The interviews also suggest that Children's Hour provided an important and functional space, especially for mothers involved in other home work, most commonly meal preparation:

Yes, between five and six o'clock it was Children's Hour. After they had come in from school, they really used to look forward to it. Sometimes their friends would come round and they'd watch it together. When they were younger I used to watch some of it with them – in the days of the 'toddlers truce' that was.[37] But as they got older, I was usually busy in the kitchen when Children's Hour was on, it was useful, because you knew what they were doing.[W]

Many of the interviews also revealed however, that outside the 'safe' confines of Children's Hour, children's viewing was clearly regulated and controlled in a number of ways. Several accounts noted that access to particular TV programmes was used to reward children's good behaviour: 'staying up late' to watch with parents became a treat and, by corollary, the denial of such access was also used as a punishment.[38] At a general level, it became clear in the discussions that all of the households had a strong sense of a divide between what was, and was not suitable for their children's viewing, and that this division was negotiated during this period.

Two types of recurrent reference were made here. On the one hand there was anxiety about 'adult exposure', in particular, that TV would show children scenes of sexuality – references were made here to early TV plays and their 'risqué' reputation:

I don't think I let the children watch in the evenings very much, except perhaps at weekends. We were quite strict about what they could and couldn't watch – nothing too adult – not that there was a lot of sex on TV then![W]

On the other hand, some interviewees recalled their concern that their children should watch programmes that they defined as 'good for them' in cultural and educational terms and hence that their children's leisure time with TV should be productive. I have already noted the positive references made to nature and wild-life documentary series in this context. More generally, the interviews provide some evidence that children's viewing, outside of designated children's programmes, was monitored and that parents felt that they should be concerned about it. This was most marked when evening television viewing clashed with school work, or other pursuits defined as more valuable or important. In one case, for instance:

It wasn't so bad in the winter, but I remember in the summer evenings it used to upset me – I'd come in on a lovely evening and I can remember it now, all the curtains would be drawn and they'd [two boys and a girl aged between five and nine years, in the late 50s] be sat in the gloom, glued to the set. I often got annoyed and turned it straight off – 'get out in the fresh air' I used to say.[M]

Most interviewees remembered arguments with children, especially those approaching teenage years, about programme choice and domestic control of the set.

The ways in which the women and men interviewed spoke about their memories of television and their children crystallised a more general set of issues concerning gender relations and television. In this context for example, I have already referred to the masculine 'technical ownership' of early sets. The role of controlling childrens' viewing appears, on the basis of these interviews, to have been predominantly the responsibility of the mother, an associated part of the domestic division of labour which designated the management and care of children as primarily mothers' work. Very few of the women I interviewed had independent employment outside of the home in the period. As a result, their relationships to TV viewing differed from that of their husbands. In particular, the interviews do suggest that women's viewing in this period was often in tension with other household labour and obligations. For men, the leisure space of the typical evening was 'time *after* work', a formally 'free' space, consisting of leisure options within and outside the home. For the women I interviewed, TV viewing generally was a way of temporarily 'breaking off' from ongoing housework and home-based responsibilities, often in fact accompanied by sewing, knitting, ironing and other types of activity that could be combined with viewing.

Two themes may be significant here. First, women interviewees were more likely to talk in terms of the 'companionship' of television, indicating that TV provided them with a valued means of diversion, an antidote against domestic isolation in the evenings:

Well, when he was away travelling with work, I used to watch it more – it gave me something to look forward to in the evenings – and then when we had the children, it was important for me in the evenings when he went out.

The second theme concerns the ways in which women interviewees often made reference to television viewing as an activity which could divert them from housework:

You'd start off watching something early in the evening – *Emergency Ward Ten* was a particular favourite of mine, or something like that – and if you weren't careful, the whole evening would be gone and you'd done nothing. If there was something on that I really wanted to watch I'd have to get the children off to bed and finish off tidying up after tea before I could settle down. I used to do that for the plays, *Play of the Week* I remember.

Implicitly, this kind of comment seems to reveal a sense in which time spent viewing for women could be a potential source of domestic guilt, given other household priorities. At least, women's responses in the interviews often indicate a process of 'preparing' for a valued programme: as one put it, 'clearing the decks' in order to enjoy uninterrupted viewing. This clearly lends some historical support to recent work on gender and styles of viewing,[39] in that the men interviewed did not appear to recall the activity of viewing as being either dependant upon, or related to, the completion of work in the home. In fact, several of the men talked about the value of television viewing as a relaxation after their day's work outside the home, and other leisure activities outside the home were more likely to compete for their attention. In this way the interviews seem to confirm that men and women, because of their positions within a conventional, patriarchal familial division of labour, developed structurally different relationships with television during this period.

I was concerned to develop this aspect of the research and to examine whether memories of television programme preference indicated some of the kinds of differences revealed in David Morley's work on 80s audiences. In general, I found that men's remembered viewing preferences tended to foreground television actuality – news, current affairs, documentaries and films. Women were more likely to recall dramas, either single plays or historical series, serials and films. Televised sports coverage is remembered as the preserve of men. Situation comedies and light entertainment or variety shows seem to be remembered as common viewing spaces in the schedules. Developing this aspect of the research more fully and precisely forms a major objective for future work.

A final issue I discussed with the interviewees concerned the implications of television's entry into the home for other leisure pursuits. Most interviewees noted that from the late 1950s onwards, television viewing had become a major way of spending their leisure time. In brief, most of those interviewed were able to document in some detail the kinds of 'pre-television', domestically based, pastimes that had, they felt, been displaced by TV. References here were most commonly made to a decline in playing cards and other kinds of games; less radio listening and reading of books; declining involvements with musical instruments, hobbies and so on.

Interviewees also recognised that leisure involvements outside the home were also gradually changed by television's appearance in the period. Many of the accounts noted in this context that their involvements in a whole range of non-domestic, sporting and social activities had undergone significant changes. Cinema-going was often singled out as something that had declined considerably. For some of the interviewees, television was perceived as a cause of widespread change in the nature of social gatherings in pubs, clubs and other social meeting places. In many cases however, changes in their own family relationships, notably in the form of children, had important consequences for their available leisure time during this period.

I hope in this rather schematic and exploratory account to have started to suggest some of the ways in which an important missing dimension in the history of British television needs to be addressed. After what has in effect been a pilot project, more carefully designed and considered work is required. In part, such work should be concerned to extend our understanding of the constitution and dynamics of particular domestically based viewing cultures from the 1950s and early 1960s onwards, and to understand how television viewing has developed as a 'naturalised' and integral component of household life and situated culture. Furthermore, increased understanding of the domestic conditions and cultures which govern personal television viewing and use has a vital part to play in gaining greater critical insight into the shifting historical and contemporary significance of television and other communication technologies in the transformation of post-war British culture.[40]

Notes

1. Hermann Bausinger, 'Media Technology and Daily Life', *Media, Culture and Society* vol. 6 no. 4, 1984.
2. Twenty-one interviews form the basis for this discussion, eleven of these were carried out in South Wales, six in North Yorkshire, and four in Kent. I used family and friendship contacts and networks to arrange the interviews, and on these terms, all of the interviewees were known to me in some capacity. The majority of interviews were with married couples (eighteen) and all of the interviews were tape recorded and took place in the interviewees' own homes (on three occasions with their video recorders recording programmes that were on at the time). Interviews lasted for approximately one hour. I used a combination of directive and non-directive questions (see M. Hammersley and P. Atkinson, *Ethnography: Principles in Practice* (London: Tavistock, 1983), ch. 5. All of the interviewees were white, British, sixty years old or over and in terms of social destination, middle-class professional householders. Where necessary, [M] and [W] identify the gender of the interviewee. On methods of oral history see P. Thompson, *The Voice of the Past: Oral History* (Oxford: Oxford University Press, 1978), and J. Tosh, *The Pursuit of History* (London: Longman, 1984). For an import-

ant discussion of interviews and research practice see E. Seiter, 'Making Distinctions in TV Audience Research: Case Study of a Troubling Interview', *Cultural Studies* vol. 4 no. 1, January 1990.

3. See, for example: Ann Gray, 'Reading the Audience', *Screen* vol. 28 no. 3, 1987; David Morley, *Family Television: Cultural Power and Domestic Leisure* (London: Comedia, 1986); Ellen Seiter, Hans Borchers, Gabriele Kreutzner and Eva-Maria Warth (eds.), *Remote Control : Television, Audiences and Cultural Power* (London: Routledge, 1989).

4. Alan O'Shea, 'Television as Culture: not just texts and readers', *Media, Culture and Society* vol. 11 no. 3, 1989.

5. David Chaney, 'A Symbolic Mirror of Ourselves: Civic Ritual in Mass Society', *Media, Culture and Society* vol. 5 no. 2, 1983. See also David Cardiff and Paddy Scannell, 'Broadcasting and National Unity', Ch. 7 in J. Curran *et al.* (eds.), *Impacts and Influences* (London: Methuen, 1987).

6. Radio and Television broadcasts of the Coronation on 13 June 1953 produced the largest domestic audience of viewers and listeners recorded to that date. BBC research suggested that 88 per cent of the adult population of the United Kingdom saw or listened to some part of the service. Furthermore, the event is widely regarded as the first broadcast event when viewers outnumbered listeners. BBC research indicated that 37 per cent of the broadcast audience listened to radio, predominantly in their own homes. The TV audience, on the other hand, was estimated at 51 per cent – approximately 20 million viewers. Over half of these watched in the homes of friends, relatives or neighbours, while at least 1.5 million viewed in public places: halls, shops, cinemas or pubs. See for summary, Robert Silvey, *Who's Listening?: The Story of BBC Audience Research* (London: Allen & Unwin, 1974), p. 165. Also Asa Briggs, *The History of Broadcasting in the United Kingdom, Volume 4: Sound and Vision* (Oxford University Press, 1979). Many of the interviewees I spoke to recalled watching the event on television in either domestic situations or these types of public location. I also spoke with one couple who were amused by my assumption that they would recall aspects of the televised event. From their home in Kent, the televised coverage was decidedly rejected in favour of attending and participating in the 'real' celebrations in London.

7. See for example Grace Wyndham Goldie, *Facing the Nation – TV & Politics 1936–76*, (London: Bodley Head, 1977); Leonard Miall (ed.), *Richard Dimbleby – Broadcaster* (London: BBC, 1966); Robin Day, *Television: A Personal Report* (London: Hutchinson, 1961).

8. See for recent summary: Ellen Seiter *et al.* (eds.), *Remote Control.*

9. Robert Silvey, *Who's Listening?*, p. 154. See also Asa Briggs, *Sound and Vision.*

10. Asa Briggs, *Sound and Vision*, pp. 187, 204.

11. Ibid., p. 161.

12. BBC, *The Public and the Programmes* (London: BBC, 1959). R. Silvey, and B. Emmett, 'What makes viewers choose', *New Society* no. 24, 14 March 1963, pp. 11–14.

13. See H. Himmelweit, A. N. Oppenheim, and P. Vince, *Television and the Child* (Oxford: Oxford University Press, 1958); Knight Committee Report, *Television and the Family* (London: HMSO, 1960).

14. See P. Barwise, and A. Ehrenberg, *Television and its Audience* (London: Sage, 1988). Also, J. Mallory Wober and Barrie Gunter, 'Television Research at Britain's IBA', *Journal of Broadcasting and Electronic Media* vol. 30 no. 1, Winter 1986.

15. Shaun Moores, 'The Box on the Dresser: Memories of Early Radio and Everyday Life', *Media, Culture and Society* vol. 10 no. 1, 1988.

16. See David Morley and Roger Silverstone, 'Domestic Communication – Technologies and Meanings', paper presented to the 1988 International Television Studies Confer-

ence. Subsequently published in abridged form, *Media, Culture and Society* vol. 12 no. 1, January 1990, p. 31–55.

17. Todd Gitlin, 'Televisions Screens: Hegemony in Transition' in M. Apple, (ed.), *Cultural and Economic Reproduction in Education* (London: Routledge and Kegan Paul, 1982).

18. Michael Chanan's discussion of the earlier emergence of the visual 'sights' and 'sites' of film in early cinema is useful and suggestive here. See *The Dream that Kicks* (London: Routledge Kegan Paul, 1982).

19. Jan-Uwe Rogge has recently used the term 'media career' to refer to the patterns of media contacts which characterise and constitute particular phases and stages of life, from childhood and through adulthood. See 'The Media in Everyday Family Life', ch. 9, in Seiter, E. *et al.* (eds.), *Remote Control*.

20. BBC 2 began regular colour transmissions in July 1967. This was extended to BBC 1 and ITV in November 1969.

21. In this context, Richard Dyer has provided a useful framework for the analysis of the 'internal dynamics' of television. See *Light Entertainment* (London: British Film Institute, 1974).

22. On this and other aspects of the economics of television growth see A. D. Bain, 'The Growth of Television Ownership in the UK', *International Economic Review* vol. 3 no. 2, May 1962.

23. A point noted in Bain's analysis, ibid., pp. 157–9.

24. The design, marketing and promotion of the domestic television receiver during this and subsequent periods provides an important area for future analysis. On design, see D. Chambers, Ph.D.Thesis, University of Kent, 1984, *Design and Designers: A Sociological Study of the Processes and Meaning of Product Styling*, pp. 229–271.

25. Source: Robert Silvey, *Who's Listening?*, p. 188.

26. Jennifer Bryce (cited in Morley and Silverstone, 'Domestic Communication') has developed a distinction that is relevant here, between 'monochronic' and 'polychronic' time orientations that characterise modes of family-TV relations. The monochronic form relates to planned, attentive viewing; the polychronic to unplanned viewing in tandem with other domestic activities. See J. Bryce, 'Family Time and TV Use' in T. Lindlof (ed.), *Natural Audiences* (Newbury Park: Sage, 1987).

27. Paddy Scannell, 'Radio Times: The temporal arrangements of broadcasting in the modern world', paper presented to the 1986 International Television Studies Conference.

28. For Raymond Williams, 'the central television experience is the fact of flow. . . . hardly anything is ever said about the characteristic experience of the flow sequence itself. It would be like trying to describe having read two plays, three newspapers, three or four magazines, on the same day that one has been to a variety show and a lecture and a football match. And yet in another way it is not like that at all, for though the items may be various the television experience has in some important ways unified them'. *Television: Technology and Cultural Form* (London: Fontana, 1974), p. 95.

29. Relations between 'liveness' as constructed on television, history and subjectivity have been recently explored by Mimi White, 'Television: A Narrative – A History', *Cultural Studies* vol. 3 no. 3, October 1989, pp. 282–300.

30. D. Morley and R. Silverstone, 'Domestic Communication', p. 13.

31. Pierre Bourdieu and Jean-Claude Passeron, *Reproduction in Education, Society and Culture* (London: Sage, 1977), p. 40. See also, Pierre Bourdieu, *Distinction: A Social Critique of the Judgement of Taste* (London: Routledge and Kegan Paul, 1986), ch. 3.

32. Mike Featherstone, 'Lifestyle and Consumer Culture', *Theory, Culture and Society* vol.

4, 1987, p. 64. See also, Graham Murdock, 'Class Stratification and Cultural Consumption; Some Motifs in the Work of Pierre Bourdieu (1977)', ch. 7. in F. Coulter, (ed.), *Freedom and Constraint : The Paradoxes of Leisure* (London: Routledge/Comedia, 1989).

33. Technically this choice was dependent upon domestic ownership of a new set capable of two channel reception and, as James Curran and Jean Seaton note: 'At first this was a tiny fraction of the total audience. Even as late as 1960 the ITA estimated in its annual report that fewer than 60 per cent of licence holders had two channel sets'. *Power without Responsibility: The Press and Broadcasting in Britain* (London: Routledge, 1988), p. 179.

34. Keith Bartlett, 'British Television in the 1950s; ITV and the Cult of Personality', paper presented to the 1986 International Television Studies Conference, p. 23. For additional analysis of the role of the Television Personality, see John Langer, 'Television's "Personality System" ', *Media, Culture and Society* vol. 3 no. 4, 1981, p. 351–65.

35. See for summary, Robert Silvey and B. P. Emmett, 'What makes Viewers Choose', *New Society* no. 24, 14 March 1963, pp. 11–14.

36. In this context, many of the interviewees specifically referenced 'Bronowski programmes' – *Insight, The Ascent of Man*.

37. The 'toddler's truce' referred to the 6–7 pm slot in the BBC schedule during which time there were no programmes transmitted, in part to make it easier for parents to persuade their young children to go to bed. The 'truce' ended in February 1957 when, under pressure from ITV to use this strategic slot, the BBC introduced *Tonight*, the current affairs news magazine programme. See Grace Wyndham Goldie, *Facing the Nation*, p. 209.

38. This theme should perhaps be taken to apply not only to children's viewing. More generally, television viewing and access to particular programmes entered the domestic 'reward structure' of the household. See for recent discussion of this idea: Geoff and Stella Hurd, 'The Centring Space', ch. 7. in Philip Simpson, (ed.), *Parents Talking Television: Television in the Home* (London: Comedia, 1987).

39. See David Morley, *Family Television*, ch. 6., and Ann Gray, 'Behind Closed Doors: Women and Video Recorders in the Home', in H. Baehr and G. Dyer (eds.), *Boxed in: Women and Television* (London: Routledge and Kegan Paul/Pandora, 1987).

40. My thanks to Hugh McKay and Shaun Moores for their comments on earlier drafts of this paper. I should also formally acknowledge the patience, goodwill and interest of those who talked to me about their memories of television in the period under review.

'Grandstand', the Sports Fan and the Family Audience

GARRY WHANNEL

A key characteristic of television form is the magazine nature of many of its programme forms. The magazine programme, the collection of discrete items linked by a presenter, has been a standard form in many areas of television. Stuart Hall argues that television is a hybrid medium, in which studio situations characteristically mix the modes of transmission, and that sport programmes like *Grandstand*, which combine live, studio, and filmed inserts are television originals, with nothing quite like them in any other medium. Consequently attention should be paid to that feat of 'collective socio-technical co-ordination and control', the assembly process.[1]

In relation to sport, three variants of the form, all of which emerged during the 1950s, have proved remarkably resilient. These are the Saturday afternoon programme, the Saturday evening highlights, and the mid-week magazine. These programme forms construct, out of a diversity of different events, and different items, a unity: the unity of the world of sport. Our entrance into this world is mediated by the presenter – our guide to the programme and its events.

The presenter provides the articulating point for the set of representations that the programme assembles. He (and to date it is invariably 'he') articulates the discourse that enables the seamless suturing of a range of discursive elements into the unity of the programme form. The unity produced is the unity of the 'world' of sport, separated from the real world of social and political conflict. The mode of address employed to hail us to this world has to accomplish two conflicting points of identification. First, a range of enthusiasts for different sports have to be positioned as generalised sports fans, willing to take an interest in all sports. Second, television's need to win and hold a large heterogenous audience means that the address must also hail and position both sports fans and the general audience. The conflict between expert and popular modes of representation has to be negotiated.

In this article, having first made some remarks about the earliest forms of sports broadcasting, I want to focus on three key phases of development. First of all, on the formats of *Sportsview* and *Sports Special* as pioneering programmes of the mid-50s; then, and centrally, on *Grandstand* as the BBC's highly successful formula for Saturday afternoon coverage; finally, on the competition offered by the ITV network.

The magazine form of sports coverage has a significant pre-history in radio and in the early experimental period of television between 1936–39.[2] As a result of the development and refinement of the multi-source technique (constructing radio programmes from a number of separate sources), and the expansion of the Outside Broadcast (OB) Department resources, it became possible to launch in 1934 the first 'afternoons of broadcast sport'. They involved fairly rapid shifts from one sport to another – cricket, tennis, rifle shooting, and speedboat racing, for example; or football, rugger, hockey and boxing, 'without loss of continuity, so as to give the listener a total experience, not confused but blended'.[3]

This marks the first point at which broadcasting so clearly identified Saturday afternoon with sports. There were to be a number of radio variants of the magazine form, *Sports Review*, *Calling all Sportsmen*, *Sports Special* (a pre-war radio programme not to be confused with the 50s TV programme of the same title), *Tomorrows Sport*, *National Sportsreel*, *Sporting Record*, *Saturday Sports Report*, *Sports Round-Up*, and *Sports Forum*.[4]

In television too a monthly sports review, *Sporting Magazine*, appeared as early as 1937.[5] This however would appear to have had less influence, as it was not until four years after the 1946 re-launch of television that a magazine format appeared in the shape of *Television Sports Magazine*. This is not to say, however, that the forming of programmes out of collections of items was an unused method in the 40s. An early feature on golf, an outside broadcast from Moor Park on a Saturday afternoon, featured a brief history of the club, a lesson by the club professional, some views of members in play, and a demonstration by three professionals.[6]

The practice of surrounding major events with preview and *post-mortem* material also began to develop in the early years of television as this extract from a memo makes clear:

3. Wembley Preview.
I have told Madden that we can concoct something to follow the Newsreel on Cup Final morning. The programme will not show crowds collecting but will show the interior of the stadium and will include some interviews with stadium staff and some discussion of the teams' prospects.[7]

Foundations: 'Sportsview' and 'Saturday Sports Special'
It was in the years between 1950–58 that three of the most basic forms of sport programme – the Saturday afternoon coverage, the Saturday night football highlights and the mid-week magazine, all found their place in the schedule. The process began with *Television Sport Magazine*, which appears to have originated in a proposal from outside the BBC in the late 1940s. George McPartlin and William Latto of the CCPR suggested to Peter Dimmock a 'Television Sport Club', for which they produced a detailed proposal. It was on the air fortnightly from various locations, starting from summer 1950. Twenty-one editions were produced between 1950 and 1952. The programme was aimed at 'people already interested in sport or who might become so. The first thing therefore is to attract and hold attention.'[8]

The programmes were to feature a wide variety of items, including demonstrations of technique, quizzes, personality profiles, actual competitions, items on jobs to do with sport, reviews of sports publications, making of sports equipment. Head of Sport, S.J. de Lotbiniere emphasised that 'the material must be interesting and as universal as possible'.[9] In a publicity handout for the programme by editor Berkeley Smith, it is obvious that the programme was attempting to put together an audience combining sport fans and casual viewers:

> In *Television Sport Magazine*, we are aiming to cater not only for the great body of knowledgeable sports enthusiasts in this country, but also for the thousands of viewers who have been introduced to sports through their television screens.[10]

This characterisation of the target audience could be seen as a fundamental principle underlying much television sport, and as a key factor in the development of its particular mode of address. Television always has to fight to assemble heterogenous audiences, and in sports coverage the conflict between expert and popular modes of address always has to be handled. The programme had a degree of success, although the Controller of Television appears to have desired to end the run after the first six editions.[11]

In a new proposal for a sport magazine programme, Kenneth Wolstenholme argued that *Television Sport Magazine* lacked topicality, and suggested a programme that would mix the past, the present, the future and the controversial.[12] But the 'controversial' was always likely to be marginalised. Alec Sutherland, in a 1951 memo, suggested an item on the soccer players' struggle for better conditions.[13] This was rejected by Lotbiniere because of the delicate state of negotiations over TV football. The tendency of sport to attempt to insulate itself from social and political conflict was already marking television. Like any specialist journalists, the dependency of the BBC Outside Broadcast department upon good relations with their suppliers, the sports organisations, was inevitably going to hamper any attempts to establish a tradition of investigative reporting.

Television Sport Magazine proved to be only a trial run for the BBC's longest running regular programme, *Sportsview*, (assuming that one regards *Sportsnight* as a continuation of the same programme with a different title). The programme that was to establish the Wednesday night sports slot began originally as a fortnightly programme, but its success meant an early change to weekly output. From the start, the programme was intended to win a large audience – it was aimed consciously at the family audience:

> Mother may not be especially interested in sport, but we still want her to enjoy *Sportsview* if possible.[14]

The expert/popular distinction is frequently displaced onto a male/female one. The sports fan, as possessor of knowledge, is implicitly male. Just as 'family audience' denotes the general audience as opposed to the 'sports fan', 'mother' represents lack of knowledge and competence, which is assumed to be the domain of masculinity.[15]

There is no doubt that *Sportsview* made a major impact when it arrived in

Spring 1954. Apart from *Panorama*, it is the sole survivor from the pre-ITV era of television:

> First a fortnightly, then a weekly series, it reflected not just an interest in sport, but an exhilarating relish for the professional opportunities now being opened up fast by new technical facilities. Dimmock and McGivern got the management of the day to spend far more resources on a single programme than any half-hour programme had had before. It was the first series programme to operate independent of a department. Within two months it was clear that something quite new and exceptional had arrived. It was no coincidence that when *Panorama* went weekly it also began to mingle outside broadcasts, film, studio techniques, and to develop a *Sportsview*-type style of presentation in which a very strong unified editorial drive and command was apparent.[16]

Many of the BBC's major successes in the 50s – *Panorama*, *Sportsview*, *Tonight*, *Monitor* – were variants of this magazine assemblage. The *Sportsview* style rested on immediacy, slick presentation, and a focus of attention on sporting personalities. There was an emphasis on 'the latest news', the programme was described as living 'by its topicality' and there was a stress on 'what's going to happen'.[17] The BBC *Annual Report* for 1954–55 boasted that almost every sporting personality of note was interviewed in the course of the year. It was the first BBC programme to have its own full-time production unit. With the approach of competition the stakes were high. In the autumn of 1955, as ITV was launched, *Sportsview* staged a two-hour special, and devoted a whole programme to women's sport in an effort to attract more women viewers.[18] But the almost entirely male BBC Sport department, together with the male dominance of the organisation, performance, and cultural context of British sport, ensured that women's sport remained a marginal element.

Sportsview grew along with the expansion of the OB department, which spent much of the 50s pressing for greater resources. In 1955 Dimmock was pressing for an increase in the film allowance to a minimum of one thousand feet per week (around twenty-five minutes). He also wanted a full-time film editor, assistant, cameramen and sound cameras assigned to the programme. In 1956, when the average actual weekly costs of the programme were between £1200 and £1600, requests were made to raise its official weekly allocation from £1250 to £1600.[19]

In 1955 *Sportsview* was placed in an 8.30–9.00 pm slot on Wednesday night. Dimmock regarded this as the best of both worlds – not late enough to have to pay overnight expenses to participants, and yet late enough to permit the inclusion of an afternoon football story. The programme's place in the schedule was a cause of continual discussion. Paul Fox referred to the need to balance the start-time between being late enough for film reports while early enough, in summer, for live open air OBs, and suggested 8.30 or 8.45 pm.[20]

It was, then, upon a combination of organisational, professional, and technical advance, that *Sportsview* attempted to win a general audience, and became the first fully successful magazine format programme. The fact that it had its own independent production team meant that it established many of the practices and conventions for subsequent developments in BBC sport.[21]

In 1954–55 *Sportsview* used film extracts of football matches, usually lasting two to three minutes in length. The plan was then made to launch a new Saturday evening programme, with filmed highlights from three matches, news and interviews of football generally, and items on other sports. The new Saturday evening schedules contained two sport slots, *Todays Sport* at 7.10–7.25 pm, and *Sports Special*, from 10.00–10.30 pm. The latter programme presented considerable logistical problems. Film had to be flown by plane or helicopter back to London and rushed by high-speed motorbike, while high-speed cars transported commentators and producers from the airport to the studios.[22] This process was emphasised in the programme's publicity:

> Tonight at 10.15 *Sports Special*, the first edition of a weekly series is on the air. The BBC *Sportsview* unit, with the assistance of studios and film cameras, and live outside broadcasts from key centres throughout the British Isles, will present up to the minute coverage of the best in today's sport. Aeroplanes, a helicopter and a fleet of cars and motorcycles are standing by to rush personalities to the studios. Tonight's programme is introduced by Peter Dimmock.[23]

Sportsview Unit editor Paul Fox stressed the need for slickness and punch and strict time-keeping, and emphasised the importance of the regional contributions in the competition with ITV.[24] The introduction to the first show (10 September 1955) made a point of addressing the sports follower more specifically than *Sportsview*:

> Good evening and welcome to the new programme. Its title is *Saturday Sports Special*, and it is especially for sports enthusiasts. I do stress this, because with the *Sportsview* programme on Wednesday night, we try to include something to interest all the family. But with this programme we aim to give you, with film reports and personality interviews, a complete picture of the day's news in sport.[25]

The opposition here between the 'sports enthusiast' and 'all the family' provides a distinction between two different ways of addressing the audience. It also references again the implicit 'maleness' of the concept of sports fans – no direct reference is made to gender, but our knowledge of cultural codes links sports fans and maleness. The assumption, implied in the opposition between sports enthusiast/all the family, is that the sports enthusiast being addressed is male.

Sports Special was well received by the press, although there were great technical problems, with timing and co-ordination of various regional contributions. Controller of Television, Cecil McGivern, was also unhappy that there was far too much talk and not enough action. He called for a programme with at least 95 per cent film and telerecording of the day's sport.[26] In reply to Dimmock about this demand, Fox pointed out that even 30 per cent film was straining the resources. The programme had only six cameramen, three editors and two writers, but even if extra staff were available, there were no extra cameras (sound cameras were at that time hard to obtain) and there was not enough cutting-room equipment.[27]

McGivern was still unhappy about the amount of action in the programme and said, 'I feel that this present *Sports Special* is wrong and will NOT achieve a majority audience. And a majority audience is from my point of view its purpose.'[28] Dimmock replied that the programme now had twenty minutes of film. To show more would require greater camera, sound, editing, transport, and laboratory facilities. Agreements with the Football League only allowed fifteen minutes of football. Cost prohibited film coverage from Scotland, so their contribution had to be live (and therefore, basically, news and interviews), and the whole staff situation was desperate.[29] It is, however, clear that during this period the amount of action in the programme was increased, and the pressure made the programme aware of the need to win a broad audience. In other words, the segmented mode of address – explicitly pitching the programme at 'sports enthusiasts' – was not seen as a viable strategy in the era of competition.

Three features of the programme are worthy of note. The emphasis on slickness points to the growing importance of technical professionalism and to the practice of achieving transparency, a seamless representation in which audience awareness of technical intervention is minimised. The emphasis on pace, immediacy and action shows the commitment to the production of excitement as a prime entertainment value. In some ways the contradiction between realist style and entertainment value is here resolved under the sign of 'slickness, pace, and immediacy'. The initial target audience, the sports fan, in itself to a degree a television construct, has to be modified in the light of pressure to win the 'majority' audience too.

The Winning Format: 'Grandstand'

As sport coverage expanded during the 50s, the BBC had regular outside broadcasts on Saturday afternoons, sometimes from two or three separate locations. It made increasing sense for these OBs to be grouped together under a programme heading.[30] Taking this further, using a studio presenter to link the various OBs would make it possible to handle fluctuations in timing or problems of weather. It would also be possible to include a constant flow of up-to-date news. Early in 1958, Dimmock asked Bryan Cowgill to produce proposals for a Saturday afternoon sports programme. Cowgill's original proposal is in fact a close description of the form the programme eventually took.[31]

The programme would run for around four hours with at least three separate OBs, concluding with results and reports. Racing was expected to have prominence as the one major sport regularly available during the October–December period earmarked for the experiment. Cowgill stressed the project as an opportunity to present multiple OBs in 'a much more attractive package than has been achieved before'. The studio and technical facilities needed were to be important to the success of the programme – teleprinters, extra telephones and operators, telecine for 16mm and 35mm, and omnibus talkback between the studio control room and the various OB points.

After a meeting of OB members in April 1958, and further discussion, Cowgill produced a more detailed proposal, which was more specific about problems of timing and the need for new technical facilities – notably access to an Ampex video recorder, the first video recorder, and only recently commercially available.[32] He stressed the importance of team-work and said it would be desirable to have the same camera crew for at least six weeks, particularly at the start of the programme's run.[33]

It was decided to go ahead, but there were many problems during the development of the programme. The major one was that the proposed schedule, even revised to finish at 5.00 pm, meant cutting Children's Hour back to forty-five minutes. This was strongly resisted and the BBC hierarchy insisted that *Grandstand* finish at 4.45 pm, despite strong protest from Paul Fox:

> Quite frankly, unless we can give the results AS THEY COME IN and stay on the air until 5.00 o'clock to present them in tabulated form the programme is not worth doing at all. I see this as a sports news programme and I do not see how we can go off the air at the very moment THE news of the day is happening.[34]

At stake here was a struggle between two different attempts to construct the audience through scheduling. The BBC has always played a part in the construction of childhood and its associated rituals, through such programmes as *Listen With Mother*, Children's Hours and through scheduling devices like the 'toddler's truce'; but the sanctity of Children's Hour was now challenged by a rather different project, that of inscribing Saturday afternoon as the domain of sport. The only way *Grandstand* could be given its full power as a winner of audiences was to allow the programme to finish with a comprehensive results service providing a strong reason for viewers to remain tuned, as well as helping to service the gambling industry.

It was only after *Grandstand* had been on the air for a while that Fox's argument carried the day. Other battles took place over the installation of teleprinters, the financial allocation to the programme and the need for new technical facilities, particularly an Ampex video recorder and a Lawley fast film developer. It was less than three weeks before the programme went on the air in autumn 1958 that Fox got Dimmock to agree to the title *Grandstand*, in preference to Dimmock's own suggestion, 'Out and About'![35] The launch of the programme made great play of the immediacy with which the results and news would be brought to the screen and the human and technical system was described in detail:

> Around Peter Dimmock, who will introduce the programme for the first few weeks, there'll be gathered all the machinery that goes with high-speed sports reporting. Batteries of tape machines, a giant sized scoreboard, the

David Coleman introduces a 1959 edition of *Grandstand*.

sub-editors table – they'll all be on view in the studio so that not a moment is lost in passing the latest sports news on to viewers at home.[36]

Indeed the programme has always made a point of including the apparatus of fast news in the picture, so sub-editors can be seen in the background, presenters have news handed to them while on the air, and of course the football results were eventually to be displayed as they arrived on the teleprinter.

A great stress was placed by Fox and Cowgill on the need for technical slickness, particularly in the constant hand-overs between studio and outside that were a feature of the programme's style.[37] The introduction of the programme – with a menu elaborated with brief appetite-whetting visits to the OB sites – was, in 1958, similar to the present form.

Once the programme format was established it was clear that the BBC had a success. It remains in some ways the most complex regular programme – being four and a half hours of predominantly live television using multiple outside sources. Originally it was felt that the special technical and presentational problems would require the use of the same studio crew each week, but it gradually became a matter of routinised professionalism.[38]

For all that, the programme placed great demands on the professionalism of the crew, particularly producer and presenter, and Cowgill stressed the crucial importance of organisation and teamwork.[39] Similarly, presenter Frank Bough stressed the importance of preparation and future planning:

> ... the homework, the meticulous preparation, the problems of timing, of mixing the *Grandstand* programme so that it never droops in the middle, of making sure events do not clash ... the programme's groundwork is laid way in advance when contracts are signed with the various sporting bodies. Some events therefore we can block into the programme schedule months, even years in advance. Rugby Union internationals, the Cup Final, the Boat Race, Wimbledon, the dog race meetings, the Test Matches – they have all been negotiated and paid for, so we know they're there.[40]

Bough talks of the need to produce information rapidly and faultlessly, the need for producer, editor, and presenter to 'get used to each other's professional habits', and the difficulties of working with a talkback system through which the presenters hear the combined voices of everyone in the control room, the VT engineers, vision and sound engineers, and production assistants checking timings. Indeed it may well be a mark of the thorough and complete professionalism needed to operate a programme like *Grandstand*, that both Cowgill and Fox subsequently rose to managing director level with Thames and Yorkshire respectively. *Grandstand* firmly established the concept of Saturday afternoon for sport.

Like *Sportsview*, *Grandstand* refined the whole process of articulating diverse elements into a unity, by establishing a strong overall programme identity, linked to a personality presenter, giving the assemblage a strong coherence. A technically ambitious programme, it required a routinised professionalism in which technical slickness was paramount and immediacy foregrounded as a point of identification within the mode of address.

So in just four years between 1954 and 1958, the BBC established the basic shape of regular sports broadcasting. *Sportsview* founded the concept of the regular midweek magazine, becoming *Sportsnight* after a brief period as *Sportsnight with Coleman*. ITV opened with a mid-week sports magazine *Cavalcade of Sport*, which was not a success. Their subsequent attempts to challenge the BBC in sport have, as noted elsewhere, been handicapped by the ITV structure and the in-built strengths of the BBC. It is worth noting that when Cowgill shifted to Thames Television in 1978, his first move was to hire Sam Leitch from the BBC as Head of Sport, and they began drawing up plans for a regular mid-week sports programme. This plan met opposition from the network committee, particularly from ATV and (ironically) Yorkshire, who were only interested in the programme when it featured football.

Grandstand established the link between Saturday afternoon and sport on television, and ITV reciprocated in 1965 with *World of Sport*, after again some tension between the network companies as to whether sport was the best way of winning viewers to this slot. More recently, the increase in Sunday sport has led to an increasing number of multiple OB programmes, a pattern acknowledged by

190

the BBC in 1981 when they launched a summer magazine on BBC 2 called *Summer Grandstand*.

While *Sports Special* nominally featured a variety of sports, the pattern it established was for weekend football highlights. With the development of video technology, Anglia launched an evening highlights programme in 1962. The BBC, caught on the hop for once, followed up with *Match of the Day*, originally started in 1964 on BBC 2 in the early evening, and eventually moved to BBC 1 at around 10 pm. ITV began regular football highlights programmes like *The Big Match* on Sunday afternoons from 1965. So the period from 1954–58 saw the establishment of the main variants of the magazine format as far as sport was concerned.

Bough discusses the difference between the *Grandstand* and *Sportsview* formats:

> *Grandstand* of course is the great events programme. It is about action, fast moving pictures, horses tearing across the screen, motor cars roaring in every direction, sixes being struck in top class cricket. There is a pace about *Grandstand* which dictates that a slow, quiet, thoughtful piece of reporting is really quite out of place.
>
> But in *Sportsview* each Wednesday for thirty-five minutes or so you could vary the pace and change gear in much the same way as we do in *Nationwide*, another magazine programme. There was room for, say, an action report on the Monaco Grand Prix, well shot on film the previous Sunday, well cut for the best pictures with me diving about the pits getting lap by lap reaction from drivers and mechanics as well as a background piece shot on the Berkshire Downs about the training of a great race horse.[41]

But what is more revealing here is the similarity: the impulse in both cases to produce a programme that constructs from a heterogeneity – the followers of various sports, and the casual viewer – a homogeneous audience of 'sport fans'. *Sportsview*'s mode of address was at its most successful when motor-racing fans could be induced to watch the showjumping, when showjumping fans watched the grand prix, and when casual viewers lapped up both.

ITV's Challenge: 'World of Sport'
The BBC's attitude towards the appearance of a competitor has been characterised as complacent. The Outside Broadcast Department, however, is generally regarded as an exception to this. Despite the rapidly rising fees being demanded by sports organisations, who, seeing the approach of ITV, realised they were in a stronger position, the BBC endeavoured to secure a number of long-term contracts with sports. Their success in this was to make it difficult for the new commercial companies to make progress in sports coverage.[42]

This was certainly recognised as a problem within ITV. Bill Ward, who had been with the BBC since 1936, joined ATV in 1955 as Head of Light Entertainment, and he later commented on this period that Dimmock was the only man at the BBC who thought ITV would succeed, and he actively tried to make life as difficult

191

as possible.[43] Dimmock also employed key staff on a contractual basis, with large increases in pay to discourage them from going to ITV.

Because of the federal system, the early plans of ITV were diffuse. Four different companies, with separate bases and orientations, each had their own ideas of how to provide the service. It was only after the first few years that the stabilising mechanism of the network system began to impose a greater co-ordination and hence homogeneity upon the programme output.

None of the first four companies seem to have had sport as a very high priority.[44] ATV's base in entrepreneurial show business made them ill-suited to relate to the amateur paternalism characteristic of British sport organisation, as suggested by the story that Lew Grade, overhearing an ATV staffer phoning the Amateur Boxing Association and the Amateur Athletic Association, sternly told him that ATV wanted no dealings with amateurs, only professionals.[45]

Associated Rediffusion's (AR) approach, based upon straightforward populist commercial principles such as 'give the people what they want', was no closer to the dominant traditional values of the sports administrators:

> Lets face it once and for all. The public likes girls, wrestling, bright musicals, quiz shows, and real-life drama. We gave them the Halle Orchestra, Foreign Press Club, floodlit football, and visits to the local fire station. Well, we've learned. From now on, what the public wants, it's going to get.[46]

Granada and AR had no access to weekend slots, and while AR attempted a sport magazine, *Cavalcade*, Granada never made sport a priority. The weekend companies, ATV and ABC, were more active. ATV valued the world of entertainment more highly, with sport occupying a relatively low place, while ABC from the start saw the importance of OBs to their two day output.[47] These two companies together spearheaded the attempts to outbid the BBC during the 50s.

Several factors mitigated against strong ITV competition over sport. First, the BBC was consolidated in the field. They had developed over many years expertise, equipment, contacts and contracts. They had much of the available production talent under contract, and, thanks to Dimmock, most major sports under long-term exclusive contracts.

Second, the regional structure prevented ITV from benefitting from the economies of scale. No single company was large enough, or had a big enough audience, for it to be worth investing substantial capital in OB facilities, and no single company could muster large bids for exclusive contracts. ABC, as a weekend company, had most incentive, and did make a determined but unsuccessful bid to get the rights to televise league football in the 1950s. Each company had its own set of priorities. Competition with the BBC required co-operation between the companies, and this was hard to establish with the network system itself only gradually taking shape in an *ad hoc* manner. Had the ITA opted for franchises based on programme type, rather than region, a commercial contractor could have been in a considerably stronger position to challenge the BBC. Similarly, had the companies opted to establish, along with ITN, a nationally based, jointly owned sport company, ITV sport would have been in a stronger position.

Third, sport was not in the mid-50s an obvious audience winner. The Olympics and The World Cup had yet to become major television events, and in the days before colour, action replay, slow motion, video editing, and communication satellites, sport was yet to become a major source of television spectacle. Only showjumping and tennis were seen as reaching both sexes effectively, and ITV did indeed compete with BBC in covering Wimbledon during the late 50s. The regional structure continued to present problems:

> The toughest battles are about the weekend: no one seems able to agree what the network should put out. While London Weekend puts up ambitious plans for more culture, Sir Lew Grade at ATV clamours for more variety and films, especially on Saturday afternoons when the commercial network tries to outdo the BBC in sport. Since the BBC have long been the prime network for sports, Sir Lew would happily leave the games to the BBC and offer a movie on ITV. 'We've never really resolved it,' admitted one network controller. 'Our plans for Saturday have never come off, which is one reason the BBC does so well at weekends.'[48]

The ITA was unhappy about the situation during the early 60s. They pressed for greater competition over sport, and continually expressed concern about professional wrestling, regarded as unrespectable in sporting terms:[49]

> There had been almost continuous concern about ITV's coverage of sport since the summer of 1962, when serious attention had to be given by ABC and ATV to the failure of the Saturday afternoon sports programmes to compete with any success at all with the BBC's *Grandstand*. Eventually ABC came forward in 1964 with plans for a new approach which led to the launching in association with ATV of *World of Sport* in the autumn of that year.[50]

In 1965 ATV and ABC had launched *World of Sport* as a joint operation, and in 1965–66 they contracted with the Football League to televise football highlights on a Sunday. However, the ITA were still pressing for improvements in sports coverage.[51] Various attempts were made to re-jig *World of Sport*, but by 1967–68 the ITA were still sounding apologetic:

> Although the overall standard of the events broadcast in this programme was not consistently high, in terms of either importance or general popularity, they covered a wide range of tastes and interests in the sporting field.[52]

The programme was considerably revamped after the franchise reallocation of 1967–68. LWT took over the London weekend, ATV going to the midlands, and ABC becoming the dominant partner in Thames, in effect taking over Associated Rediffusion. The dominant weekend companies were now LWT and ATV, but in fact LWT from now on assumed the initiative, taking over *World of Sport*. They introduced *On The Ball*, the football preview, into *World of Sport*, and in 1969 the racing was placed into one, integrated, segment of the programme. There appeared to be a feeling that the fragmented approach of BBC's *Grandstand* did not work for ITV, either because of the lesser appeal of some of their sports, or because of the advertising breaks:

> The long standing method of Saturday afternoon sports coverage was out-dated; far from satisfying the viewer, it was causing annoyance and frustration. That method meant watching for three or four hours to catch maybe half an hour of the one sport the viewer wanted to watch.[53]

It is clear that the programme form of BBC's *Grandstand* itself acted as a constraint on ITV. Unable to copy it, they had to define themselves against it. The structure of *World of Sport* was now in five sections: On The Ball, Racing, International Sports Special, Professional Wrestling, and the results sequence. LWT also introduced in 1968–69 a more elaborate football highlights programme, *The Big Match*, on Sunday afternoons.

A significant move for ITV was the decision in 1966–67 to establish a central sports unit, which would be responsible for acquisition of transmission rights and planning of sports programmes on behalf of the network.[54] In August of 1967, a Director of Sport was appointed and transmission rights for the Football League Cup, the Gillette Cup, and Brands Hatch motor-racing were acquired. The ITA commented that, 'in general there were encouraging signs of a new impetus in the presentation of sport on ITV'.[55]

The basic priorities for Independent Television Sport, as the central unit became known, were to secure rights to more of the major national sporting events and to improve the production and presentation of sport by building up a strong team of producers and commentators and acquiring more sophisticated equipment. Acquiring rights caused problems:

> with increasing competition from the BBC – strongly entrenched for many years in sports such as swimming, athletics, cricket and rugby – there was little doubt that the task of attracting a majority of the sporting audience to Independent Television would be a long one.[56]

Indeed, despite the more recent acquisition of exclusive contracts for British athletics, from 1985, and the Football League, from 1988, ITV remains unable to dislodge BBC from its dominant position, firmly established by the 1960s. Consequently, television sport remains firmly marked by the production practices, representational styles, professional ideologies and programme forms that had their formative period in the BBC OB department between 1950–1970.

I would like to thank the BBC Written Archives Centre for permission to quote archive documents, and the staff at the Centre for their invariable helpfulness and patience.

Notes

File numbers beginning with T all refer to files in the BBC Written Archives Centre at Caversham.

1. Stuart Hall, *TV as a Medium and its Relation to Culture* (Birmingham: CCCS Stencilled Paper, CCCS, 1975), pp. 95–96.
2. David Cardiff, 'The Serious and the Popular', in *Media, Culture and Society* vol. 2 no. 1, January 1980, pp. 29–48.
3. Asa Briggs, *The Golden Age of Wireless* (London: Oxford University Press, 1965), p. 119.
4. See Asa Briggs, *The History of Broadcasting in The United Kingdom, Volume 4: Sound and Vision* (London: Oxford University Press, 1979), p. 849; John Snagge and Michael Barsley, *The Vintage Years of Radio* (London: Pitman, 1972), pp. 78–84; and Eamonn Andrews and Angus MacKay, *Sports Report* (London: Heinemann, 1954).
5. Gordon Ross, *Television Jubilee*, (London: W. H. Allen, 1961), p. 53.
6. BBC: Notes on meeting to discuss programme, 15 December 1948 (T14/487).
7. BBC Memo from Lotbiniere, HOB to HTelP, 17 April 1950 (T16/128).
8. BBC note on proposed Television Sports Club series, S. J. De Lotbiniere, HOB, 20 June 1950 (T14/1178).
9. Ibid.
10. Publicity note for *Television Sport Magazine*, Berkeley Smith, BBC, 1950 (T14/1178).
11. BBC Memo from HOB to CTelP, 7 November 1950 (T14/1178).
12. BBC Memo from Wolstenholme to Dimmock, 3 September 1951 (T14/1178).
13. BBC Memo from Alec Sutherland, 6 July 1951 (T14/1178).
14. Paul Fox, quoted in K. Baily, (ed.), *The Television Annual for 1956.*
15. Garry Whannel, 'Sit Down With Us: TV Sport as Armchair Theatre', in Sue Glyptis (ed.), *Leisure and the Media* (London: Leisure Studios Association, Conference Papers no. 16, 1983).
16. Peter Black, *The Mirror in the Corner* (London: Hutchinson, 1972), p. 132.
17. Briggs, *Sound and Vision*, pp. 850–852.
18. Ibid., p. 853.
19. BBC Memo from OB organiser to HPP Tel, 9 March 1956 (T14/1192/2).
20. BBC Memo from Fox to HOB Tel, 4 May 1956 (T14/1192/2).
21. Garry Whannel, 'Televising Sport: The Archaeology of a Professional Practice', in Judy White (ed.), *Leisure: Politics Planning & People Vol. 5: The Media And Cultural Forms*, (Brighton: Leisure Studies Association, 1986).
22. Ken Wolstenholme, *Sports Special* (London: Sportsmens Book Club, 1958), pp. 28–35.
23. Announcement for *Programme Parade*, 10 September 1955 (T14/1182/1).
24. BBC Memo from Paul Fox, September 1955 (T14/1182/1).
25. Programme Script for *Saturday Sport Special* (BBC), 10 September 1955 (T14/1182/1).
26. BBC Memo from CtelP to HOBTel, 12 September 1955 (T14/1182/1).
27. BBC Memo from Fox to Dimmock, 16 September 1955 (T14/1182/1).
28. BBC Memo from CtelP to HOB Dimmock, 30 September 1955 (T14/1182/4).
29. BBC Memo from HOB Dimmock to CtelP McGivern, 7 November 1955 (T14/1182/4).
30. BBC Memo AHOB Alan Chivers to *Radio Times*, 23 March 1958 (T14/493/1).
31. BBC Memo Cowgill to Dimmock, 10 April 1958 (T14/493/1).
32. Notes on meeting, 14 April 1958, re Saturday Sport, BBC (T14/493/1).
33. BBC Memo Cowgill to Dimmock, 21 July 1958 (T14/493/1).
34. BBC Memo from Fox to Dimmock, 1 August 1958 (T14/493/1).
35. BBC Memo from Dimmock, 29 August 1958 (T14/493/1).

36. Note for *Radio Times*, 22 September 1958 (T14/493/2 File 1b).
37. BBC Memo from Cowgill, 24 September 1958 (T14/493/2 File 1b).
38. Ross, *Television Jubilee*, p. 204.
39. David Coleman, (ed.), *Grandstand TV Book of Sports* (London: BBC, 1960), pp. 163–69.
40. Frank Bough, *Cue Frank* (London: MacDonald Futura, 1980), p. 64.
41. Bough, *Cue Frank*, pp. 46–47.
42. Black, *The Mirror in the Corner*, p. 130.
43. Bill Ward in *Broadcast Special*, 22 September 1976, p. 14.
44. In 1954, as a water-testing exercise, the ITA asked for applications from interested parties and among twenty-five, one offered to provide a supply of sport programming (see Black, *The Mirror in the Corner*, p. 71).
45. See Bill Ward in *Broadcast Special*, 22 September 1976, pp. 12–16.
46. Roland Gillett, quoted in Black, *The Mirror in the Corner*, p. 21.
47. See Howard Thomas, *With an Independent Air* (London: Weidenfeld and Nicolson, 1977), p. 157.
48. Timothy Green, *The Universal Eye* (London: Bodley Head, 1972), p. 108.
49. *ITA Annual Report* 1964–65, p. 22.
50. Bernard Sendall, *Independent Television in Britain, V2 1958–68* (London: Macmillan, 1983), p. 238.
51. *ITA Annual Report* 1965–66, p. 23.
52. *ITA Annual Report* 1967–68, p. 25.
53. *ITA Handbook*, 1971.
54. *ITA Annual Report* 1966–67, p. 22.
55. *ITA Annual Report* 1967–68, p. 25.
56. *ITA Annual Report* 1968–69, p. 17.

All Bark and No Bite
The Film Industry's Response to Television

EDWARD BUSCOMBE

A full-page advertisement in the *Guardian* on 27 November 1989 featured a large picture of John Wayne. Underneath was the heading, 'Some people strive all their lives for an Oscar. We've just picked up 122.' Following a touching account of how the Duke broke down in tears when he was finally awarded his Oscar for *True Grit*, the advertisement announced that British Satellite Broadcasting would shortly be going on the air with movies boasting over 100 Oscar awards between them:

> We're actually spending $750 million in Hollywood acquiring TV rights to over 2,000 screen gems from Columbia, Warner Bros., MGM/United Artists, Universal, Paramount and Orion. This means that BSB's Movie Channel can screen full-length feature films at 6.00, 8.00, 10.00 and 12.00 every night.
>
> And, as we've already explained, these won't be any old films.
>
> We know (because we asked you) that the films you really wanted to see were recent releases.
>
> On BSB, six nights a week, you'll be able to see films never before shown on British television.
>
> For these 20-odd first-run films a month, we intend to ask less than £2.50 a week.
>
> Not bad when you consider that it could cost around £40 a month to hire as many 'new' movies on video.
>
> To ensure the films really are bang up-to-date, we've even bought the rights from major studios of films that haven't been made yet.

Only towards the end of the advertising copy are we given, much more briefly, details of what BSB will show on its other four channels. The launching of BSB more than doubled overnight the number of officially sanctioned television channels in the UK. Clearly there was little doubt in the minds of BSB executives about what would be the major appeal of the new service. With an irony that would no doubt tickle Marshall McLuhan, we find that all the dazzling state-of-the-art technology which BSB will employ, including its revolutionary D-MAC transmission system promising sharper pictures than ever before, will be devoted to programming works originally produced for a medium whose last major technical innovations, sound and colour, were introduced over sixty years ago.

197

Not that we should doubt the wisdom of BSB's advertising strategy. The evidence of the ratings on established channels is plain. Movies do indeed constitute a major attraction on television. Though they rarely oust from the pinnacle of the charts the domestic and imported soap operas which dominate the ratings, they form a major weapon in the scheduling wars, particularly at seasons of maximum audience attention such as Christmas. TV Times, dedicated to the promotion of the programmes on the two commercial channels, regularly gives movie stars precedence over the lesser lights of television on its front cover, and both TV Times and Radio Times devote several pages to the couple of dozen or so film offerings without which the television schedules are now unthinkable.

And yet, it was not always thus.

From the earliest, pre-World War Two days, film companies were loath to sell their wares to television. The first feature film ever shown on the BBC, on 14 August 1938, was The Student of Prague, a German silent classic. Virtually the only films the BBC could get in the pre-war and immediate post-war period were foreign; that is, non-English speaking. Examples included Les Enfants du paradis, The Cabinet of Dr Caligari and The Blue Angel.[1] Before the war, only the Disney studio in Hollywood had been willing to co-operate; Disney had released several shorts to the BBC, and a Mickey Mouse cartoon was the last thing seen on BBC television before the wartime shutdown. After the war, the hostility of both the British and American film industries towards the new medium increased. The supply of Disney productions was cut off when the studio agreed with the American Federation of Musicians not to sell its films to television.[2] Terrified by the threat which television posed to its audience, the film industry closed ranks to prevent television using its own product to compete against it.

The refusal by film companies to sell broadcasting rights to the BBC was not confined to the feature film. It extended to newsreel material as well. The BBC was slow to realise the opportunities for news presentation which television presented, and initially intended to rely on the well-established Wardour Street newsreel companies for footage. Only when it became clear that this would be denied did the BBC organise its own department to produce a regular programme of visual news. Film industry representatives at a meeting with the BBC, frightened at the prospect of competition, had seriously proposed that transmission of any 'televised versions of outside events' should be delayed for forty-eight hours to allow the cinemas time to distribute their own newsreels, but were persuaded that this was hopelessly unrealistic.[3] BBC Television Newsreel first appeared on the air on 5 January 1948.[4]

The rapid decline and eventual demise of cinema newsreels proved that television could more than hold its own in this area of programming. But neither television's budgets nor its technology were any match for the glamour and production values of the feature film, as carried to the peak of technical perfection and audience appeal by the post-war Hollywood film industry and its epigones in Britain. The production of fiction on television was a very different matter from producing news. Television in the late 1940s was still a Cinderella service, disposing of very small resources in comparison to radio. There was no possibility at all that the BBC could produce its own dramas on film in a style to compete with cinema productions. Live productions of studio-produced plays, with all their in-built handicaps, were the only kind of drama the BBC could make for itself. (Videotape was not introduced until the mid-1950s).

Curiously, though it is hard to credit now, at the same time that television wanted to put the cinema on to its tiny screen, the cinema was making overtures to television, hoping to capture the excitement which the live televising of real events could alone provide and to deliver this on a large-screen format to its theatrical audiences. In 1947 there were discussions between the BBC hierarchy and J. Arthur Rank, the most powerful figure in the British film industry of the time. The talks were held under the auspices of the Television Advisory Committee, a body which reported periodically to the Postmaster General, the government minister in charge of broadcasting. Rank, canny as ever, did not make it entirely clear to the BBC exactly what it was that he wanted to do with television. Did he wish simply, as at times he suggested, to distribute cinema films to theatres via electronic means? Was the intention to use television mainly as a way of presenting live coverage of sports events to paying audiences? Or was the ultimate goal the securing of a foothold in the provision of the full range of television entertainment? The BBC had little doubt that it was the latter.

Rank had expressed an interest in relaying some of the BBC's own programmes to his cinema customers, presumably as a novelty. (By the end of 1947 only 34,000 television sets were in use, and only 0.2 per cent of homes were equipped.)[5] The BBC had no particular objection to this, as long as the cinemas were willing to pay, but an internal memo of the time makes the BBC's suspicions abundantly clear:

> In the end it is the televising of their own studio productions, and not BBC studio productions, in which the film organisations will be interested. Moreover, although this may be mere conjecture, if the television public ultimately grows to ten million licence holders, the effects on the economics of the film industry will be profound. The cinema profits at present are no more than marginal, and if audiences were to drop by 10 per cent, it is likely that the industry would cease to make any profit. If such losses occur, the film industry will certainly seek the ready source of profit and will strive to enter the home with financially remunerative sponsored television programmes.... It is therefore the Corporation's view that the film industry wishes to get its foot into television: a) as a hedge in case television develops in some way inimical to film interests; b) so as to have a vantage-ground from which to sap the public service and keep its programmes within bounds.[6]

Despite its hostility to Rank, the BBC felt it was politic to make a few concessions to his demands, and so decided to raise no objections to the proposals for television relays of sporting events to cinemas. Yielding on this point opened up the possibility that there might be a *quid pro quo*, namely a relaxation of the film industry ban on selling television rights to cinema films. Not, the BBC hastened to add, that it intended to fill its schedules with substantial numbers of feature films:

If full concession were given to documentaries, supporting films and a limited number of feature films, the BBC would not wish to take wholesale advantage, since it is no part of the Corporation's intention to convert the BBC Television Service into a home cinema, showing mainly commercial films. It has a far more serious responsibility.[7]

In respect to the productions of the film industry the BBC was, as always, quick to occupy the high moral ground:

Television, which will eventually go into almost every home in the country, will be developed by the BBC as an instrument of education and information as well as of public entertainment. The BBC has the same conception of its duty here as it has in sound broadcasting. It aims to use television as an additional means of helping to bring about an informed democracy and generally to raise public standards. A compromise with the film industry would gravely damage this work. Commercial interests will become uppermost and the box office drive down standards.[8]

In its turn, the film industry accused the BBC of being out of touch with the public. In a speech in 1946 Rank had remarked acidly that, 'I always think the BBC is my best business friend and drives more young people into the cinema than anything else in the country.'[9] Rank's right-hand man, John Davies, never one to mince his words, told the BBC hierarchy at a dinner that film critics on the BBC were élitist and took no account of mass taste.[10]

The objections to showing films on television came not only from those anxious to preserve the BBC's Reithian mission to raise cultural standards and uphold its educational function. There were a number of thoughtful commentators who took the view that showing films on television was a betrayal of the new medium's true potential. Writing in 1952, Jan Bussell singled out the immediacy of television:

Film and television are quite different media and to borrow is a confession of weakness. Television should rejoice in its limitations, and exploit them. .... I maintain that even in the cleverest trickery it is always possible to detect the canned deadness of a piece of film. This may be because of the slight change of quality in the picture, but I prefer to believe it is psychological. There is something vital about the present moment that the photograph cannot catch, the magic of sharing this moment of creation with the artist, whose performance becomes in some indefinable way more sensitive, knowing his moment is shared.[11]

Other writers agreed that television's capacity to give an instantaneous picture gave it a privileged relation to reality:

What are the qualities [television] holds peculiar to itself? These are, I think, a sense of immediacy, a sense of reality close to the reality of life as it is known to the mass of people. Or, to put it another way, television is not merely a substitute for the theatre or cinema which hold up a mirror to life: it is rather an open window on life.[12]

The idea that television's ability to transmit a picture instantly meant it could show reality unmediated was to become an unquestioned axiom in professional thinking about the medium, its most celebrated manifestation being the famous sub-title of the BBC's flagship current affairs programme, *Panorama – A Window on the World*. Similar things were being said on the other side of the Atlantic. No less an authority than Gilbert Seldes told prospective television writers in 1952: 'The essence of television techniques is their contribution to the sense of immediacy . . . [audiences] feel that what they see and hear is happening in the present and is therefore more real than anything taken and cut and dried which has the feel of the past.'[13] Other commentators preferred to stress not the inherent property of the medium, but the different viewing conditions, which dictated a different pace and style:

> It is doubtful if there exists a cinema film of any appreciable length that is ideally suited to the television screen. In the first place, the commercial film is made essentially for a mass audience, not a group in the sitting-room. Secondly, because it is for a mass audience its tempo is much faster, with a quick-cutting technique that can be disturbing when viewed at home.[14]

Maurice Gorham, a former head of BBC Television, agreed:

> Unless television as a medium is to throw away its greatest advantage, its prime audience will always be a home audience, and a small group in the living-room will demand a different tempo and a different feeling in their television programmes from what they will welcome when they visit a theatre on their evening out. . . . The stridency of the musical openings to many films would blow viewers out of their armchairs, and it is hard to imagine the typical film trailer, all explosions and superlatives, raising anything but a laugh in the home.[15]

In the event, the BBC was successful in heading off these early film industry attempts to get into television. In its evidence to the Beveridge Committee on broadcasting in 1950, the BBC reaffirmed its view that television's 'real future would lie in the home.'[16] When it appeared, the Beveridge Report referred somewhat lamely to what it called 'the interesting problem of the relation of television in the home to television in the cinema', but declined to make any firm recommendations, which suited the BBC admirably. Not until the advent of commercial television later in the decade would the film industry renew its attempt to secure a stake in its rival, and this time it would be through buying into broadcast television, not by attempting to transform the nature of television itself.

Unfortunately, when the film industry lost interest in the possibilities of relaying television to its theatres, the BBC lost its only bargaining counter in the struggle to persuade the film companies to sell them television rights to their product. Despite its lofty dismissals of the vulgarity and commercialism of the cinema, the BBC could not lightly renounce the attractions which cinema films offered. There were repeated meetings with film industry bodies to try to get the ban lifted, but to no avail. In 1950 the BBC proposed a history of British cinema in collaboration with the British Film Institute, but the Cinema Exhibitors Association (CEA) refused permission for the three-minute extracts from feature films which were requested.[17] In 1953, at a meeting with several film trade bodies, the BBC listed its film requirements: sixty-six features a year for afternoon programmes, plus one feature a month for evening showing.[18] Increases in broadcasting hours were making the need for films even more pressing. There was a slightly desperate note in a memo from the Director of Television Broadcasting to the Director-General in April 1953:

We must seek celluloid outside this country. I would like to send a member of our staff to Europe, North America and India to buy film, with . . . at least £25,000.[19]

So eager was television to get just a taste of film industry glamour that it was willing to countenance programmes that were little more than shameless plugs for new Hollywood releases. As Burton Paulu recounts:

During 1954 and 1955 there were programs of dance sequences from several Rita Hayworth films, ending with a section from *Sadie Thompson*, which was then opening in London; forty minutes of clips from Doris Day musical films, preceding the London premiere of her *Lucky Me*; and an hour-long compilation of Bing Crosby films, from *The Big Broadcast of 1932* to *White Christmas*, at the time of the latter's first London showing.[20]

Part of the problem was that the BBC could not afford to pay much. In America, NBC paid $500,000 for a showing of Olivier's *Richard III* in 1956; at that time the BBC was offering only £400–£500 for an evening showing of a feature, and could manage no more than a fifteen-minute trailer when the film opened in London cinemas.[21] The film industry thus had no incentive to open its vaults to the BBC, at a time when it was becoming clear to all that television was making substantial inroads into the cinema box office.

Following the huge success of the televising of the Coronation in 1953 and the advent of a new, commercial, channel in 1955, the number of viewers rose steeply. And the number of cinema admissions declined with equal rapidity.[22] Both the BBC and the new ITV companies were eager for feature films, but, as its economic future got worse, the film industry dug in its heels. It was becoming clear, however, that the appeal of even the relatively small sums which British television could offer might eventually become irresistible to some film producers in a declining theatrical market. One reason for the perennial weakness of the British film industry in the face of economic threat was that it had never been able to speak with one voice, since the interests of the film producers were so often at variance with those in exhibition. This was never more apparent than over the question of film sales to television. Though in the long term the interests of both producers and exhibitors united in the need for a healthy box-office, it also increasingly seemed possible, as Keynes famously remarked, that in the long term they might all be dead. Meanwhile, television was waving bank-notes in the faces of film producers who were sitting on cans of old films which no one would ever pay to see in the cinema again. It was all very well for exhibitors to say that if these films were sold to television, people who would otherwise go to see new films at the cinema would stay at home, and so eventually cinemas would close, which would assuredly affect the producers' revenues on films not yet made. The film industry had never been noted for its readiness to take the long view. A bird in the hand, especially your own hand, was a lot more enticing than two in someone else's bush. It was hard to expect film producers to sacrifice cash in hand in exchange for the long-term collective benefit of the industry. This was against all the ingrained habits of an individualistic industry.

British companies such as Ealing, Rank and Alexander Korda's London Films had already begun selling films to American television as far back as 1948. Though initially the American majors had been as implacably opposed to television as their British counterparts, by the mid-1950s the floodgates were starting to open in the USA. In 1955 740 RKO features were made available to the networks, and in January 1956 Columbia offered all its pre-1948 features to television. Warner Bros. followed suit in March and 20th Century-Fox in November. Eighteen months later, Paramount also sold its pre-1948 library to television.[23] By now it was clear that only drastic action would prevent things going the same way in the UK. Indeed, in December 1957 the BBC was reported to have acquired a hundred films from RKO.

Finally a plan was conceived. The two halves of the industry, production and exhibition, for once joined forces to fight the common foe. Four trade associations were involved: the Cinema Exhibitors Association, the British Film Producers Association, the Federation of British Film-makers and the Association of Specialised Film Producers. The plan was for a levy on cinema admissions of one farthing per seat. The fund that this would create would be administered by a new organisation, to be named FIDO: the Film Industry Defence Organisation. FIDO would approach film producers and offer them money to sign an undertaking not to sell their films to television. Cinema owners would, in effect, be paying the producers what they might have expected to receive from such sales. FIDO itself would not actually acquire the rights, but the films would be taken out of circulation.

It was a sign, perhaps, of desperation that such a fragmented industry could unite around such an unlikely scheme, a plan that could only work if substantial sums could be collected and if there were no breaks in the ranks. FIDO was reported in the trade press to have got off to a good start. By May 1959 it was collecting £9,000 a week. It had negotiated fifteen covenants with film producers, and another thirty-one were in the works.[24] Spiros Skouras of 20th Century-Fox praised the scheme and remarked that the Americans should follow suit.[25]

The two major producers in the UK, Rank and ABPC, operated a policy of co-operation with FIDO, without actually taking part in the scheme. They did not apply for FIDO's money, but neither did they sell films to television. This was essential to FIDO's objectives. British films were of crucial importance to television, because the number of American films that could be shown was limited by the quota which the BBC and ITV both applied to foreign material. The American majors in Britain also co-operated unofficially during the early years of the scheme, despite the fact that back in the USA they were by this time selling hundreds of films to the networks.

After eleven months, FIDO had taken fifty-seven films off the market, and was negotiating for eighty-eight more.[26] A strict code of secrecy was preserved. The Association of Independent Cinemas, which remained sceptical about the scheme, repeatedly asked for the films to be named, but William Speakman, the Secretary of FIDO, refused to list titles. The policy was not to acquire any films made before 1938 unless they were acknowledged classics, but in principle FIDO was prepared to pay for any films of a later date, regardless of quality. Short films and documentaries were also eligible, though these could hardly have been much of a counter-draw to the cinemas if shown on television.

There were occasional cracks in the united front. In September 1959 the BBC paid $50,000 for twenty-two films from the Selznick company, including *Rebecca*, *Spellbound*, *Nothing Sacred* and *The Prisoner of Zenda*.[27] The CEA, which was the most militant of the bodies supporting FIDO, immediately recommended a boycott of Selznick films in its theatres. American film interests in Britain, though sympathetic, were quick to point out that they could not collectively refuse sales to television, since their parent bodies in the US might face legal action if they were to become involved in any actions that could be deemed in breach of anti-trust legislation. Such was the dependency of all sectors of the British industry on the Americans that FIDO backed off from an official boycott, though the CEA continued to urge its individual members not to book Selznick films.

In November 1959 there was a further threat of a boycott when *High Noon* was sold to the BBC and the CEA wanted to black its producer, Stanley Kramer. Carl Foreman, the film's scriptwriter, who was based in Britain, wrote to the CEA protesting that Kramer had in fact sold the film to another company, National Telefilm Associates, before FIDO had come into existence.[28]

A more serious breach occurred at the beginning of 1960. Associated Rediffusion, one of the ITV contractors, bought a package of around thirty films from producer Daniel Angel for £5,000 each.[29] It also bought fifty-five films from Romulus Films, whose chairman was John Woolf. These films included such well-known titles as *The African Queen*, *Richard III* and *Moulin Rouge*.[30] Woolf claimed to the trade press that he was never approached by FIDO; FIDO retorted that the films were never offered to them. A first-class row ensued. The CEA banned exhibition of any of the producers' films, and Sir Tom O'Brien, secretary of NATKE (National Association of Theatrical and Kinema Employees) threatened that his members would refuse to work for either Woolf or Angel.[31] The two producers took out an advertisement in *Daily Cinema*, claiming that 300 films had been shown on television over the past year, and making the telling point that some of these had appeared on Granada Television, which was of course owned by the Granada cinema chain.[32] The film unions protested that FIDO had failed them, and demanded a new body be formed to keep films off television.[33]

FIDO, however, soldiered on. By the beginning of May 1960 it boasted that it had signed covenants for 297 films, having just paid British Lion £400,000 to keep seventy-six of its films off the television screen.[34] Eighteen months later, in October 1961, it announced that over £1 million had been dispensed on 665 films.[35] Among them was a package of thirty from London Films Productions. This deal, agreed in July 1961, included some of the most prestigious British productions ever made: *The Four Feathers*, *The Private Life of Henry VIII*, *The Scarlet Pimpernell*, *The Thief of Baghdad*, *Sanders of the River*, and *The Shape of Things to Come*. The sum paid was £45,000.[36]

By 1964, FIDO reported that it had removed 925 films from the market, at a cost of £1,954,354.[37] But FIDO's very success had sown the seeds of its own decay. Its policy amounted to bidding for television rights in competition with the television organisations, and this inevitably resulted in driving up the price that television had to pay. Some producers eventually found the lure of television money irresistible. In August 1964, ITV networked *Room At The Top* and achieved number one in the ratings.[38] Around the same time, ATV paid half a million pounds for just fifty films from the Goldwyn company.[39] In September, Paramount sold 140 pre-1948 films to the BBC.[40] In an apparent attempt to shore up the defences by regrouping around a smaller redoubt, the CEA said it would no longer object to films more than five years old being sold to television. This change of tack 'rocked' the industry, according to *Kine Weekly*.[41] The CEA, no longer breathing fire, conceded meekly that 'with the passage of time, circumstances, including in particular the attitude of the public to television, have changed . . .'[42] This appeared to mean that they were throwing in the towel.

The next month, in October 1964, 100 Warner Bros. pictures were sold to ATV.[43] In a few weeks it was all over. At the end of November FIDO announced that the levy to support the scheme would end in January.[44] Writing in the *Evening Standard* on 10 November 1964, Alexander Walker pronounced the obituary: 'FIDO was always a better name for a house pet than a guard dog, and its policy of boycotting producers who sold films to TV has been all bark and no bite.'

Probably the scheme was doomed from the start. It took funds from a constantly declining revenue base, the cinema box-office, and used them to compete in the market with a rival whose economic strength was increasing with every year that went by. ITV advertising revenues were soaring in the mid-1960s,[45] while the advent of the £5 surcharge for the colour licence in 1968 would give a significant boost to the BBC's finances. Sooner or later, the sums which television was prepared to offer would have outstripped the level of finance which FIDO could raise from the exhibitors. And it would have become increasingly hard to sell the scheme to theatre owners when box office receipts continued remorselessly on their downward spiral, whether there were films on television or not.

There was something depressingly predictable about the British film industry's response to the challenge of television. Despite the enthusiasm of Spiros

Skouras for FIDO's plan, it is doubtful that such an idea would have been tried in America even if anti-trust laws had not ruled it out. In the first place, there would not have been the required collectivist spirit. But more important, perhaps, the instinct of American business was not so negatively defensive. The response of Hollywood to the threat posed by television was various. On one level, the strategy was to attack by developing a superior product: CinemaScope, stereophonic sound, colour, bigger spectacles, more sex, whatever the public could not get from television. At another level, the response was to co-operate. 1951 saw the first filmed production for American television, *I Love Lucy*, shot in a Hollywood studio. In the same year Columbia Pictures launched Screen Gems, a subsidiary to produce filmed material for television. Before very long Hollywood had become the major production centre for American television. Admittedly the structure of television in the UK made it more difficult for the film industry to get involved at the production level. But its instincts were always restrictive and defensive rather than expansionist. The American film industry, despite being faced with the most powerful television system in the world, has retained its theatrical base by means of a huge programme of investment, relocating from the decaying inner cities to the suburban shopping malls. The British film industry spent little on new facilities, but instead adopted a stance which derived ultimately from King Canute. Their results were somewhat similar to his.

Notes

All quotations from BBC documents are taken from material stored in the BBC Written Archives Centre, Caversham Park, and are used by permission. My thanks to Jacqueline Kavanagh, BBC Written Archives Officer. The records of FIDO are held in the Library of the British Film Institute. My thanks to the staff of the Library.

1. John Swift, *Adventure in Vision* (London: John Lehmann, 1950), p. 186.
2. Maurice Gorham, *Television, Medium of the Future* (London: Percival Marshall, 1949), p. 28.
3. 'Television Advisory Committee: Third Report to the Postmaster General', Second Draft, TAC 97, p. 4.
4. Swift, *Adventure in Vision*, p. 188.
5. See Asa Briggs, *The History of Broadcasting in the United Kingdom, Volume 4: Sound and Vision* (Oxford: Oxford University Press, 1979), p. 242.
6. 'Television and the Film Industry', Draft Paper for the BBC Board of Governors, p. 2, 11 July 1948.
7. Ibid., p. 13.
8. Ibid., p. 14.
9. Reported in BBC memo to Television Advisory Committee, 14 November 1946.
10. BBC memo, 10 October 1951.
11. Jan Bussell, *The Art of Television* (London: Faber and Faber, 1952), p. 55.
12. Arthur Swinson, *Writing for Television* (London: Adam and Charles Black, 1955), p. 21.
13. Gilbert Seldes, *Writing for Television* (Garden City, New York: Doubleday, 1952), p.

32; quoted in Lynn Spigel and Henry Jenkins, 'Same Bat Channel, Different Bat Times', in Roberta Pearson and William Urricchio (eds.), *The Many Lives of the Batman*, (London: BFI, 1990).

14. Swift, *Adventure in Vision*, p. 186.

15. Gorham, *Television – Medium of the Future*, p. 31.

16. Quoted in Briggs, *Sound and Vision*, p. 386.

17. Memo from Controller, BBC Television, 13 July 1950.

18. BBC Memo for a meeting with representatives of the BFPA, CEA, KRS and Association of Specialised Film Producers, 1 January 1953.

19. Director of Television Broadcasting to Director-General of the BBC, 17 March 1953.

20. Burton Paulu, *British Broadcasting* (Minneapolis: University of Minnesota Press, 1956), p. 279.

21. Paulu, p. 277.

22. Television licences had climbed to 2,142,452 by 1953 and to 4,503,766 by 1955. See Briggs, *Sound and Vision*, p. 240. Cinema admissions slumped from 938.8 million per year in 1954 to 452.2 million in 1959, and down further to 375 million in 1960. See John Spraos, *The Decline of the Cinema* (London: George Allen and Unwin, 1962), passim.

23. *Screen Digest*, April 1988, pp. 87–8.

24. *Kine Weekly*, 7 May 1959.

25. *Kine Weekly*, 14 May 1959.

26. *Daily Cinema*, 31 August 1959.

27. *Daily Mail*, 17 September 1959.

28. *Daily Cinema*, 27 November 1959.

29. *Financial Times*, 2 January 1960.

30. *Daily Telegraph*, 5 January 1960.

31. *Daily Mail*, 8 January 1960.

32. *Daily Cinema*, 13 January 1960.

33. *Daily Cinema*, 14 January 1960.

34. *Daily Cinema*, 2 May 1960.

35. *Daily Cinema*, 11 October 1961.

36. Letter from William Speakman, 25 July 1961, in the FIDO files.

37. *Daily Cinema*, 11 May 1964.

38. *Financial Times*, 20 August 1964.

39. Ibid.

40. *Motion Picture Daily*, 2 September 1964.

41. *Kine Weekly*, 17 September 1964.

42. *Variety*, 16 September 1964.

43. *Variety*, 7 October 1964.

44. *Daily Cinema*, 27 November 1964.

45. ITV revenues went from £58,359,000 in 1959 to £93,276,000 in 1961. See Barrie MacDonald, *Broadcasting in the United Kingdom* (London: Mansell, 1988), p. 74.

Index of Proper Names and Programmes

A for Andromeda, 17, 109, 114–123
Adam, Kenneth, 95, 96
Adventures of Robin Hood, The, 39
Anderson, Lindsay, 48
Andrews, Eamonn, 62
Armchair Theatre, 36
Arthur Haynes Show, The, 75

Baker, H. W. and Kemp, W. D., 34, 36
Barry, Sir Michael, 3, 4, 126
Bartlett, Keith, 173
Baverstock, Donald, 7, 150, 154
BBC *Quarterly*, 25, 28, 30, 34, 36
Beadle, Gerald, 7
Beveridge Report, 5, 6, 201
Beyond The Fringe, 148
Big Match, The, 191, 194
Bird, John, 150
Black, Peter, 14, 48, 77
Blessed, Brian, 141
Bough, Frank, 190, 191
Bourdieu, Pierre, 173
Boy Meets Girls, 100
Bridson, Geoffrey, 49
Briggs, Asa, 26, 160
Brown, Ivor, 27
Burns and Allen Show, 81, 86
Bussell, Jan, 200

Cadbury, Peter, 9
Cartier, Rudolph, 34, 110, 111
Casey, Albert, 135–7
Cathy Come Home, 18, 142
Chambers, Iain, 102
Children's Hour, 175, 188
Christie, Julie, 114
Churchill, Winston, 3
Clements, John, 36
Cock, Gerald, 22–4, 38
Coleman, David, 189, 190
Collins, Norman, 76
Comedy Playhouse, 80
Contrast, 25, 33, 37, 38, 132
Cook, Jim, 79

Cool for Cats, 91
Compact, 128
Corbett, Harry H., 81, 86, 87
Coronation Street, 17, 18, 127, 129, 136
Cowgill, Bryan, 187–190
Cutforth, Rene, 46, 47

Daily Express, 47
Daily Mail, 48
Daily Mirror, 9
Daily Sketch, 9, 47
Dial M for Murder, 28
De Lotbiniere, S. J., 184
Dig This!, 100
Dimbleby, Richard, 57
Dimmock, Peter, 183, 185, 187, 188, 191
Dinwiddie, Melville, 26
Dixon of Dock Green, 130, 131, 139
Double Your Money, 9, 63
Douglas, Josephine, 93, 96
Dr Finlay's Casebook, 139
Duff, Sir James, 152

Eaton, Mick, 80
Ellis, John, 72
Educating Archie, 77
Emergency Ward Ten, 177
Entertainers, The, 55
Expresso Bongo, 70, 71

Face to Face, 64–6
Faith, Adam, 100
Featherstone, Mike, 173
Fox, Paul, 185, 186, 189, 190
Freeman, John, 64–7
Friendly, Fred, 44
Frost, David, 145, 155
Frost Report, The, 155

Galton, R. and Simpson, A., 77–80, 82, 86
Gielgud, Val, 28
Gillet, Roland, 15
Good, Jack, 91, 93, 96, 100, 101, 104

Goon Show, The, 78
Gorham, Maurice, 201
Grade, Lew, 192, 193
Grandstand, 9, 18, 187–191
Greene, Hugh Carleton, 10, 38, 39, 114, 126, 149, 153
Grierson, John, 40
Grossberg, Lawrence, 103

Haley, Sir William, 14, 26
Hall, Stuart, 182
Hamer, Robert, 34
Hancock's Half Hour, 8, 75–87
Harding, Gilbert, 60–72
Harris, Roy, 50
Harty, Russell, 68
Hennegan, Alison, 67
Highway Patrol, 127
Hill, Charles, 90
Hobson, Dorothy, 80
Hoggart, Richard, 9
Home, Sir Alec Douglas, 145, 156
Hood, Stuart, 125, 126, 137
Hopkins, John, 125, 130, 135, 137, 139
Housing Problems, 44, 45
How Do You View?, 76, 81
Howerd, Frankie, 86
Hoyle, Fred, 114–16, 119

I Love Lucy, 12, 77, 79, 82, 83, 206
In Prison, 50–52
It's A Square World, 75
Ingrams, Richard, 152

Jacob, Ian, 75
Jacobs, David, 101, 102
James, Sid, 82
Jenkins, Peter, 37
Jennings, Humphrey, 52, 53
Johns, Stratford, 141
Jones, Elwyn, 126, 135
Journey's End, 29
Juke Box Jury, 17, 101–103

Kemp-Welch, Jane, 91
Kennedy Martin, Troy, 32, 127–9, 131–3, 136, 139–42
Kneale, Nigel, 108–10

Lang, Don, 95

Levin, Bernard, 151, 156
Lewis, Peter, 132
Life With The Lyons, 76–8
Listen to Britain, 53
Listener, The, 31, 37, 54, 130
Lloyd, Selwyn, 6, 11
Loach, Ken, 142
Look In On London, 56–8
London Town, 57

Macmillan, Harold, 121, 145, 154
Madden, Cecil, 30
Maigret, 39
Main Wilson, Dennis, 96
Martin, Millicent, 151
Maschwitz, Eric, 99
Match of the Day, 191
McGivern, Cecil, 43, 44, 84, 96, 99, 186, 187
McGrath, John, 127–9, 131, 133, 136, 139–42
Michelmore, Cliff, 7, 8
Midwinter, Eric, 87
Miller Jones, Andrew, 151
Milne, Alasdair, 91
Mitchell, Denis, 43, 47, 49–58
Morley, David, 177
Morning In The Streets, 49, 52–4
Murdock, Rupert, 35
Murray, Pete, 93, 96, 102
Murrow, Ed, 44

New Statesman, The, 48
Newman, Sidney, 135
1984, 34

Off The Record, 90
Ogilvie, Sir Frederick, 3
O'Shea, Alan, 159
Oh Boy!, 17, 96–101

Panorama, 12, 201
Paulu, Burton, 202
Percival, Lance, 151
Picture Post, 44
Pinto-Duschinsky, M., 1
Plater, Alan, 139
Prior, Alan, 126, 135
Pilkington Report, 9, 10, 135
Play Of The Week, 177

Quatermass series, 17, 109–14, 122–3

Radio Times, The, 12, 25, 27, 29, 30, 35, 129–31, 135, 198
Rank, J. Arthur, 199, 200
Ready, Steady Go, 103
Reid, Robert, 44
Reisz, Karel, 48, 53
Reith, Lord, 5, 6, 11, 14, 36
Richard, Cliff, 60, 98
Robertson, Ker, 91
Robin Hood, The Adventures of, 163
Rose, David, 135, 136
Rotha, Paul, 42

Samuel, Raphael, 71
Sarnoff, David, 37
Saturday Sports Special, 183–7
Scannell, Paddy, 46, 169, 170
Seldes, Gilbert, 201
Shubik, Irene, 108
Sherrin, Ned, 150, 151, 153–5
Silvey, Robert, 160, 162
Simon and Laura, 70
Six-five Special, 8, 17, 90–104
Sloan, Tom, 93
Snow, C. P., 119
Spain, Nancy, 67, 73, 102
Spare Time, 52
Special Enquiry, 43–9
Spitting Image, 156, 157
Sportsview, 78, 183–7
Steptoe and Son, 71, 81, 126, 135
Sunday Night at the London Palladium, 9, 36, 77, 104
Sunday Pictorial, The, 10
Sutton, Shaun, 139, 142
Swallow, Norman, 43–9

Swift, John, 31–2

Take Your Pick, 9, 63
Taylor, Don, 33
Television Sport Magazine, 184
Terry-Thomas, 76, 81
That Was The Week That Was, 17, 71, 75, 145–57
That's Life, 64
This England, 55
Tonight, 7, 8, 12, 13, 91, 148, 149, 153
TV Times, 12, 25, 101, 198
Tynan, Kenneth, 62

Waldman, Ronnie, 76
Walker, Alexander, 205
Walton, Kent, 91
War Game, The, 18
Ward, Bill, 191
Warner, Jack, 130
Wedding on Saturday, 55
Wham!, 101
What's My Line?, 4, 16, 26, 62–64
Williams, Raymond, 171
Willis, Ted, 131
Wilson, Harold, 1, 121
Woffenden, Bob, 103
Wolstenhome, Kenneth, 184
Wood, Duncan, 77, 80–84, 86
World In Action, 54, 58
World of Sport, 191–4
Worsley, T. C., 139–42
Wyatt, Woodrow, 10
Wyndham Goldie, Grace, 8, 13, 108, 149, 150, 153, 154

Z Cars, 17, 125–43, 171
Zoo Quest, 9